Goethe's Other *Faust*

THE DRAMA, PART II

Goethe's Other *Faust*

THE DRAMA, PART II

JOHN GEAREY

University of Toronto Press
Toronto Buffalo London

© University of Toronto Press 1992
Toronto Buffalo London
Printed in Canada

ISBN 0-8020-2808-X

Printed on acid-free paper

Canadian Cataloguing in Publication Data

Gearey, John, 1926–
Goethe's other Faust : the drama, part II

Includes index.
ISBN 0-8020-2808-X

1. Goethe, Johann Wolfgang von, 1749–1832.   Faust.
2. Theil.   I. Title.

PT1940.G43 1992   832'.6   C92-093350-5

For Francis

There is no reason why an hour should not be a century in that calenture of the brain that can make the stage a field.

Samuel Johnson
Preface to Shakespeare

Contents

Contents

Preface

The Goethe who began *Faust* was not the poet and thinker who completed the work some sixty years later. Not only had he himself developed in an astonishing manner in his own right, but developments in the politics, thought, science, and literature of his times were in turn of a broad and radical nature. One tends to assume that the forces that seem so compellingly to move our world are the product of that world, and we look no further for their origins. One hears that the upsetting changes that have occurred in our century in the world of art are the product of a fragmented view of life, and that view itself is the product of overwhelming contemporary advances in science. In the moral realm, our confusion of values is attributed to devastating experiences of the recent past that have undermined a clarity of purpose. But the great force for change in art and in the way of perceiving reality that marks our world came not at the beginning of the present, but the previous century, the period in which Goethe conceived, struggled with, and completed his *Faust*, Part II. The conception, the struggle, and the meaning of the 'strange construct' that resulted are the subject of this book, and its purpose the illumination of an idea.

Goethe did not, as one might expect, revise and alter his *Faust* over the years to fit each new stage in the development of his own understanding. Rather, he retained, added, and accumulated, with virtually no revision, and so produced in the end an evolving work whose theme itself became evolution.

In the early stages he acted out, as it were, the idea of evolution in his very manner of creating, in the variety of forms he adopted and adapted as his needs changed, in his willingness and ability to grow

as the work grew, in his instinctively developmental rather than ide-
ologically purposeful approach to life and to art. What had been originally conceived, apparently, as a monodrama in the rough, 'woodcut'
form of verse, the *Knittelvers*, that evoked the sixteenth-century setting
of the legend became a drama of high passion and profound thought
as it adapted the alchemical and mystical urges of that earlier age to
the impulses of the newly developing Romantic movement of its own
time. What, in turn, threatened now in its own right to become a mere
poetic agglomeration of profundities and internal and external dramatic
conflicts with little order or clear purpose was itself put to constraints
and comprehended within the majestic philosophical framework which
the 'Prologue in Heaven' finally provided. After almost three decades
of thought and composition, Goethe had created the rationale for the
series of associated perceptions, experiences, and powerfully dramatic
motifs that he seems more freely than in a planned manner to have
conceived and executed over the years. By that time he had also conceived, and broadly outlined for himself, a scheme for a second part,
a new drama that would take up the themes and problems that had
evolved in the limited real world, the *kleine Welt* of Part I, and re-
envision and resolve them in the greater context of the world of mind
and of history, the *große Welt* of Part II. What was intended to come
to an end had only prompted a new beginning. I have attempted to
describe the unique dynamics of the earlier undertaking in my *Goethe's
'Faust': The Making of Part I*.

Part II occasioned a confrontation. No longer did the idea that informed
the work function simply as a guide to its creative impulses, it now
had become wholly conscious. This was in part a matter of maturation,
in the work and in the author. The drama itself had moved from action
·to vision, and the author from apprentice, if apprentice of great genius,
to master during its writing. More important, the age as a whole in its
thought and perceptions had changed, struggled, and come to define
itself in large part in and through this same idea. Evolution is only the
definitive word we use in describing a phenomenon that an earlier
time – when it first gained the perception – distinguished simply as
process, organic as opposed to foreseen design, becoming as opposed
to being. I deliberately use the word 'evolution' in this study more
often than the word 'development,' since the former suggests, at least

to my mind, a process less conscious and more instinctive than does the latter. I do not say unconscious, since we are concerned here with a creative process.

Darwin marked the culmination, not the beginning, of a new development in thought. It was, to be sure, his great scientific achievement to have discovered in natural selection a *mechanism* that could account for the evolution of man and animal, but it was the earlier discovery of the antiquity of the earth that provided his theory with the necessary amount of time to account for a process that could only have occurred over a formerly unthinkable span of years. The concept of an evolving world has its roots not in the biological sciences, but in geology. The discovery in the earth's strata of evidence for its gradual formation over eons not only put to rest the biblical accounting of Creation but created an entirely new concept of the world in which the human being was imagined to be housed. Goethe was still alive at the time of the publication of Lyell's *Principles of Geology* (1830), itself the culmination of earlier research in which he too was privately active; he lived and formed his thought in an intellectual climate that produced the *Principles* and *On the Origin of Species*.

These distinctions between preordained and evolutionary creation, between essentialism and gradualism, between, in general, being and becoming, were precisely the distinctions that separated the eighteenth from the nineteenth century in the essential matter of perceiving reality and thus in the matter of representing reality in art. Significantly, the earliest plan for a *Faust*, Part II, undated, can be traced to the years 1797–1800. The impact of the concept of evolution on the objective form of art that is drama is thus the idea at the center of this study.

When the artist at the beginning of the twentieth century attempted to put on canvas not simply what he saw but also what he knew, he was forced to disrupt the plane of reality and juxtapose images that he might see before him with those that might be in his mind. I will speak of literary cubism, of disjunction and juxtaposition, in discussing *Faust*, Part II. But the writer at the beginning of the nineteenth century who wished to represent in dramatic form a process, or becoming, that entailed in its history much more than could ever be placed in sequence in a single play would be confronted with a similar dilemma and likewise forced to an extreme solution. The forms of art in the Western tradition, grounded as they were in the models from the classical Greek world, rested on the assumption that the varied, individual, distinctive life and reality they presented were merely particulars that more importantly reflected an organization and laws that were universal, eternal, and unchanging. To reflect these laws was the object of art. But the evolutionist vision that was now brought to bear on the content of art no less than of history and the life of man knew no fixed and absolute designs but only the laws, procedures, and dynamics of change. With the turn of the eighteenth century came the turn away from absolutism toward historicism, toward a thinking in layers of development – to use again the analogy with geology. To understand more deeply one no longer looked above to abstract principles but behind to the endless sequence of time and events. Yet no artistic form was at hand that might express, and represent in its being, the new understanding.

Faust, Part II created, or rather evolved, such a form. It was its great, radical, and largely misunderstood and ignored achievement to have done so. The misunderstanding derived from the very attempt to see the strangeness and otherness of the work in the light of the past and not as the product of circumstance and necessity that had combined to create the beginnings of something new. For the evolution of its form was only possible in and through the faith in evolution. Goethe did not create in *Faust II* a literary vehicle to accommodate his changing and developing concept of the theme, rather he allowed his new and changing concept to create the vehicle. But he could not have allowed the concept to dictate the form without the belief now emerging in the age that artistic form itself was an evolving phenomenon and not the absolute and ideal entity that an earlier time, and he himself in an earlier, distinctive period of his development, had believed it to be. *Faust II* is an act of evolution, not merely its depiction and reflection. It represents a triumph of content over form; hence its otherness. But the triumph of content over form is the triumph of evolution.

Part I exploded, and became more free in form, as it absorbed the clamoring emotion and thought that accrued to its hero and its theme; Part II *im*ploded under the pressure of an understanding that had grown too great and too broad for the traditional strictures of art and yet would not be denied. The implosion is evident in the esthetic disjunction on its surface, in what I see as a kind of literary cubism. The remarkable evolution that Goethe himself underwent in his own right and his own time brought him forward to a point where the problems he eventually faced in his art were those that would only begin to be broadly confronted a century later. He too was forced to break the surface of reality in order to see beneath and beyond to the structures and causes that he and a new generation knew now to lie in the deeper nature of things and yet were not presented to the mind by the traditional forms of art. I have attempted to trace the antecedents of the new mode of thought reflected in Part II to the developments in science to which the literary and the artistic movements of our own century are related. That accounts for the title of the second chapter, 'Faust II and the Darwinian Revolution.' To show what I believe were the broader and deeper forces at work in the age that produced this unique drama, this 'strange fruit,' as Goethe on another occasion called the work, I have also included a chapter that places Schiller beside Goethe in their moment in time.

Yet, for all the necessity of creating a new form to express the new understanding, it was circumstance that in the end made the esthetic leap possible. An evolutionary mechanism was present in the evolution. Magic, an element indigenous to the Faust theme and employed by Goethe in the first part of his drama mainly to colorfully and atmospherically effect what could have come about by natural means, becomes in the second part, in the realm of the 'great world' of mind and of history, the device by which he joins, disjoins, and juxtaposes the things that exist layered in human consciousness but are separated in the real world and in time. Magic, itself the product and the symbol of a prerationalistic era, served now in what was gradually becoming a postrationalistic age to again break the chain of causal reasoning, but on this occasion to express what the science and scientific thought of a new age had come to know. It was as if magic lay in Faust like a mechanism of literary and artistic evolution waiting for the historical moment to be put to use. In this one respect, the evolution of Faust as a work of art parallels precisely the strict scientific application of the word as Darwin intended it. I use the word 'evolution' throughout this study, however, in the more general, pre-Darwinian sense.

The result of this meeting of fantasy with reality was a world drama which moved ever deeper into the motive forces of nature, history, culture, and society, and amassed the ingredients of actual human experience as it seemed to range the farther into myth, symbol, and erudite allusion. The towering figure of the blinded Faust, who stands in the last act against a background of death and impending failure and yet proclaims his anticipation of the 'highest moment,' has not simply traversed to this point realms of individual imaginings and desire but has relived and borne witness to the cultural development of Western man. What he has inherited in and from this culture, he has also earned through rehearsing its history. The multiple juxtaposed images of *Faust II* are the broken mirror of this development. Without its reflections, and our reflection upon its reflections, neither the earthly resolution in the play nor its otherworldly ending has real substance, significance, or foundation.

I have tried to bring to the surface, and to order, the allusive, associative, imaginative, in a word poetic, thought that lies submerged beneath the surface of the text and which forms the great thematic whole of the completed *Faust*. This complete *Faust*, this other *Faust*, is the play that is lost when the poem is read as dramatic action alone and its supposed learned meanings left to scholars. But that play is a play in its own right, though of the mind. It has its own development and ultimate resolution, more painful and disconcerting, but more meaningful in our time, than the ordering of things that obtains when the usual *Faust* is read.

Again I quote from the English translation of *Faust* by Anna Swanwick, though I have been questioned on the use of this translation in my earlier study. In the meantime an excellent, unrhymed translation by Stuart Atkins has appeared, to which I refer on occasion in preference to Swanwick. But Part II is not only above all a poem rather than a drama, it can also be said to force us to *think* poetically rather than in terms of logical causation, and for that I continue to believe that rhyme serves best. In the earlier study I cited mainly English titles for further reference. The most important work on *Faust II* in the recent past, however, when this latter part of the drama recaptured, or perhaps captured for the first time, imaginative scholarly attention, has been in German. Of necessity I refer more often to this scholarly work, although, where feasible, I note English titles as well. Specifically, the essay by Max Kommerell '*Faust II*: Zum Verständnis der Form' (first published, 1939) has proved central in my own understanding and I have adapted from him the concept of 'spheres of existence' – *Daseins-*

kreise – to describe the separate worlds that come together so magically attached in the drama.

In quoting the original in footnotes I use the line numbering that is standard in modern editions of *Faust*. Citations from letters, conversations, and texts other than *Faust* are from the Artemis edition of Goethe's works. Unless otherwise noted, translations from these texts are my own.

J.G.
October 1991

Goethe's Other *Faust*

THE DRAMA, PART II

CHAPTER ONE

Prelude: Schiller and Goethe

Like the great works of literature themselves, the events of literary history take on new and different aspects with time. So with the relationship between Goethe and Schiller.

Their friendship long stood as a monument to humanism. It seemed to provide in the real world an example of that communion of sentiment and thought which was assumed to occur in the imaginative realm in the meeting of the individual mind with the great work of art, with the great work of intellect. The two poets were possessed of quite different kinds of genius and enhanced each other more in contrast than through similarities, but that only confirmed the sense of freedom in diversity that underlay the tradition they were meant to represent. Schiller was more political and moral, Goethe more psychological, in the analysis of human conduct, so that even where they differed they became joined, in that the side of experience which tended to be emphasized in the work of the one was perfectly complemented by the emphasis in that of the other.

It was Schiller who noted this deep complementary difference in his essay on *Naive and Sentimental Poetry* (1795). He saw in Goethe 'a poet in whom nature functions most purely' and in himself one who must strive for the natural in his art through unending conscious effort.[1] And since Schiller identified Goethe in his 'naive' poetic inspiration with the poets of the ancient world and himself in his reflective mode

---

1 Schiller speaks of Goethe as a 'poet in whom nature functions most faithfully and purely than any other, and who, among modern poets, is perhaps least removed from the sensuous truth of things' (in the English edition and translation by Julius Elias [New York, 1966], p. 138).

with the condition of the modern writer, a further constellation suggested itself. Not only was the present here connected to a glorious past, it also pointed to a future as to a paradise regained, as to a second coming of Art.

This view of the two poets as the composite embodiment of an ideal persisted the longer for having struck roots in a culture which itself sought identity in part through the example of their lives and works. The influence of so-called Weimar Classicism on subsequent German life and thought was immeasurable.[2] But the view precluded a proper awareness, at times indeed a simple recognition, of the forces at work in their times and on their art that posed a serious challenge to humanism. Yet these were the forces that determined the real future, the future which in fact came to be in literature and in thought. Not that the preclusion was willful; nor is our present, better awareness of the forces of potential change in their times the result of increased objectivity. Rather, the developments in art and in intellectual history over the past century have been so extreme as to throw the achievements of the preceding era not only into new, but radical perspective. What might have seemed unimportant or aberrant to an earlier view could now appear as directly significant, as formative of new lines of progression. More important, the past as such began to surrender part of its influence as agent of understanding and measure of accomplishment to the undefined but attractive concept of a *becoming* world.[3]

Faust, Part II, itself both the product and the conscious artistic reflection of this new evolutionist mode of thought, stands out unique but awkward against the literary past and only gradually finds company, gains contours, in the context of more recent developments. It is as if we were observing the work as it moved from an initial displacement to a position of order and beauty in a future time, though we know that it is not *Faust II* but we that are moving.

We are concerned with Goethe alone. But the inclusion of Schiller

2　See, for example, H. von Treitschke, ch. 1, 'Die goldenen Tage von Weimar,' in *Kulturhistorisch-Literarische Bilder*, vol. 2 of *Bilder aus der deutschen Geschichte* (Leipzig 1914).

3　A striking reflection of this change in perspective is the tendency today to characterize new movements as post- rather than neo-, as in post-modern, post-industrial. This marks, I believe, a broad urge to see the new not as a repetition of the past altered only on its surface, which is the classical and traditional mode of perception, but as part of a becoming process.

at the outset is meant to provide more than simple background or convenient contrast. Schiller in fact experienced the same artistic dislocation in his times as Goethe, and at a similar stage of his development and under comparable circumstances. This fact remains obscured, however, by his death at a point where he seemed to have reached an epitome of accomplishment and thus to have described, not a jagged line of evolution, but a perfect arc of development. The view in which he and Goethe were held presupposed just such a classical progression from chaotic creative beginnings to the clarity and balance of maturity that, itself representing the ideal, required no further change. Yet Schiller had a part in aligning his own development. Whereas Goethe responded to the forces of the age in a manner that caused him radically to enter upon his career and, with *Faust II*, radically to end it, Schiller at one point hesitated.

The hesitation came in *Wallenstein*. The forces of the age, the great undercurrents that will become the waves of a future time, pressed upon Schiller no less than Goethe. They shared a *Sturm und Drang*. But that, as it were, was for the sharing. The same upheaval in art and thought that caused the eruption in their early years only to subside into order and maturity, like a calm *after* the storm, partook of the deeper currents that gave rise to the movement of Romanticism and, as a later perspective makes more and more clear, to a development that has yet to culminate. At this deepest level, where changes in the structures and forms of art have their origins, the concept of development as such began to exert itself as a commanding principle of thought against the earlier notions of absolute or transcendental values and preordained designs. Process was replacing the idea of simple progression. When Darwin, later, demonstrated the principle of evolution in the animal kingdom, he gave scientific expression and confirmation to what had already been sensed, anticipated, and, in its own way, formulated in the realm of ideas. *Faust II* gave artistic expression to this same sense. To the extent that its essential form or structure, its mode of presentation, dislodges our own mode of literary perception, to that extent our experience of the work repeats the experience of the author in *his* age. For *Faust*, in both its parts, is not a drama of ideas but of experience, the very novelty of the experience, its otherness, requiring an otherness of form. To the extent that *Wallenstein*, conversely, remained within the broad development of traditional dramatic forms, to that extent it was compelled to conceive and realize its meanings against the past, as *Faust* its against the future.

Wallenstein, for all its monumentality, represents a path not taken. The monumentality itself, paradoxically, was the result of compromise. Schiller was forced for the first time in this play to reconcile his modernist sense of history with his classical concept of tragic drama. The resulting tension gave rise both to the imposing genius of the work and the enigmatic or diffused quality at its core, in the form of its central figure. For the new sense of history demanded what the traditional sense of tragedy would not allow. The emphasis that was placed by the former on event and circumstance as the determinant in human action undermined the investment of the latter in the conscious freedom of the individual, even if that freedom was merely conscious and not actual or real.[4] In *Wallenstein* Schiller had little choice of emphasis. If ever a historical occurrence demonstrated the hegemony of event over character, of circumstance over will, it was the Thirty Years War in which his play had its setting. The greater the weight of event, the less the stature and will of the individual. If Schiller the dramatist, standing on the threshold of the nineteenth century (he completed *Wallenstein* in 1799), hesitated to take the step which the historian in him could readily have taken, it was perhaps because he sensed what was to follow. The future development of drama reveals a systematic, seemingly inevitable, weakening of its heroic center and a strengthening, though not ennobling, of the forces that surround and contain it. By the middle of the twentieth century the process had resulted, or at least could result, in a virtual paralysis. The final exchange of words in *Waiting for Godot: A Tragicomedy* (1952) is between two protagonists who can speak, but spiritually cannot move, with so much around them 'unmeaning' and unknown. '*Vladimir*. Well? Shall we go? *Estragon*. Yes, let's go. (They do not move.)'

I offer these generalizations as part of a critique, not as criticism. Tragedy by default may be the only tragedy we have left to us in our day. Rather the point is to suggest that the traditional concept of the

4 Goethe also saw as central in modern tragedy 'our presumptive freedom of will which clashes with the ineluctable course of events' – 'die prätendierte Freiheit unsres Wollen, [die] mit dem notwendigen Gang des Ganzen zusammenstößt' (*Zum Shakespeares-Tag*, 1771 [Artemis, vol. 4, p. 121]).

hero was undermined long before the advent of what we think of as modern drama and that Schiller, looking to history, to the fountainhead of circumstance, in order to lend classical objectivity to his art, had produced in Wallenstein a modern hero, apparently against his intent. The outside had overwhelmed the inside in his play. The relevance of this point to Goethe, again in contrast, is that it suggests how much greater for him in *Faust* were the challenge and the necessity to alter and eventually to break the forms of conventional dramatic art in order to reflect the vision that the new concepts of the age had engendered in him, though through the medium of science. This question will concern us directly in the next chapter. But, to repeat, the contrast is not merely convenient. History played the role in Schiller that nature and science played in Goethe. When he began *Wallenstein* Schiller had already behind him two historical works, *The Revolt of the Netherlands* (1788) and *The Thirty Years War in Germany* (1791/93); he had been appointed professor of history at Jena on the strength of the former.[5]

The task that Schiller set himself in *Wallenstein* was to form an unwieldy mass of historical event into a coherent action which would not only serve as background to his play but become an integral part of it. It was his purpose, his mission as a dramatist, one might say, to restore event to a prominence that it had not enjoyed in tragedy since ancient times and so create a classical conflict within a modernist understanding of life. In Schiller history becomes fate, not in the sense of an inscrutable, but a determining and defining influence. The characters that surround or confront the central figures in his plays represent not so much persons who act in their own right as individuals who by disposition or from vested interest embrace, exemplify, and perpetuate the attitudes that dominate in the society and determine the social and political order. Being persons of rank, their decisions become events. Yet their actions for all that are not free but merely the repetition in the present of similarly taken actions in the past. Nor are the central figures themselves, the heroes and heroines, free. Their presumption of freedom derives simply from the fact that as central

5 Schiller did not perhaps make actual contributions in history comparable to those of Goethe in science, but see Lesley Sharpe, *Schiller and the Historical Character* (London, 1982), which shows that Schiller's historical perspective has found more and more support among contemporary historians; see, especially, pp. 35–7.

characters the weight of the action devolves upon them, and in their need to make decisions they assume they are free to decide. They fall, as they must, in and through this illusion of freedom.

If Schiller intended to create a modern classical tragedy in *Wallenstein*, as I believe he did, he succeeded in producing something both less and more. He was unsure of his subject matter from the beginning and questioned its suitability for tragic drama. Only 'a certain bold faith' in himself [6] led him to continue. His faith proved not only justified but triumphant. The form that *Wallenstein* took under his hand is imposing, ordered, and 'classical,' despite the range of events it comprises. For Schiller presented his material not only in a dramatically effective but also a symbolically representative way. Upon a simple base that was yet fully suggestive of the broad, motley character of the historical setting, he erected a gradual concentration of persons and events which itself, pyramidlike, culminated in decisive action. History was articulated through the acts of individuals in the play, but not so much outwardly in the epic manner as inwardly, toward a center, in the manner of tragedy. One might even sense in the coming-to-a-head of its action the point of the dagger that assassinates the hero.

Yet the logic and inevitability in the action of the play, which lent structure to its material and dignity to its passions, tended to diminish its central figure. He cannot be brought to act. The events that present themselves to us in such ominously logical progression present themselves to Wallenstein's mind in the same way and rob him of his sense of individual will and purpose. No delusion of freedom lures this hero to act, but not because of his realism, as is so often claimed in an attempt to distinguish him from the more typically idealistic hero in Schiller, but because of his intelligence. He is not a man out of his element, a general in love, let us say, an Antony with a Cleopatra, but a general in war, and his fall partakes more of his profession and position than of his humanity.[7] *Wallenstein* is a historical tragedy in the true sense, a tragedy of history, not merely of a person in history.[8]

6 In a letter to Goethe, 13 November 1796.

7 The historical Wallenstein's stature as a general is unquestioned; see, for example, Francis Watson, *Wallenstein* (New York, 1938).

8 For a most balanced and thorough analysis of the tragedy in *Wallenstein* see Walter Hinderer, *Der Mensch in der Geschichte* (Königstein, 1980). Hinderer sees

When we think of *Wallenstein* as the imitation of an action, it is true
that character, will, and individuality appear subordinate to event and
circumstance. But when we regard the play as a paradigm of experience,
which we are more inclined to do from a later perspective that throws
the presuppositions of the past into new relief, the outward world, like
nature, seems almost grandly or nobly to contain rather than diminish
the individuals. It was not the realities of the Thirty Years War alone
that caused Schiller to see his hero as constrained, and ultimately rendered powerless, by the course of events. The concept of history in his
own times presupposed just such a constraint upon historical persons
once thought to act autonomously. Nor was the moral disdain with
which he came to regard Wallenstein, both the historical figure and
the character he had created in his play, a logical consequence of this
view. It resulted rather from his applying a traditional ethical standard
to a hero conceived and developed within a newly imagined human
and historical context, a newly imagined world. And Schiller himself
had created both the hero and the world, though he based both on
history. In other words, when confronted with what appeared to be a
threat to humanism in the new emphasis on the natural, cultural, political, and all but ideal or absolute grounds for human action, he seems
instinctively to have sought a solution in the light of the past. For what
satisfied the historian in Schiller and, if my view of the play is correct,
must have satisfied the dramatist did not satisfy the idealist and mor-
alist – the eighteenth-century man in him.

Most significantly, after *Wallenstein* the encroachment of history upon
morality ceases and Schiller, in full retreat, one feels, turns to romantic
drama in *The Maid of Orleans* (1801), to deliberately stylized tragedy
in *The Bride of Messina* (1803), to legend and epic theater in *Wilhelm
Tell* (1804). *Mary Stuart*, begun immediately after *Wallenstein* in 1800,
seems almost a betrayal of the earlier achievement. Schiller brought
the same genius for historical dramatization to this play and again
extracted his tragedy from the composite mind of the times he had
created. But he also introduced a personal conflict between his central

---

Schiller as similarly pressed in the matter of form and moving toward an epic
theater that anticipates Brecht (pp. 33–4).

figures that he had not found in history and that, while serving to
'humanize' their motives, at the same time tended to lower them.
Though Mary and Elizabeth had in fact never met, Schiller makes the
very center of his play a confrontation between them. A tragedy of
history had become a tragedy *ad hominem*.[9] Yet we remember that
drama has traditionally been a conflict between persons, not of forces
perceived through them. The important point with Schiller is that his
particular genius combined with his times produced a challenge to that
tradition and its concomitant esthetic by offering a vision of tragedy
depersonalized, as it were, but not dehumanized. The significance of
the challenge lay in its incorporating in the vision a sense of the contingent nature of human action which the tradition in its insistence
that tragedy take place in the soul of the individual had effectively
denied. What both *Wallenstein* and *Faust II* suggest through their dramatic action, though in wholly different ways, is a concept of the
individual as a participant in tragedy but not as its mover.[10] Just as
the age in general had begun to picture man within new contexts,
which no longer served merely as backdrops to his struggle in the
world but at the same time as templates of his nature and his being
in time, so the drama of the age was pressed to reflect the new images
in its own domain. Like Goethe, who when confronted with the
'monstrous'[11] extremes of form toward which his subject matter in
Faust was compelling him, put his classicism aside in order to complete
the work, Schiller in *Wallenstein* seems for once to have accepted the
amoral implications of the tragic action he had created. In both actions
we sense the times at work in the author and not the author in the
times. In fact, it is surprising that the only apparent point of contact
between the two greatest works from the greatest period of German
literature should be from their anomalous side. But it is for that reason

9 On completing *Wallenstein* Schiller wrote to Goethe of his 'need' and 'desire' to
turn 'to a freely imagined ... and purely emotional and human subject matter' –
'zu einem frei phantasierten ... bloß leidenschaftlichen und menschlichen Stoff'
(19 March 1799).

10 In *Wilhelm Meister's Apprenticeship* Goethe had distinguished the dramatic hero
from the hero of a novel by the *handelnd* ('active') nature of the former and the
leidend ('suffering' in the sense of undergoing experience or misfortune) nature of
the latter (bk. 5, ch. 7).
This distinction would no longer apply in *Faust II*.

11 'Monstrous,' 'barbarous,' 'strange' are words that he used to describe the form of
Faust; see below p. 17.

that they are contrasted here. The seemingly aberrant and displaced has begun in the light of later developments to take on the signs of progression.

Goethe was not concerned in *Faust* with history in the factual sense. The reflections of the past and of the real world present themselves in this work poetically, fantastically, symbolically, phantasmagorically. Nor do they offer themselves chronologically. They are pictures from the mind, not from reality.

Yet they are not for that reason the less, but the more, indicative of the deeper reality in the play. They are the template of the action, the guide to its meaning. The fantasy is not there as a poetic means of displaying what can be seen in the real world, the symbolism not there as a substitute for something that can otherwise be known, the phantasmagoria not there to compensate for the confines of the theater, but all are there to suggest the workings in the mind of culture and history internalized. If Schiller was forced in *Wallenstein* to strain the limits of traditional drama in order to reveal the nature of historical tragic action modernly conceived, Goethe was forced in *Faust II* to alter the form beyond recognition, to create a new form. His task was not only to reclaim for tragedy the broader forces at work in the objective world, which a hero-oriented tradition had tended to neglect or ignore, but to uncover beneath the surface reality of the objective world a more inevitable dynamics, a law or laws of nature, in the manner of science. It was in this special sense that I spoke of science playing the part in Goethe that history played in Schiller.

But therein lay the dilemma, if also the challenge that gave rise to the unique product that is Part II. For just as Schiller expressed the new mode of historical perception in the action of his dramas, in their fabric, and not merely in words, Goethe stated his new insights into nature, and the position of man in nature, artistically, poetically, and not simply as thought. 'I have ideas too,' he once remarked typically, 'but I give only the results.'[12] In no way, however, could the dramatic tradition supply him with a form to express his vision, if only because the essential question he raised about the human position in nature and in the universe had not been asked in the tradition. The answer

12 Conversation, Jean Paul, 19 [November or December] 1797.

was presumed to be known and thus presupposed in the background of any human action, in drama as in life. Goethe, and the age, were developing a different view. In one way or another, he would have to construct a form to accommodate and demonstrate the new view.

It was not a matter of choice. Not only was his commitment to the Faust theme in drama and not in another form, but his vastly more important commitment to the salvation of his hero, which tapped perhaps the deepest instinct in the age, brought other responsibilities. Faust could not be saved within a conventional moral framework, the limits of which his actions in Part I had far transgressed; and the creation of a new morality in which he could be justifiably redeemed required the identification in nature, history, and the human condition of antecedents to moral and tragic action unimagined and uninvented in the dramatic tradition, because unneeded. *Faust II* is a compendium of these antecedents poetically presented.

How Goethe arranged his poetic material, motivated his dramatic action, created or developed his characters in the second part of his work so differently than in the first, and why, are questions that will concern us throughout the analysis of the play. Why is the question that is pressed in the next chapter.

But it should already be clear from even a superficial reading of the text, and perhaps most clear from just such a reading, that the complexities on its surface cannot be unrelated to the workings of its inner structure. The variety of verse forms, the constantly changing modes and moods, the diverse action, the disparate concerns can hardly be reflections of a harmony or order hidden from our view. They seem, and surely are, signs of a development which far from resolving itself in terms of ever greater order, grew, with time, not clearer but more creative. *Faust* had its own evolution. It not only objectified, or sought to objectify, the unruly, subjective elements and urges of its earlier beginnings in a final, 'classical' conclusion; it also began, on the same principle, to encompass the conclusions themselves in broader frames of reference, in more comprehensive images. The classical allusions and classical verse forms which might seem to project an ideal vision of life, and the ideal means to express it, prove in contrast with the other projected worlds in the play less transcendent than passing, less ideal than historically determined. This applies as well to the Catholic heaven which opens up at the very end and which also proves a phase in an evolving vision, another attempt to 'fix in lasting thought / What appears in flux in the world around,'[13] despite its ultimate position. The display of poetic amplitude, which might seem on the surface of the work an impressive, but merely an impressive, mastery of forms, proves in light of its inner structure a complex invention born of a new and complex necessity. It is Goethe the master who writes Part II but not, as we are sometimes led to believe, Goethe the detached master serenely dispensing his wisdom just as, in contrasting tumult, he had given vent to his feelings in the *Sturm und Drang* of the earlier part of the tragedy. Rather it is the consummate poet who, in the mastery of his art, dares to confront the images and follow the paths that the particular genius of his work presents to him. We said that the monumentality of Schiller's *Wallenstein* derived in part from compromise in that his hesitation with his subject matter and its artistic and moral implications led him to press a traditional form – to its limits, to be sure, but not beyond. *Faust II* breaks the form and wrenches from the tradition a poetic product as unique in character as it seems inevitable in its times. The signs of this wrenching, then, are evidenced on its surface. The esthetic dislocation on the surface, in turn, is the reflection of a moral dislocation underneath.

For the question, ultimately, is not one of form. My point in comparing Schiller and Goethe in their later developments has not been to demonstrate that the two greatest proponents of German classicism were in fact other than classical in their two greatest works. It has been to suggest, however, that it is from their anomalous side, the side which seems better to have absorbed and reflected the deeper influences of the age, that their greatest achievements present themselves to our day. From this perspective, they offer an esthetic that is challenging and a humanism and morality that, if less reassuring, are more useful in our time.

13 Und was in schwankender Erscheinung schwebt,
  Befestiget mit daurenden Gedanken. (ll. 348–9)

CHAPTER TWO

Faust II and
the Darwinian Revolution

In a footnote to the Introduction of his *Origin of Species*, Darwin cites Goethe as among those earlier thinkers whose views in one way or another had anticipated his own. 'It is rather a singular instance of the manner in which similar views arise at about the same time, that Goethe in Germany, Dr. Darwin [his grandfather] in England, and Geoffroy Saint-Hilaire ... in France, came to the same conclusion on the origin of species, in the years 1794–95.' That is precisely my point. Whatever the differences in the concept of evolution that Goethe and Darwin separately espoused, and however significant those differences would eventually prove to be in subsequent scientific thought, they nevertheless partook of the common revolution in thinking that was occurring in the age.[1] Darwin refers here, of course, to Goethe the scientist,

---

1 The meaning of the word 'evolution' is itself evolving. It is thus perhaps best to speak of the concept as an 'evolutionist sense,' as does Günter Martin in a recent article, 'Goethes evolutionärer Sinn' (*Goethe-Jahrbuch*, vol. 105 [1988], pp. 247–69). Martin suggests that the difficulty we have in distinguishing between the strictly scientific and the more philosophical implications of the concept derives from the modern tendency to falsely separate the human from the physical sciences, thus obstructing understanding of an earlier age when this was not so clearly done. Goethe believed in what would later be called epigenesis, a theory of development that envisions a chain of new formations from a common beginning; the Darwinian theory envisions evolution as a series of mutations. The German words *Neubildung* and *Umbildung*, 'new formation' and 'transformation,' perhaps make the distinction most clearly. Before Darwin, the 'theory of evolution' was understood as a development or expansion of a pre-existing form (in effect, a homunculus) and was also called Preformation, a term which relates the idea of evolution to concepts dating back to Empedocles. Caspar Friedrich Wolff (1733–94) was the first to propose the theory of *Epigenese* against *Preformationstheorie* in Goethe's

but we note that he chooses to single out for recognition not any particular accomplishment of his early contemporary, but his general method or approach. The equivalent in art of method or approach in science, however, is form. While the scientific thought of the age played an important role in the creation of *Faust* almost from the beginning, it is to the form rather than the content of that thought that the second part of the work owes its unusual genius and with which the present chapter, for the most part, is concerned.

Darwin said of Goethe: 'He has pointedly remarked that the future question for naturalists will be how, for instance, cattle got their horns, and not for what they are used.'² We ask how *Faust II* came to have its form and not what purpose it served.

The question may seem idle, just as when applied in the scientific realm its implications are not at first clear. But the same distinction between the concept of creation by design and by adaptation that caused a revolution in thought when brought to bear in the natural world has a bearing also in the world of art. Not that the future question for criticism should be how a work of art got its form. Creation by design has been so persistent an assumption in the tradition that it seems almost a definition of art. It is only when a distinct departure from the norm takes place in a radical assertion of content over form that we can speak of a true variant having come into being and meaningfully ask the question.

Faust II provides such an opportunity, perhaps unprecedentedly. For the sense of form is the product of tradition, and what deviates significantly from the tradition will appear unformed and thus unartistic, unless, establishing itself, the deviant in turn becomes absorbed in a

---

time and that surely had something to do with the satire in Act II. Yet Goethe saw the human being as the crown of creation, for all that he may have regarded nature and the surrounding world of culture, politics, and art as eternally evolving. This is in contradistinction to Darwin and to Nietzsche. See, e.g., George Wells, 'Goethe and Evolution' (*Journal of the History of Ideas*, vol. 28 [1967], pp. 537–50). For Goethe's writings in geology and morphology, see Douglas Miller, ed. and trans., *Goethe: Scientific Studies* (New York, 1988).

2 This note appears in the second edition of *On the Origin of Species*. Darwin does not quote Goethe directly, but from Karl Meding, *Goethe als Naturforscher in Beziehung zur Gegenwart* (Dresden, 1860). Goethe does not in fact make his own analogy with cattle and their horns but rather in scientific terms which Meding obviously rendered more familiar in the interest of popularization.

new progression which gradually identifies, clarifies, and justifies its existence. This was the case with Romanticism. The tradition creates form and form is created by the tradition, after the fact. There are, to be sure, exceptions. One thinks of Dante's *Divine Comedy*, a work which no more evolved formally (its content is another matter) from a literary past than it produced a new poetic medium for the future. But Dante was creating within a framework of inherited moral and metaphysical values which he accepted, and reflected in his poem. Without the guide of form his meanings can be surmised from the suppositions underlying his work. Goethe was attempting in *Faust* to create a new set of values from a new set of suppositions. Here structure emerged not as a vehicle for the expression of ideas but as a mode of experience outside of which the new suppositions and values were not to be conveyed. It has been said of *Faust* that it does not express a philosophy so much as it creates a modern myth.

We have *Faust II* in transit. If we read the work against the past it seems propelled by its otherness away from the tradition and yet not toward any subsequent development that might serve to identify its purposes and explain its differences. This, again, is in regard to form, not matter. If there have been developments in art that throw *Faust II* into new perspective, they have come not from drama, or for that matter from literature, but from the visual arts. Here the revolution in form has succeeded not only in creating but in establishing new modes of perception. A kind of literary cubism does in fact suggest itself in the interrupted sequences and broken surfaces of *Faust II*. Goethe was conscious of this problem of re-creating reality in art: 'Since much of our experience does not allow itself to be expressed directly, I have long since used the device of conveying more hidden meanings by juxtaposing images one against the other and as it were mirroring themselves.'[3] It was as if the deeper currents in the age, or the deeper potential of the Faust theme which was its herald, had already prompted in the late Goethe a development that would subsequently emerge as a general and broad concern: the imitation in art of reality perceived, not by the eye but in the mind.

Goethe did not plan an original or experimental design for *Faust*. He placed little importance on originality, which he was more likely

---

3 In a letter to the Islamic scholar K.J.L. Iken, 27 September 1827.

to see as mannerism. Experimentation of the kind that the early German Romantics championed in their esthetic theory, if less in poetic practice, he scorned. His own originality derived not from novelty but from the ability to express wholly and truly what in others almost invariably appeared fragmentary or forced. The fundamental nature of his genius rested upon this wholeness of mind which we admire more than we can imitate. In his experimentation he also shunned novelty, choosing his models from classical or traditional, folk or popular literature. Rarely did he look to innovate. Only in his early, *Sturm und Drang* period do we find exceptions.

But how to account for the dramatically disjunctive structure of *Faust II*, for its apparent lack of wholeness, if it is not the product of originality or experimentation? It is the result of an evolution. The work from its inception seems to have followed an inner law or laws that more than considerations of art determined its course. Goethe often spoke of the work as if it had a life of its own. In a letter to his publisher, it is a 'witches' creation' – *ein Hexenprodukt*.[4] At the height of his classical period, which *Faust* spanned, as it spanned all other stages of his development in its long years in the making, he could refer to it in a letter to the art historian Hirt as a 'barbarism' from which he would happily be free.[5] To the end the work remained 'the strangest the world has seen or will see,' as he wrote to the composer Zelter.[6] And while Part II, with its five-act format and its verse forms derived from classical traditions, presents itself superficially as a balanced conclusion to a tumultuous beginning, in fact it represents a far more radical departure from the norm than Part I and gains its balance only through a revision, a re-seeing, of the dramatic form at a depth that meter, rhyme, and the division into acts do not touch. Yet the departure and the newly discovered vision were not the product of design so much as the result of demands and constraints upon the work that, gradually but inevitably accumulating, had somehow finally to be confronted and resolved. The form of *Faust II*, one might say, is what remained after all other matters had been settled except the matter of form.

Yet the play is not formless. 'Content brings form with it; form is never without content,' Goethe himself wrote in the plan of 1800.

4 To Cotta, 2 January 1799.
5 To Alois Hirt, 25 December 1797.
6 Karl Fr. Zelter, 6/7 June 1828.

Moreover, he held to this tenet, if that is what it may be called, this fact of art that becomes apparent and gains meaning only in the event of a mutation in form. Such an event was *Faust II*, a triumph of content over form which yet brought form with it.

How this occurred, and how it was possible, are questions that will concern us in general and in detail throughout this study. For the triumph of content over form, as I say, is the process of evolution itself. In citing Darwin and the evolutionist mode of thinking I was not merely using modern concepts to describe a phenomenon as easily understood simply as development and change, but seeking to identify the matrix of thought that produced both *Faust II* and *On the Origin of Species*, a revolution in art and a revolution in science.[7]

The age as a whole had eaten of the tree of scientific knowledge. Not only Goethe, who practiced science, but the poets of his and the later generation that his lifetime spanned show a remarkable awareness of the scientific developments in their times.[8] Remarkable, because we are often inclined, wrongly, to think of this era that we call Romantic as distancing itself from the world of science. We think rather of the *philosophes* of an earlier generation as joining the poetic and the scientific in their thought. But it was in natural history, as we noted at the outset, that the great advances of the age occurred, so that the so-called Romantic poets and writers in pursuing the subject that was in fact their characteristic concern – Nature – had their science where their interest lay. An affinity in structure rather than in content of thought again suggests itself in the separate fields. Thus, Schiller, who was exceptionally unconcerned with science, seems nevertheless through sheer application of his contemporary intelligence to have uncovered in history, and in the analysis of history in his dramas, the same kind of developmental contexts that were emerging in science to explain the phenomena of the natural world. The moral dilemma posed by the new understanding was the distinctly modern feature he brought to the concept of tragedy and yet, with its implications of determinism, historicism, and relativism, the feature that repulsed him. The dilemma

7 See Gertrude Himmelfarb, *Darwin and the Darwinian Revolution* (Garden City, NY, 1962). Her title suggested my chapter heading.
8 See Alexander Gode-von Aesch's excellent *Natural Science in German Romanticism* (New York, 1941).

drove him back, as we noted in the preceding chapter, upon an ideal-istic moral position, a position prevalent *in* the age but, by its absolutist nature, not truly *of* the age. Similarly, Herder, who gained that title he is sometimes accorded of 'father' of modern history precisely through the importance he placed on historical development as a determinant in human action, failed to draw new moral conclusions from the base he had newly conceived for human behavior. Herder, it is true, was a pastor and his moral precepts were tied to religion. But it is also true that he did not write dramas, which is a form of expression, a mode of discourse that demands a moral resolution in a way that history and science do not.

In *Faust II* Goethe fully absorbed the implications of the science and thought of his day and drew the ultimate conclusions. It was not that his science went deeper than that of his literary contemporaries, though surely it did. But whereas Balzac, for example, cited the work of the celebrated naturalists of the era, Buffon, Cuvier, and Geoffroy Saint-Hilaire, as analogous to his own great undertaking in *The Human Comedy*,[9] Goethe made the bridge with science in principle. The extent to which the form of *Faust II* deviates from the dramatic tradition is a measure of the depths at which his thought conflicted with the view of human action on which the traditional dramatic forms were pred-icated. There is no suggestion of such a departure for the novel in *The Human Comedy*.[10] Nor do we find in general in Goethe a radical mo-rality radically portrayed. *Faust* is alone in pressing the question,[11]

9 In the preface (1842) to the series of novels under that title. In *The Wild Ass's Skin*, ch. 1, is the remark: 'Is not Cuvier the greatest poet of our century?' The contrast with the English Romantic poets is interesting. 'Much of the new poetry tended to devote itself to revealing man's inner nature ... This position tended to make po-etry and science antagonistic, or to render one a continuation of, or development from, the other. The former point of view was supported by Coleridge and his followers, who regarded these spheres as entirely antithetical. Wordsworth, on the other hand, felt that even "the remotest discoveries of the chemist, the botanist, or mineralogist, will be as proper objects of the Poet's art if the time should ever come when these things shall be familiar to us ... as enjoying and suffering beings" ' (Ralph B. Crum, *Scientific Thought in Poetry* [New York, 1931], p. 129). See also Frederick Burwick, *The Damnation of Newton: Goethe's Theory and Roman-tic Perception* (Berlin and New York, 1986).

10 Balzac does *plan* a series of 'études analytiques,' 'études philosophiques,' 'études des moeurs,' which were to illustrate the *principles* of human behavior.

11 *Die Wahlverwandtschaften* also derives a radical morality from a scientific premise, but the novel is not radical in its artistic form.

though less in its capacity as a philosophical poem than in the condition of its being. The pact, or wager, it concludes with the Devil requires that it demonstrate in its action what it presumes in its thought, and that thought was different from any thought that had come before.

The Renaissance has been described as a secularization of an essentially religious frame of mind inherited from the Middle Ages.[12] Goethe, as if in an inevitable next step, sought a naturalization of the abstract moral and metaphysical principles of the preceding age through the scientific understanding that was the mark of his own age. His view did not preclude what had come before, rather it reinterpreted or, better, co-interpreted the ways of God to man in terms of the laws of nature. The Prologue in Heaven of Part I had already set the pattern. From the higher vantage point it afforded, but now in the physical sense, Goethe was able to effect the transmission of his science into poetry by the description from eternity of the earth in its turbulent, almost violent atmosphere that was the arena in which the action would play itself out. The description is as physically accurate as it is poetically striking and dramatically relevant. The point is not its scientifically conceived accurateness, however, nor its expressive beauty, but its reminder that the physical and the poetic are one, or, at least, they strive to be one. Goethe in the essay *On Morphology* stated: 'One forgot that science had developed out of poetry; one did not consider that after a revolution in time the two might again meet on a higher plane, to their mutual advantage.'[13]

Appropriately, then, *Faust*, Part II begins with what has been called a 'prelude on earth.'[14] The contrast helps to relate the two parts – an impression Goethe attempted to reinforce in any minor way as he faithfully developed the theme in his work at the expense of its dramatic continuity. But the importance of this second prologue lies again in its physical, and thus philosophical, positioning of man. The Faust who, standing on earth, looks to heaven, to the sun, in order to know and to see, must turn away blinded, as if in a scientific confirmation

---

12 Robert Ergang has written that 'the secularization of life, thought and culture is the essence of the Renaissance' (*The Renaissance* [New York, 1967], p. v).

13 *Zur Metamorphose der Pflanzen. Schicksal der Druckschrift*, 1817 (Artemis edition, vol. 17, p. 90).

14 Stuart Atkins in his discussion of Pleasant Landscape in *Goethe's Faust: A Literary Analysis* (Cambridge, Mass., 1964), p. 101.

of the religious or philosophical concept that certain truths are not allowed to man. Faust turns his back to the sun so that he may see by its reflected light: 'So let the sun behind me stand.'[15] This position of man in the universe, in 'die große Welt,' which is the composite world of times and places in the play, determines the nature and development of its action just as the glimpse of the turbulence in his physical setting anticipated the inner life of the individual in 'die kleine Welt' of Part I.

A transformation and naturalization of morality also occurs immediately in Part II. The Faust who has sinned so greatly in the Gretchen tragedy is not made to repent and so proceed as hero and protagonist in a new action. He is made to sleep. Sleep 'removes the burning shaft of keen remorse,' as does repentance; sleep 'bathes him in the dew of Lethe's stream,'[16] restoring him to life, as if nature were causing with time what morality causes through sentiment. Not that the transforming of the philosophical and the moral into the physical and the natural introduces a new vision in which the scientific grasp or basis of reality would substitute for the abstract and diffused concepts in earlier thought. *Faust* in fact ends with a religious epilogue. But the religiously colored ending is no more a concession to the historical setting of the theme than is the biblically allusive Prologue in Heaven, as fitting as both might be. Nor, conversely, does it represent a final, transcendent vision. Like the poetic and the scientific, the moral and the natural, it is yet another metaphor, a co-interpretation.

The structure of Part II is designed to bring the audience or the reader, but not Faust, to that recognition. 'Everything transitory / Is but a metaphor,' as the Chorus Mysticus says in summary at the end of the play. His progress will be the reliving of the deeper antecedent experience that brings him to an ultimate resolution, a 'final wisdom' in his time, as if he were a child of the collective unconscious. Our progress is a growing awareness of that process.

Faust II is there more for us, as *Faust I* was there for the hero. At times we observe with him events in which he himself has little active

---

15 My translation of 'So bleibe denn die Sonne mir im Rücken' (l. 4715).
16 'Entfernt des Vorwurfs glühend bittre Pfeile' (l. 4624) / ... 'Dann badet ihm im Tau aus Lethes Flut' (l. 4629).

part. The action itself, by its nature, is almost always at one remove, for us in the sense that we are experiencing illusion or poetry, for him in that he knows that the substance of his life is not 'real' but the product of magic. When he attempts to make real his union with Helen of Troy, initially at the end of Act I and again at the end of Act III, his attempts are frustrated. If we in turn try to grasp an objective reality behind the symbolism in the play, or behind a physical reality a metaphysical truth, we will be similarly misled. These terms will have become metaphors, and magic will have joined their ranks. Magic is here another word for poetry, which also creates from nothing.

Yet, as allusive, imaginative, recondite, and, at times, playful as *Faust II* may be, its underlying theme is that of time and place. This is not the time and place of traditional drama, to be sure. Nor is it the time and place of historical fact, which would have compromised the purpose of the play in moving its hero through different worlds of thought and states of mind. For these worlds were conceived not simply as products of earlier causes in a continuity leading to a present but as truly evolving, with a life and development in their own right, and in that sense free. The fantastic countenance of the work, its literary cubistic aspect, reflects the need that Goethe felt to keep these worlds distinctly separate so that they would better tell against one another and against the world and state of mind that would ultimately obtain for Faust in his moment of decision in *his* time and place. That was the purpose: to resolve within a single sphere of existence a problem separately and differently resolved in other spheres in the play; to frame the moral choice within always deepening and broadening contexts.

What these contexts were will be discussed when they emerge separately. I mention here time and place only to suggest that Goethe's poetic rendering of the past has less to do with poetry and fantasy than with his understanding of history as influencing the unconscious no less than the conscious actions of men, that is, his understanding of history as culture. In this understanding lay an answer to the question that had initially been raised in *Urfaust*, that is in the early period of revolt when Goethe himself, like Faust, saw little use in a knowledge of history, if indeed it were attainable. There the past seemed 'a book with seven seals' and our attempts to explain other times a futile effort resulting in a mere reflection of our own times.[17] Part II, through the medium of poetry, breaks the seal and penetrates the past in a way that it may be known and absorbed. When we enter the world of classical antiquity, for example, we hear the steady and measured rhythms of greek tragedy, the iambic trimeters; when Helen joins Faust in the modern world she notes its rhymed speech, that symbolic expression of a state of mind poised between remembrance and anticipation – the modern, the romantic state. The two worlds are there in their very verse forms.

How did the work come to have its form? I repeat the question, not rhetorically with a view to summarizing the answers already stated or implied, but in order to make a final point. For while our present discussion has indicated the many reasons why traditional forms could not serve Goethe as his drama took on more and more the colorings and suppositions of a new era in thought, still it has not suggested what form could and did serve.

Faust II, we said, is not formless. Yet its structure in depth, its juxtaposing of material and motifs in abrupt and unforeseen sequence, casts the whole into such extraordinary and unique relief that we are made, not so much to see its content in a new light, as to alter our mode of thinking in order to be able to 'see.' It is not surprising that when the work first appeared, in 1832, it was not judged with much understanding. Instead it was viewed against the past, and a manner of thinking born of the past was used to judge it. The lack of dramatic cohesion in the play was attributed to the waning powers in the aged author who had after all brought himself to complete his *Faust* only in the last years of his life.[18] An inversion of this critique found willfulness rather than lack of clarity (though both might be symptoms of senility) in the face that *Faust II* presented and, in recognizing the multiplicity of perspective afforded the work by its apparently total

17 In the original version: 'Was ihr den Geist der Zeiten heißt, / Das ist im Grund der Herren eigner Geist, / In dem die Zeiten sich bespiegeln' (ll. 224ff.).
18 Otto Pniower, in 'Fausts zweiter Teil,' *Dichtungen und Dichter: Essays und Studien* (Berlin, 1912), p. 74, is most dogmatic on this point. Wilhelm Emrich sees this approach to the question as typical of nineteenth-century German criticism of *Faust II* (*Die Symbolik von Faust II* [Bonn, 1957], p. 66).

freedom of form, at the same time denied that freedom as such to art. 'Every work of art must convey its infinite meaning in finite form.'[19] Nor did later critical literature on *Faust II* answer the questions raised by the initial reaction. The tendency was to resolve the problems presented by the text within the larger frame of reference that is Goethe himself in his works and total development. The censure was gone but the sense of esthetic displacement, which is the initial and persistently striking feature of our experience of *Faust II*, remained.

For the challenge from the beginning was not to uncover a hidden design either within or outside the work that would create new and elaborate harmonies. The challenge, I believe, was to pose the question that was impossible to pose from within an esthetic that presupposed design and purpose as the beginning and the end, the goal, of creativity. Not why *Faust II* took its unique form, but how, was to be the question. For, once posed, an answer would lie close to hand.

The answer lay in the motif of magic. The element of magic, so indigenous to the theme and in such potentially radical opposition to the concept of order as to attract the young *Sturm und Drang* Goethe when he first conceived *Faust*, grew as the work itself grew. What had served mainly as accompaniment to the action in Part I became its mover and shaper in Part II and thus its dramatic expression. From the background in the play, magic emerged as foreground and altered the mode of perception. One senses Goethe himself attempting to resist this poetic development as he time and again plans and then abandons scenes and motif which would have created links with logic and traditional thought. It was as if he had deliberately to suppress those conceptual instincts that were part of his times and his literary heritage in order to allow creative urges that anticipated the future to hold sway. The transition from the 'little' to the 'great world' required more than a mere extension of time and place, as it proved. The relation of cause and effect had also to be adjusted if a new sense of life and view of things were to emerge. In true evolutionary fashion, the element of

---

19 Friedrich Theodor Vischer acknowledges the 'Unendlichkeit der Perspektive' in *Faust II*, but warns: 'Jedes Kunstwerk soll in endlicher Form die unendliche Bedeutung tragen, keinem soll diese Perspektive fehlen; bei Goethes "Faust" aber springt das Auge über Vordergrund und Mittelgrund jeden Augenblick weg, um sich in dieser unendlichen Aussicht zu verlieren ...' (quoted in Karl R. Mandelkow, *Goethe im Urteil seiner Kritiker*, vol. 2 [Munich, 1977], p. 180).

magic in the play both allowed and forced this adjustment. It provided the freedom to create patterns and juxtapositions of reality that exist in the mind but not in time, while establishing in the process an order of thought from which there was no return in the play.

Goethe does not use magic to account for the unaccountable in *Faust II*. So employed, the motif only reestablishes the order it is designed to upset. So employed, nothing changes in the world in which magic has occurred and the perception of that world remains the same. But Goethe was intent on altering perception. Mephistopheles alighting in the first scene of Act IV in seven-league boots that would account for the great distances he is supposed to have traversed is the exception. The rule is the fate of Helen. Evoked as a phantom by Mephistopheles, she then materializes in her own realm, only to vanish literally into the air when she takes leave of Faust. Magic giveth and magic taketh away. Not that the inexplicability, the mystery, of these occurrences was the purpose in their design. Nor was the transitoriness of things their intended meaning. The world of *Faust II* is presented in abrupt disjunctions, phantasmagorically, but not on the assumption that there exists in essence outside the work a world similarly designed. The play is not an imitation, a representation. Yet it is also not a fantasy. The past, or rather the pasts, it evokes are meant as real, as realities in poetic guise, and it is only against the background they form that the final resolution in the play gains its true significance. But the presentation of this past is unusual in that it offers neither a continuous action, in the manner of history, nor a concentrated action, in the manner of drama. It presents rather the past contained in the present, multilayered, as it exists in the mind, as it exists in culture.

Magic made possible the transfer of this vision to the stage.[20] But

---

20 Goethe contradicts himself on the question whether *Faust II* was intended for the theater, at times speaking of the effectiveness of certain motives or scenes when imagined on the stage, at others seeming to dismiss the possibility of a performance of the play. ('Almost unthinkable,' to Eckermann, 20 December 1829.) He speaks directly of an 'audience' and of 'the performance' in his 'Ankündigung' to the *Helena*, which might more easily have been staged. On the question of performing the whole work, he says to Eckerman, 20 December 1829, 'Geht nur und laßt mir das Publikum, von dem ich nichts hören mag. Die Hauptsache ist, daß es geschrieben steht.' On the problems and challenges of staging a modern performance of *Faust II*, see, e.g., Jocelyn Powell, 'Reflections on Staging *Faust*, Part II' (*Publications of the English Goethe Society*, n.s., vol. 48 [1978], pp. 52–80).

in the process, and in the necessity, of suspending time and the laws
of cause and effect, which magic by its nature prescribes, it also replaced
the sense of history or life or drama as progression by a new sense or
experience of the constant emergence of things within a context. By
evoking the past within the present, realities within a reality or, if one
will, illusions within the illusion or fiction that is the work of art itself,
magic created or induced a way of seeing no longer compatible with
the traditional view (whence the disjunction) but suggestive of the
altered mode of thought in the new age. Magic effected here in the
realm of poetry what the new concept of time had brought about in
the science of the day, an opening onto a world of the past vastly
expanded in its relation to man, a 'große Welt.' I am not speaking of
Darwin and the specialized concept of evolution but of the more generalized development that had occurred earlier and created what we
called at the outset of this chapter the structure or form in the thought
of both Darwin and Goethe, and in the poetic no less than the scientific
writings of the latter. The phenomenon of emergence in the physical,
plant, and animal worlds was his concern from the beginning in his
scientific work and it found its least sober, perhaps, but most illumi-
nating expression in his search for a plant primeval from which all
plant life had emerged, his *Urpflanze*. Yet life as constant emergence
within a context was a model of thought he had encountered as well
outside the realm of science, in the realm of history. The concept of
history as culture that we associate with Herder and further identify
in Goethe is an evolutionist concept simply in its view of the unfolding
of events not as progression but as process. In its modern, laboratory
sense the word 'culture' means growth in a medium.

The form or structure of *Faust* as a whole, to repeat, evolved. The
very fact of a second part to the work was less the result of design
than necessity. It was not the desire to explore a universe newly measured and history newly conceived that prompted the journey into the
great world. The central action alone, the issue of good and evil, when
re-seen and developed within the new mode of thought produced of
itself the kind of expanding contexts not found in earlier forms of drama
because not present in earlier forms of thinking. Like the phenomena
of nature, good and evil were no longer to be conceived abstractly or
absolutely, created once and for all in the nature of man as the universe
itself had been created once and for all at some beginning in time. A
Faust drama in one part was not to be written any more, as it were.

Just as magic had emerged from its mainly poetic and atmospheric role to transform the conceptual and perceptual character of the play, the moral issue, newly conceived, transformed the concept of the hero and the nature of the dramatic action. There is every evidence that the Faust of *Urfaust* was not conceived as a representative hero, as a symbol of Western man, which he became only later. The great world was not created as an arena for the actions of a representative Faust, therefore, so much as he became that figure by his presence and his actions in that great world. The moral issue determined the dramatic development, not the dramatic the moral, which is the case in traditional drama that offers objective reality as a confrontation in which the actions of the hero or heroine are tested and not, as here, as a context in which they are understood. This distinction becomes more important when we attempt to define the moral character and justify the salvation of Faust, whose actions are too often seen simply as the product of an individual will rather than the expression at a given stage of a cultural evolutionary process. The proliferation of dimensions that comprises *Faust II* reflects this process; and to read only its last act as a fitting conclusion to Part I, which is often done when the work is read in translation and one seeks its 'essential meaning,' is to miss the point.[21] Its meaning, and its drama, if a different type of drama, lie in the comprehensively imagined worlds that surround and define the action and project it beyond. *Faust* does not come to a conclusion so much as it reaches a point that can be declared a present. It brings us to where we are in time, which is the only conclusion possible in an evolutionist mode of thought.

Goethe did not need Darwin in order to carry out his evolutionist intention in *Faust II*. An awareness of the mechanics of evolution, which was the achievement of Darwin and alone rendered the theory scientific,[22] might well have hampered him. The fantastic creatures, half-

21 It was also one of the reactions in the misunderstanding of the work when it first appeared: 'Für die Geschichte Fausts an sich, dramatisch genommen, könnten vielleicht die vier ersten Akte ganz wegfallen' (quoted in Mandelkow, *Goethe*, vol. 2, p. 68). This contention is repeated in effect by Heinrich Rickert in *Goethes Faust: Die dramatische Einheit der Dichtung* (Tübingen, 1932).

22 Manfred Wenzel makes this simple and most important point at the beginning of his extensively thorough study 'Goethe und Darwin: Goethes morphologische Schriften in ihrem naturwissenschaftshistorischen Kontext' (Dissertation, Bochum, 1982).

man, half-beast, who pass through the Classical Walpurgis Night in
playful tableau might have lost their suggestive powers had they been
made to resemble a scientifically imagined reality. Instead, Goethe
adapted, he 'naturalized,' myth. He placed his sphinxes, centaurs, griffins, pygmies, and other legendary creatures in a perspective that was
concerned with the emergence of earth forms and physical beings and
thus included them in his grand theme of a developing universe. We
think of science too often as preceding poetry in the arrival at truth
and indeed praise those poets who are even aware of its discoveries.[23]
It is rare that we can identify, as here in the example of Goethe, Darwin,
and evolution, the truer picture of a new sense of things, a 'truth,'
coming into being in separate realms in its separate ways. Not that
Goethe contributes to science with his parade of creatures from myth.
This is Goethe the poet, not the scientist, speaking. But he contributes
to the evolution of thought, as he leads us to discover in these pro-
jections of the primitive mind the element of animal interrelatedness
that will eventually become scientific theory. If science and poetry come
together in Goethe, it is because he believed they emerge from a common source. They were, after all, combined in him.

But *we* need Darwin in order to understand *Faust II*, if not in its
content, in the particulars of its form. We are dealing here with a work
that not only reflects a mode of thought but is itself best understood
within that mode. We spoke of magic as a mechanism in its evolution,
as a factor or motif given in the legend but made now to serve not
only a new but a necessary function. Magic opened up a world hidden
by the traditional imitation or representation of reality in art, the very
world or context within which the new sense of the human condition
alone could be portrayed. Or, more accurately, it reopened a world in
which the spiritual and abstract underpinnings and antecedents of experience once had their place and filled it with natural causes. The
completed *Faust* stands in that relation to the *Divine Comedy*. Paradoxically, the broadest movement in literature from Dante to Goethe
was toward a verisimilitude or realism which, at least in drama, came

---

23 In ch. V, 'Poetry Champions Evolution: Goethe,' Crum (*Scientific Thought*) looks
for reflections of the new scientific view only in Goethe's didactic poems and not
in the inner structure of his art. Since Thomas S. Kuhn's *The Structure of Scientific
Revolutions* (Chicago, 1970) we have come to see the relation of science to its
times in a new light.

to exclude more and more of the reality that was considered more and more the truly real. In *Faust II*, magic interrupted the progression to reveal a new real world.[24]

Goethe did not deliberately create a disjunctive whole in *Faust* so much as he omitted or discarded elements of dramatic and thematic continuity that would have served to 'complete' the work, but at the same time belie its content. A completed form implied a completed world. Many of the plot factors and motifs contained in the plans, sketches, notes, and verse jottings to *Faust*, as we shall see, will suggest familiar and traditional links in motivation and logic, and their abandonment an uneasiness with just such explicit design. But it was not by default alone that the great disjunction of form, and thus the great freedom of allusion, arose in *Faust II*. Rather the development in the composition of the work, its internal evolution which produced the external form, was itself the determining factor.

Long before Act I, Goethe had conceived and in part written a *Helena*, a planned 'Interlude to Faust,' which, altered, eventually became Act III. Begun in his classical period, the *Helena* was an uncompromising imitation of ancient tragedy, with a Chorus and in classical meters. Goethe had thus fashioned a separate world in its own right, which was not to be joined artistically, but only conceptually, to the other worlds in *Faust*, including the world of Part I. In the awareness of this fact and this necessity, we sense, unable to join, he began artistically and formally to put asunder. He now created each world in its own right and with its own laws of composition, each 'a little world standing on its own.'[25] He would trust, as he said when the work was finally completed, that 'the idea of the whole will present itself to the intelligent reader, though he will not be lacking in transitions to supply.'[26]

---

24 The great world that Calderon opens up in his dramas is sometimes cited as a precedent for the 'große Welt' that Goethe creates in *Faust II*, but Calderon is drawing on a world and universe already preconceived in Catholic doctrine, as we noted earlier in the similar comparison with Dante, whereas Goethe was attempting to reflect a view only newly emerging and as yet to take established form either in thought or in art. On Calderon and Goethe see, e.g., Swana Hardy, *Goethe, Calderon und die Theorie des romantischen Dramas* (Heidelberg, 1965); also Stuart Atkins, 'Goethe, Calderon and *Faust II*,' *Germanic Review*, vol. 28 (1953), pp. 83–98.

25 As Goethe said of Act IV to Eckermann, 13 February 1831.

26 To Wilhelm von Humboldt, 1 December 1831; similarly in a conversation with his

Like magic, the *Helena* had functioned as an evolutionary mechanism. The part had not been inspired and created by the design, the design was inspired and created by the part.

Yet this 'supplying of meaning,' an expression Goethe used as well in reference to *Wilhelm Meisters Wanderjahre*,[27] was to be no mere esthetic exercise. The becoming aware of what one unconsciously knows through culture, through the living but disjunctive experience of the past, was also a moral imperative: 'Would thou possess thy heritage ... render it thine own.'[28] *Faust II* brings us through the past, in its broadest and deepest human sense, to a present, but not in the manner in which we experience history, or experience knowledge that is presented already possessed and therefore not for our own possessing, but as poetry and culture are experienced. We noted above that poetry, like magic, provided an appropriate means of expressing the vision in *Faust II* of evolving views of life, views that are to be understood as changing in time. We may now say that it was the only means. For in this way *Faust* itself, as poetry, as cultural artifact, takes its place in the very development it was created to describe.

---

assistant Fr. Wilhelm Riemer, undated, 1830/31. Eckermann himself speaks of a 'set of small world circles [in *Faust*], which, enclosed within themselves, certainly affect, but have little do with, one another' (13 February 1831).

27 Quoted in Klaus F. Gille, *Wilhelm Meister im Urteil der Zeitgenossen* (Assem, 1971), p. 283.

28 From Part I: 'Was du ererbt von deinen Vätern hast, / Ewirb es, um es zu besitzen' (ll. 682–3).

CHAPTER THREE

Act I: The Prologue
in Nature

The separate worlds, or spheres of existence, that Goethe created in
Faust II are comprehended in a larger world of thought. Part I began
with a prologue in heaven. Part II begins with a prologue on earth,
although it is not so named,[1] in which, from the reverse position below,
an eternal act of the universe, the rising of the sun, is observed. Both
visions create the perspective and provide the light in which the events
that unfold are to be judged.

The prologue to Part II not only takes place on earth, it is *of* the
earth. The task of bringing Faust from the 'horror' of Part I, to use
Goethe's word,[2] to a new envisioning of the position of man in the
universe is completed by and in nature. The setting, first of dusk and
then of the rising sun, encompasses the night and the sleep which
bathe Faust in forgetfulness, so that he awakens inwardly forgiven.
'No trial is held, [as] might happen with human judges,' Goethe remarked of the scene.[3] The rebirth of the day accompanies Faust's own
rebirth and is both its cause and its symbol, the thing and what we
think of it. Faust's remark on awakening, 'You, Earth, survived this
night, as [did] I,'[4] suggests his sense of having joined with nature in
undergoing a process of which his conscious mind had not become

---

1 Reinhard Buchwald also speaks of Pleasant Landscape as a 'Vorspiel zum zweiten
  Teil' (*Führer durch Goethes Faust* [Stuttgart, 1964], p. 117).
2 To Eckermann, 12 March 1826.
3 To Eckermann, Part II, 1829/30.
4 'Du, Erde, warst auch diese Nacht beständig' (l. 4681). I follow Stuart Atkins
  (*Goethe's Faust* [Boston, 1984]) in his translation of *auch* as referring to *Erde*, not to
  Nacht, and thus relating to Faust.

aware. In default of human will, nature had provided the continuity. I leave aside the question whether Goethe succeeds in having us forgive as nature forgives. But that his intent in Part II was to naturalize and despiritualize morality, and in general to seek a generic and objective cause in the actions and will of the individual, and in events, is clear. That is where his drama lay. The development, moreover, had already begun in Part I when in its prologue 'sin,' in the context of an earth enveloped in the alternating darkness and light in which man must seek his way, was re-envisioned as error: 'Man will err so long as he strives.' Not that the new word will now be made to substitute for the old, any more than the concept and image of the river Lethe is to be replaced by the notion of time as healer or that of conscious remorse by the unconscious workings of the mind in sleep.[5] These concepts and images, to repeat, are co-interpretations. They represent the multilayered nature of reality as it is uncovered by the mind.[6]

The Prologue in Heaven, by its very title, gained access to Christian analogy. The prologue on earth was bound to nature, and for the forces of nature the Christian tradition had created no myths. When Goethe was faced with the need to invent a voice that could express the inner transformation that his hero undergoes, he had at his disposal neither a Good Angel nor, since the action was to be understood as unconscious, the conventional device of a monologue. He chose a figure from Shakespeare, Ariel. With a chorus of spirits hovering above the distraught body of Faust, Ariel leads a song which through its music and its poetry casts over the whole scene a 'cloak of reconciliation.'[7] These spirits are moved by the figure before them, 'whether he be saint or sinner.'[8]

The importance of this choice lay less in its appropriateness than in the precedent it now set. Literature could substitute for myth in the further development of Faust II. By introducing Ariel, an agent of good

---

5 'In the Platonic tradition the human being is educated *into*, in the Goethean tradition *out of* religion' (D.A.B. Kayβler, *Fragment aus Platons und Goethes Pädagogik* [1821]; quoted in Gille, *Wilhelm Meister*).
6 A similar sense of the multilayered in painting is described by Goethe in his essay on 'Ruisdael as Poet' where he speaks of the 'sukzessiv bewohnte Welt' in the painting *The Waterfall*. The world of *Faust II* is also a 'successively inhabited world.'
7 To Eckermann, 12 March 1826.
8 'Ob er heilig, ob er böse' (l. 4619).

as well as seeming evil in *The Tempest*,[9] Goethe was calling upon Shakespeare to support him in the belief in the rightness of nature beyond morality. In Act III he will personify the spirit of modern poetry in Euphorion, a figure meant to stand for Byron. These are examples from among the more apparent motifs that Goethe 'ensecreted' – *hineingeheimnisset* – in the work.[10] More important is the immeasurable variety of verse forms, meters, tones, and poetic styles that the decision to leave nothing unembodied in his grand vision entailed. For the worlds he created in that vision brought these different forms with them. The freedom of form that is so apparent on the surface of *Faust II* reflects not the desire for variety but a refusal to homogenize the experience of a changing reality in uniform verse.[11] Not only the world of Helen of Troy is evoked in indigenous form. Other worlds of thought and experience, and strands and layers of worlds within them, are heard in their own meters and forms. In Act IV the Emperor in taking council at his court will suddenly speak in the alexandrine verse that calls up the ancien régime whose spirit and influence is seen to persist into the contemporary world. The poet who has Helen remark on the rhymed speech that Faust brings with him from another realm will have us too hear different times and ages in the different voices in his poem.

Yet in the monologue that Faust now speaks on awakening, Goethe expresses a vision that goes beyond time and place in a worldly sense and touches on the universal. The monologue is written in the terza rima of the *Divine Comedy*.[12] Not through this analogy or through any abstraction from beyond does the monologue gain transcendence, but, rather, by its very rootedness in time and place in the physical world. The place and time, however, are universally human. The place, earth, as Faust watches the rising sun, establishes the inevitable and eternal

9 Ariel is the nature spirit who is the cause of a shipwreck at the beginning of the play from which all are saved.
10 In a letter to Zelter, 26 July 1828.
11 There is no universal verse form, though prose may more easily be said to remain neutral. Yet prose also surely has rhythms that belong to different ages or different strata of society.
12 On Dante and 'Pleasant Landscape' see Paul Friedländer, *Rhythmen und Landschaften im zweiten Teil des Faust* (Weimar, 1953). He quotes Marie de Flavigny: '[Goethe] qui chache sous la robe et le nom du reprouvé docteur Faust les témérités de Spinoza est le système suspect de Geoffroy Saint-Hilaire' (p. 7).

relationship of man to the source of light and of energy, that is, to life. The time, sunrise, marks the eternal rebirth of energy and the inevitable renewal of light, so that the monologue in its setting encompasses existence at an irreducible level. Yet the monologue here is first an action and only then a contemplation. The same forces that caused a rebirth in Faust after the tragedy of Part I impel him further toward energy and light. He gazes toward the rising sun, glorying in the new day – and on its appearance it blinds him! He turns away in pain – *vom Augenschmerz durchdrungen*.[13] He had been repulsed in the same way by the Earth Spirit to whom he had turned at the very beginning of the drama in hope and expectation.

The monologue cannot simply end in the repulsion from light. For Faust now to despair utterly or, reborn, to continue only blindly in his search would merely repeat the pattern of tragic action in Part I. There elation and dejection, hope and disillusion formed lesser deaths and rebirths that culminated in the attempt at suicide, itself then thwarted by nature and the coming of a new day: 'A tear wells up. Earth has me again!'[14] The Gretchen tragedy followed. If Part II was to transcend Part I it could only be in a comprehensive and comprehending absorption of what has gone before, in full honoring, as it were, of the death of Part I before it proceeds in its own rebirth. When Faust turns from the blinding sun in order now to see and know only by its reflected light – 'So let the sun *behind* me stand!' – he evokes in fact an image, which, though physically present, recalls his life in the drama to that point. The image is a waterfall which 'through rocky cleft that roars, [falls], / In thousand torrents to the depths below ...'[15] In Part I, Faust himself is the waterfall, an 'Inhuman monster, aimless and unblest, / Who like the greedy [torrent], from rock to rock, / Sweeps down the dread abyss ...'[16] But now there is the sun, and from its light *and* from

---

13 Line 4703.
14 'Die Träne quillt, die Erde hat mich wieder!' (l. 784). The equation of water with life will become deliberate in the closing scenes of the Classical Walpurgis Night.
15 Der Wassersturz, das Felsenriff durchbrausend ...
   Von Sturz zu Sturzen wälzt er jetzt in tausend ...   (ll. 4716–18)
16 Der Unmensch ohne Zweck und Ruh',
   Der wie ein Wassersturz von Fels zu Felsen brauste ...   (ll. 3349–50)
   The English translation, like the original, and perhaps both are unpremeditated, repeats a number of words in both passages: *Wassersturz, Fels zu Felsen/Felsenriff,*

the restless spray of the torrential waters, emerges, and physically alone can emerge, the symbol that joins the two parts of the work, the rainbow.

Much has been written about the symbol of the rainbow in its relation to the esthetic, philosophical, and scientific concerns and theories that occupied Goethe in the years of concentrated effort to complete *Faust*.[17] The rainbow symbolized for Goethe the scientist, no less than the poet, the very nature of reality or truth as it is experienced in the mind. 'The true, which is identical with the divine, can never be known by us directly. We see it only as reflection, as example, as symbol, in separate and in related things. We are aware of it as unfathomable – and cannot deny ourselves the wish despite that fact to grasp it. This applies to all phenomena in the intelligible world.'[18]

Pure light is not given to us, but only regiven in the colors that attach themselves to the things of the world in wondrous display. For Goethe maintained, in angry opposition to Newton and accepted theory, that color resulted from the reflection of pure light on matter, which provided the 'darkness' (*das Trübe*) of which in part it is made. But beauty also, like light, attaches to objects. Mephistopheles, the son of darkness and the enemy of light, had already deplored that fact: 'From [objects] it streams, them it makes fair.'[19] The anger against Newton, therefore, which Goethe expressed with surprising vehemence in the polemical section of his *Theory of Colors*, had less to do with pride of place in scientific matters than with the sense that his own, unmediated experience of the real world, and with it the foundations of his art, were undermined by the mechanistic view of reality represented in Newton. For Newton, according to Goethe, color existed

---

brauste/brausend. In Swanwick there is 'surge' where I have inserted 'torrent,' but Swanwick repeats the word 'shock.' In either case the image and sense of headlong action are present.

17 See Ada Klett, *Der Streit um Faust II seit 1900* (Jenaer germanistische Forschungen, vol. 33 [Jena, 1939]), pp. 27–8; also the full discussion in Wilhelm Emrich, *Die Symbolik*, under *Iris*, and in Dorothea Lohmeyer, *Faust und die Welt* (Munich, 1975), pp. 65–7; further Hans Arens, *Kommentar zu Goethes Faust II* (Heidelberg, 1989), pp. 47–53.

18 'Toward a Theory of Weather' (1825).

19 'Von Körpern strömt's, die Körper macht es schön' (l. 1355).

absolutely. Not only was it inherent in light but its specific manifestations, the colors of color, were already present in light as if from the beginning of time.[20]

Newton destroyed the rainbow. For a phenomenon that was not each time a new creation but merely the rearrangement of already created matter could not stand as a symbol of human experience, of life itself. Not in the colors of the rainbow but in its constitution lay its meaning. The rainbow that Goethe has Faust experience is hardly ethereal. It is made up of the waterfall to which the light attaches itself and, in this turbulence, produces its splendor.[21] The rainbow is also not fixed. 'An ever changeful, yet continuous form, / Now drawn distinctly, melting now away,'[22] it hovers above the restless torrent much as the spirits who through the night hovered above the restless Faust as he inwardly relived the storm of Part I. Through color it accomplishes what was accomplished there through music: reconciliation and appeasement, though here with life as a whole. The acceptance of life in the symbol of the rainbow as colorful reflection – *am farbigen Abglanz*[23] – suggests as well the new position away from the center of the universe that man had to accept for himself in the Renaissance.

But the symbol of the rainbow not only serves to reflect the endlessly conflicting energies and purposes of man that are reconciled in its glory. Its very form, which spans and overarches, suggests the role it in fact

20 '[Newton] strides directly to the conclusion that not only is color inherent in light but the specific colors are already present in light as original rays.' '[Newton] schreitet unmittelbar zu dem Schlusse, es sei die Farbe dem Licht nicht nur eingeboren, sondern die Farben in ihren spezifischen Zuständen seien in dem Licht als ursprünglichen Lichter enthalten ...' (*Materialien zur Geschichte der Farbenlehre*; Isaak Newton: Die Optik [1810]). Cf. 'Theory of Color,' in Miller, ed. and trans., *Goethe*, pp. 157–298. Albrecht Schöne quotes some fragmentary lines of verse that Goethe jotted down on this same matter: 'Einheit ewigen Lichts zu spalten / Müssen wir für töricht halten' (*Goethes Farbentheologie* [Munich, 1987], p. 214). For a full accounting of Goethe's quarrel with Newtonian theory, see Burwick, *Damnation of Newton*, pp. 9–53; for Goethe's own theory, the compact, efficient discussion by George Wells, 'Goethe's Scientific Methods and Aims in the Light of His Studies in Physical Optics,' in *Publications of The English Goethe Society*, n.s., vol. 38 (1968).
21 From l. 4721: 'diesem Sturm ersprießend.'
22 Wölbt sich des bunten Bogens Wechseldauer,
Bald rein gezeichnet, bald in Luft zerfließend   (ll. 4722–3).
23 Line 4727.

plays in joining the two parts of the work, artistically no less than spiritually and philosophically. One senses an almost magical quality in the image when its meaning for the theory of art that Goethe developed is also recalled in its light. Here the dispute with Newton again plays a part. If truth and life are given or known to us only indirectly, then art that is a reflection of life takes its place beside all other truths that are themselves only reflections. Art is redeemed in the rainbow. Art, or beauty, was now no longer an imitation, a copy of the true or the real residing in things like the colors in the light that Newton knew. Beauty, rather, was the product of the pure light that attaches itself to the matter of art from the creative mind like the eye that brings to the real world the instrument that renders it intelligible. Beauty and art are the creation of individuals in time and not the expression or reflection of an order that exists absolutely. Here Goethe breaks with the classical norm of esthetics.[24]

Not that he need have had such concerns and theories in mind when he approached the creation of the second part of his work and radically altered its form. The break with Part I, which seems so abrupt, was in fact a gradual process, and the symbol of the rainbow a confirmation of his poetic theory and not an incentive to create new forms. We might even say that the rainbow itself as a poetic inspiration was the result of the same process which then found in it assurance and the will to continue a project that had long stagnated. For the rainbow as poetry or art would contain within it the same unsettled forces it reflected as a symbol of life and so both suggest and resolve not only the hectic action of Part I but its unsettled form as well.

Yet the course that Goethe had taken in his poetic development up to this point was toward an art of a quite different kind, a classical model whose splendor derived from balance and order, from a balance through order and not, as in *Faust* and in the symbol of the rainbow, through the dynamics of conflict. If the work was to transcend, and not merely abandon, its artistic beginnings, which were now so far removed in time, it would have to be in a form that included a development that was itself already extended and complex. Not that the task was impossible, although the great hesitation and reluctance Goethe

---

24 See my Postscript to *Goethe's Essays on Art and Literature* (trans. Ellen and Ernest von Nardroff [New York, 1986], pp. 229–40).

felt at the prospect of continuing 'this strange construct' – *dieses seltsame Gebäu* – is understandable.[25] He foresaw difficulties. 'Conflict between form and formless' appears as a notation in the scheme for the completed *Faust* that he set down circa 1800,[26] almost three decades before he took up the task in earnest. But the principle on which he seems to have based the decision to continue was the principle that had informed his creative work from the beginning. 'Preference for formless content over empty form'[27] is the notation that immediately follows the notation above. Whatever the form that *Faust II* would ultimately take, it would be a form that derived its order, like the rainbow, from disorder, and reflected its meaning indirectly.

The symbol of the rainbow in its moral dimensions also spans the two parts of the *Faust*.[28] Of course, it is only when we know the final resolution that we can see in this image that pulsates between clarity and diffusion an anticipation of the outcome of the play and its tragic implications. Faust will be made to envision a perfect moment, but only as illusion. His expectations in fact are shattered, much as they were when he turned to the Sign of the Macrocosm, to the Earth Spirit, to suicide and a life of wisdom in another world, and to the rising sun[29] in the repelling clarity of which he sees the history of all his

25 In a letter to Wilhelm von Humboldt, 17 March 1832.
26 'Streit zwischen Form und Formlosen' (Paralipomena to the *Faustdichtungen*, vol. 5 of the Artemis edition, ed. Ernst Beutler, p. 541).
27 'Vorzug dem formlosen Gehalt vor der leeren Form.' Max Morris sees this notation as pointing backward to Wagner rather than to the form of the work itself (*Goethe Studien* [Berlin, 1902], vol. 2, 'Die Faustparalipomena,' pp. 153–232).
28 Only a scientific view of the rainbow could see in it a reflection of a human truth, i.e., that pure light is 'darkened' by the actions of men. The good, pure light is refracted and 'darkened' into color in human experience. But the urge to the good, i.e., life itself, is an inner urge deriving from the eternal Good which we do not know. Newton's theory, in a kind of Manachean science, would imply a presence of the 'darkened' element from eternity. Yet Goethe himself sees evil, in the form of Mephistopheles, as present everywhere and on all occasions.
29 In his suicide attempt Faust had also turned his back on the sun, but by choice, and metaphorically, not in physical repulsion: 'Ja, kehre nur der holden Erdensonne / Entschlossen deinen Rücken zu!' (ll. 708–9). The parallel between these and the later lines is not always noted, yet the difference between Parts I and II is neatly captured in the contrast and makes one wonder whether Goethe was conscious of the echo from the earlier scene as he wrote the later lines.

expectations which is disillusion: 'So it is when deep desire nears its highest hope ...'[30] It is only his death that spares him the awareness of the tragic reality that is his fate and at the same time relegates the experience to us, who know. His clarity is our diffusion. To be sure, Goethe creates for us in the Chorus Mysticus a new vision, a 'rainbow' fixed and constant in it position beyond nature and time. Here, finally, the unattainable is attained.

It is difficult to sense tragedy in the rainbow. Its image is all too redemptive. Yet that aspect of its meaning must be grasped in *Faust*. Part II has no serious justification for its unique design unless it is to present a development that leads as inevitably to tragic disillusion as to salvation and cannot otherwise be artistically presented or described. Its symbolism and magical occurrences, its literary, political, and philosophical satire could as easily have been accommodated in an action that presented a self-contained sequence of events[31] – but not its tragic vision. That required an element or position of mind separate from the reality within the paly that would share with the hero his experience but not see it through his eyes. That mind, like another protagonist, would experience the next phase or cycle in the tragic action that is denied to the hero by his death. This is not an elaborate way of describing what might simply be called an audience or reader. The reason Faust is made to stand idly by through much of the course of the action in Part II, though he emerges a towering dramatic figure in Act V, is that this action has not been designed exclusively for him. Goethe has not brought the drama to his hero, which is the traditional mode and was the case in Part I, but his hero to the drama, that is to the 'great world' that is acting out a development of its own of which he is a part. And since the other protagonist in *Faust II*, the mind that 'supplies' the links that will connect the whole, is conceived of as mind, the events in the larger framework are presented to it in a fashion that presumes assimilation, that is, disjunctively, associatively, allusively, and in the confidence that it will appropriate what Faust himself experiences and just that much more. This more that is appropriated is

---

30 So ist es also, wenn ein sehnend Hoffen
   Dem höchsten Wunsch sich traulich zugerungen. (ll. 4704–5)
31 Cf., e.g., Ibsen's *Peer Gynt*.

the tragic something that is not the concern of Faust in his time and place but our own concern.[32]

The nature of this tragic concern fully emerges only with the conclusion of the drama. But it is already clear from the action of Part I and from the terms of the pact with the Devil that the recurrent and inevitable failure of man to attain the highest goals produces the equally recurrent need to continue to strive, which is the evolutionist principle. What is tragic in the individual proves all-saving in the species: the cataract, rushing 'from fall to fall,' produces in the proper light the rainbow.

Yet it is not everyone who will see in the raging torrent crowned with glory, as does Faust, a symbol of human endeavor. It may as well suggest a colorful disguise of futility, the kind of futility that he himself will continue to experience in his pursuit of Helen and in his final grand plan to regain land from the sea. And when Goethe in the last act has him once again, and finally, reach out to the highest moment, and we observe the reality behind his illusion, the latter interpretation may indeed appear confirmed. The 'rainbow' that crowns the action in the Chorus Mysticus at the end of the play would then seem itself empty. It is as if we had come from the first scene of *Urfaust* where the beautiful vision of the Macrocosm was evoked some sixty years earlier in the composition of the work only to find another vision, equally beautiful, but again a vision only – *ein Schauspiel nur.*[33]

This deeper ambiguity will remain in *Faust* and not be overcome. It is an ambiguity already given in the symbol of the rainbow which is 'Now drawn distinctly, now melting away.' It is the breathing in and breathing out of human understanding. Even the verse form in which the symbol had its birth, the terza rima, used here for the only time in the poem, suggests a resolving and dissolving in its rhyme scheme which emerges only to fade away and reemerge. It is, further, a verse form that Goethe at the height of his classical period once contemplated using and then rejected, 'because it allows no rest ... and

---

32 Benjamin Bennett: 'Catharsis is denied us; we do not leave behind the tragedy of *Faust*; rather, the work compels us to continue living in the atmosphere of the tragic' (*Goethe's Theory of Poetry: Faust and the Regeneration of Language* [Ithaca, 1986], p. 37).

33 From *Urfaust*, l. 101.

can nowhere conclude.'[34] In that sense the opening monologue of *Faust II* in its choice of form would unconsciously function as a rededicatory poem to Faust – the restless hero no less than the inconcludable work – and to the problems it would present.

34 '... weil [jenes Silbenmaß] gar keine Ruhe hat und man wegen der fortschreitenden Reime nirgends schließen kann' (to Schiller, 21 February 1798). Today, one might be tempted to translate 'nirgends schließen kann' as 'knows no closure.'

CHAPTER FOUR

The Imperial Court

It was from Herder that Goethe first learned the significance of poetry as a reflection of a historical milieu. The *Knittelvers*, that rough-hewn, 'woodcut' verse form Goethe originally chose for *Faust*, thus suggests the sixteenth-century world of his legendary hero.[1] A verse form that suited the 'little world' was, of course, not suitable for the larger worlds or modes of thought and feeling – the *Daseinskreise* – that Faust is eventually made to explore. The result was the variety of verse forms that soon emerged. A *Faust* verse also evolved from the *Knittelvers* and formed a kind of norm.

But the principle remained. The importance of poetry in the present regard lay in fact not in what it signified esthetically, but historically. History for Herder, as for Goethe in *Faust II*, was the monitor of human experience and no longer simply the recorder of great events. The laws, customs, and rituals of a people, like its poetry and language, better reveal the broader moving forces in a nation or a time than do the actions of individuals, which often only alter the surface of reality. Yet this fact was generally ignored, by poets and historians alike. To the historian Niebuhr, Goethe wrote, 23 November 1812: 'What is in the past can seem to us directly present when it appears in the form of literary monuments, annals, chronicles, documents, memoires, etc., of the times. They transmit something immediate which fascinates us just as it is [and] which we would like to communicate to others. We do; we process the material. And how? As poets, as intellectuals! That has always been the case, and these modes of presentation are highly

---

1 'Holzgeschnitten' is the word Goethe uses to describe the character of Dürer's art in his early essay 'On German Architecture' (1772).

effective ... they fill the soul, strengthen character and inspire action. [And yet] it is a second world which has devoured the first.' The great world that Faust enters in Part II is this first world, as far as it is possible for a poet in the present to create such a world. The task now was to present the materials of former eras and of the deep past in an unprocessed manner that would preserve their immediacy without creating a second world designed to 'devour' their meaning within its own context. If *Faust II* is undramatic, as it is seemingly fragmentary, through much of its second part, it is deliberately so. The dramatic frame, like the logical sequence, is often suspended in order to allow the forces that underlie the drama and the logic to emerge. The background becomes foreground and regains its immediacy. If we remain unaware of this intention, we will look for the drama when it is not present or take what is presented for something it is not. This is understandable. Part I by its dramatic thrust and its established theme – we assume from the pact that Faust will continue to strive in all his actions toward a highest moment – leads us in one direction and Part II in another. Yet this other direction is not toward an esoterically symbolic reading of the text. Symbolism in the late Goethe is more often an *open* secret, and so obviously before us as to easily go unnoticed. 'That is true symbolism which represents the more general in the particular, but not as dream or shadow, but as immediate, living experience of the unfathomable.' 'A symbol is an idea formed in the mirror of the mind and yet identical with the object.'[2] It is through this kind of plain symbolism, which is then only another way of saying reality, that he gains his extensive meanings in Part II. The immediacy is retained and yet a world is created that can extend as far as the reality we associate with it. *Faust II* is a drama derived from poetry, not poetry derived from drama, as is *Faust I*.

Nothing could be simpler and yet more meaningful than the time at which Faust is made to arrive at the imperial court in Act I. That he

---

2 The open secret: from *Sprüche und Prosa*, '[Die Worte] mögen als offenbares Geheimnis der Zukunft bewahrt werden.' 'Das ist die wahre Symbolik, wo das Besondere das Allgemeinere repräsentiert, nicht als Traum und Schatten, sondern als lebendig-augenblickliche Offenbarung des Unerforschlichen.' '[Das Symbol ist] ein im geistigen Spiegel zusammengezogenes Bild, und doch mit dem Gegenstand identisch' (from *Maximen und Reflexionen*). On Goethe's use of symbolism in his late works, see Hans-Joachim Schrimpf, *Das Weltbild des späten Goethe* (Stuttgart, 1956).

comes to the Imperial Court, or an imperial court, is determined by
the legend, but the moment is chosen by Goethe. The moment is also
le moment in the sense that Taine used the word to mean a point in
history or moment in a culture when the factors that constitute the
essence of that time seem to converge in a single event, institution, or
accomplishment. The moment here is Carnival. The forces that together
create the world that Faust first enters in Part II are found in this single
custom or institution and in the enactment of its ritual.

The very concept of Carnival presupposes a duality in human nature
which it has been the object of *Faust* from the beginning to resolve. A
reinterpretation of the conflict between the spiritual and the physical
in man is already anticipated in the two *souls* at war in Faust, that is,
two equally strong and equally valued properties of mind and of body
neither of which in the design of nature can be properly denied. Not
that the conflict will in the end be resolved. It is not even seen as
present in the ancient classical world of Act III; and in the new world
that is envisioned at the end of the play it will take the form of a
spiritual and an active energy that join in conceiving the highest human
ideals – and yet cannot realize them.

But in the world of Act I, which is the intermediate world between
the classical and the modern spheres of existence, neither of the ruling
passions in mankind is put to useful purpose. 'It is the world as it
shouldn't be.'[3] The spiritual urge has been relegated to particular periods of time and institutionalized and specialized in customs and rites,
the natural urges indulged unthinkingly and then denied once a year
in Lent. In a kind of collective rationalization, the Lenten period that
is intended as a spiritual preparation for the holy celebration of Easter
has become a punishment, and thus a payment, atonement, and justification in advance, for the pagan revelry that will now be indulged
to the exclusion of all else. The Emperor cannot understand why 'on
this day / When we all care would cast away ... should we with state
affairs ourselves annoy,'[4] though he is about to lose his kingdom and

3 As so nicely described by Ernst Traumann, 'eine Welt, wie es nicht sein sollte'
  (*Goethes Faust* [Munich, 1914], vol. 2, p. 119).
4 Doch sagt, warum in diesen Tagen,
  Wo wir der Sorgen uns entschlagen ...
  Und Heitres nur genießen wollten,
  Warum wir uns ratschlagend quälen sollten?   (ll. 4765–9)

his empire. This is satire, but its purposes go beyond. Behind this political and social irresponsibility, this abuse of time and neglect of the world, stands a philosophy of life that has relegated the things of the earth to a position far removed in importance from the things of another world, though the latter are honored in name. In Carnival is enacted, not a moment of frivolity in the context of a dire existence, which is its rationale, but the perennial and typical postponement of reality. It is the model for the larger postponement of life to a 'true' existence in a projected world beyond.

It offers bread that is 'eaten before it is earned': the *vorgegessen Brot*[5] that comes to the table across the land and is the symbol both of the economy and the psychology of this late medieval and early Renaissance kingdom that is failing. Carnival is the act of living ahead, like the loans made against future income which are the practice of the day and are here called *Antizipationen*.[6] Even the creation of paper money against treasures buried in the earth and yet to be discovered, which is the plan that Mephistopheles devises in order to save the kingdom, not only repeats the sin of postponement but is itself postponed, the 'more merrily to celebrate the joyous carnival.'[7]

It is the justification for this last, minor particular that casts light on the flaw in the system that supports, and will ruin, the kingdom. The justification is offered by the court astrologer, who urges this delay so that 'through things above [we may] deserve what lies below' – a reference at once to the heavenly blessing and the propitious stars that to his mind must attend all human endeavor and earthly gain.[8] In the

5 'Und auf den Tisch kommt vorgegessen Brot' (l. 4875).
6 Line 4871.
7 Indessen feiern wir, auf jeden Fall,
 Nur lustiger das wilde Carneval. (ll. 5059–60)
 Here time is deliberately squandered: 'So sei die Zeit in Fröhlichkeit *vertan*' (l. 5057). My italics.
8 'Das Untre durch das Obre verdienen' (l. 5052). In Act II Mephistopheles also speaks of the 'things above and the things below,' there in a specifically Christian frame of reference: 'Die Schlüssel übt er wie Sankt Peter, / Das Untre so das Obre schließt er auf' (ll. 6650–1). In the first instance the reference may be as well to the things above and beneath the earth, e.g., treasures or gold, but I think Emrich for one goes too far when he builds an elaborate structure of symbols upon this latter assumption alone (*Die Symbolik*, 192ff.). Ehrhard Bahr, *Die Ironie im Spätwerk Goethes* (Berlin, 1972) sees political and social irony in the reference to the 'higher' and 'lower,' those 'above' and those 'below' (p. 139).

Astrologer are joined the religion and the science of the day. He is the
contemporary wise man. But his ordering is precisely wrong. It is not
through the things above in the form of astrology or magic, religious
belief or metaphysical speculation, that the things below are earned
and deserved in *Faust*, but the opposite. It is through acts in the present
that the future is formed, through deeds in this world that heaven is
gained, in whatever form it may be imagined to exist. From the beginning the movement in the drama has been away from living in the
past or living in the future and toward an existence not postponed. In
the end Faust will envision the ideal life as 'standing *alone* before nature
as a man,'[9] shorn of magic, and with magic, of all the imaginings and
manipulations of reality that he has experienced as fact and one experiences normally only in the mind. He will not attain this ideal, since
man is an imaginative animal.[10] But the world he envisions in the final
act will stand at the opposite pole from the present world in the play,
where truth is postponed in order to live for the moment, and the
moment itself abused.

Yet it is not the Astrologer after all who speaks. 'Goethe had to
motivate everything,' his assistant Riemer once remarked,[11] and that
aspect of his genius is remarkably evident here. He has Mephistopheles, in the guise of the court jester, prompt the astrologer as he utters
his words. Thus, 'The fool prompts and the wise man speaks.'[12] Not
only is the satire heightened by having the Devil profess the folly,
which the wise man in all innocence and earnestness believes, but the
specific folly itself is now identified with evil, which in the world of
Act I it is. What might simply be folly in another time and place is
here both symptom and cause of a historical disintegration. This emperor is the Emperor of the Holy Roman Empire. The mission of this
great, if intangible, religious and political institution from the time of

9 My italics.
  Stünd' ich, Natur, vor dir ein Mann allein,
  Da wär's der Mühe wert, ein Mensch zu sein. (ll. 11406–7)
10 'Why are we moderns so distracted, why challenged by demands we can neither
  meet nor fulfill?' (*The Italian Journey* for 17 April 1787).
11 'Goethe has to motivate everything and, as he once told me, there was never any
  mention or matter in his plays or novels of even a piece of chalk or the like without its having earlier been unnoticeably referred to or introduced' (Conversations
  from the years 1803–14; in *Gespräche*, vol. 22 of the Artemis edition, p. 754).
12 'Der Tor bläst ein – Der Weise spricht' (l. 4954).

Charlemagne to Napoleon was to join the spiritual and the temporal, the things above with the things below, in a union of Christian and secular virtues and powers. The reality was quite different, to be sure. But the nature, if not the success, of the enterprise is given in its name. That mission is now before us in ridiculous disarray, with its main goals askew, and with the one serving to negate the other.

It is not the knowledge of history alone that allows us to see the seriousness of this folly at court. A world is being created in Act I that anticipates, and will contrast with, the other worlds that emerge in the ensuing acts, each with its own central focus but all revolving around the question of the economy of time. The perfect moment that is stipulated in the pact pinpoints dramatically what is in fact present in a broad and diffuse manner throughout the play. If the world of Act I represents living *for* the moment, and the classical world of Act III a living *in* the moment, the envisioned new world in Act V, as if in a synthesis of the spiritual and the temporal, the Christian and the ancient, represents a living *toward* the moment, with the spiritual now reconceived as an ideal to be realized on earth. The words that Faust uses at the end of the play to condemn a spiritual life directed toward another world seem an almost intentional contradiction of the words used by the Emperor to open his court at the beginning, 'Above is written our joy and salvation.' Faust says, 'The view beyond is denied to us.'[13] Since the moment in Part II is both an individual experience and the symbol of a cultural and historical development, what Faust experiences as an individual is at the same time an inevitable progression of larger forces that will distribute themselves in such a way as to make the resolution of their conflict the resolution of his own. There is a warring of background and foreground in the structure of the play, with now one, now the other, more prominent, until both strands culminate in the action of Act V. There, with history as it were behind him, Faust emerges in an all-encompassing dramatic focus.

Here in the opening scenes at the imperial court he has mainly a passive role. We think of *Faust* as a quest but it is also an accumulation. Symbols, associations, and evocations of the simplest as well as the

---

13 'Da droben ist uns Glück und Heil geschrieben' (l. 4764). Faust will say in the final act, 'Nach drüben ist die Aussicht uns verrannt' (l. 11442). The Emperor may here be referring as well to the stars which are part of the view beyond in less theological terms.

most profound human stirrings and strivings amass in the background through its poetry and form a drama of their own. Yet this independent creation, this 'defausted universe,'[14] is not merely a backdrop to which we give the name drama, as one might say that life as a whole is a drama. It has a beginning, a continuity, and, if not an end in its evolutionist setting, a projection to the future as far as the mind can see. Yet this drama is a drama of the imagination and of magic, so that its chronology is at once a going forward and a coming back, as if we were passing through frames of reference successively inhabited by different ideas and motifs, each leaving its traces. We noted the motif of Carnival in the setting of the Holy Roman Empire as a philosophical-historical variation on a continuing theme. But of course these institutions, the smaller as well as the greater, persisted into the present. The life of the Holy Roman Empire is not only a historical fact but one that brought the theme of decline and default to the doorstep of Goethe's own time. He describes in his autobiography how as a child he visited the Emperor's Room in the Rathaus of his native city and saw how little space was left on its walls for a portrait of yet another German emperor and that perhaps the end was near. Maximilian I, he notes, had prophesied that he would be the last of the German kaisers.[15] Maximilian was the emperor at the time of the historical Faust, and in *Faust* the play the Emperor represents symbolically the failure and end of a way of life that in Goethe's time had come to be called the ancien régime.

Even the deeper reaches to the past are meant in the same way to have a real existence in the present. The classical world in Act III and its embodiment in Helen of Troy represent a phase of development that Faust and Western culture traverse in their passage to the present, while at the same time reflecting a desire to live in an ideal past in art and in thought which was the moving passion of the day. One wonders to what extent Goethe is here consciously mirroring his own development into and out of a classical phase which he overcame in the writing of *Faust*. Act IV, which is the pendant to Act I, will in fact dramatize an event in the present through an action in the past by the war against the Anti-Emperor, a concept that materialized in the person

14 Friedrich Gundolf, *Goethe* (Berlin, 1918), p. 758.
15 *Poetry and Truth*, bk. 1.

of Napoleon when he pretended to the imperial crown in 1804.[16] Act II, which fantasizes the biological underpinnings of man in the adventure of Homunculus and so uncovers deeper strata of meaning beneath history, is likewise anticipated at an even deeper level in the mythical descent to the Mothers. All this is introduced in and through the action of the opening scenes at the imperial court. Thus, the world that is created in Act I for its own sake serves also as exposition for the greater drama in the background and yet in its symbolical, associative, magical expression does not devour this first world but renders it dramatic in a new way.

Carnival provided the occasion for masquerade, and masquerade the occasion for symbolic and poetic representation, for a play within a play. Here, too, the play is the thing and is designed to catch the conscience of the Emperor. But the device is not used solely for that purpose. Given this opportunity to poetize, as we might call it, as well as dramatize, Goethe created now yet another world within his play, a pageant of manners and morals which he used not only to reflect the background against which the Emperor was to be tested and, as a harbinger of the future, to fail, but also to re-create the form in which the background had found expression in art in its time: the masque of the Renaissance.[17] The carnival scene epitomizes not only a moral but a social condition. In the action of its colorful allegorical figures we have the social order of the age.[18] Again it seems to exist in its own right, undevoured and undigested, until toward the end we recognize its place in the larger economy of the drama. If the opening monologue of *Faust II* served through its inner workings to recommit Goethe to the continuation of his work, the opportunities for fantasy and symbolism that this new development now afforded seem to have provided the sustenance for the task. The masquerade scene is by far the longest in the first act[19] and, against all logic, the longest, if the lightest, in the play.

16 He literally *pretended*, that is, through appearances, when crowned Emperor of France by the pope in 1804.
17 For an analysis of the scene in this light, see, e.g., Atkins, *Faust*, pp. 118ff.
18 See the discussion in Lohmeyer, *Faust*, the section 'Gesellschaft,' pp. 69–108.
19 Some 920 lines as against a similar total for the six other scenes of Act I combined.

Yet everything at this stage in the progression of the work was pointing toward a new, not a traditional, mode of dramatic expression. The reconception of life as reflection in the opening scene already presupposed not a continuation of the drama of immediacy and intensity that was Part I but a new drama of indirection that we now find unfolding in symbolism and allegory. As unstructured as its action of flower girls and clowns, of laborers and parasites, and of figures from classical mythology and Christian parable, amid music and dance, may appear, and as masquerade should appear, its purpose in this drama that has hardly begun is not diversion or relief. This long scene in its meanderings touches upon so much, and in so freely associative a manner, that it seems to represent life itself in its social ecology as it maintains its balance through variety and change. This is not the world as it should not be, but as it is. The court that views the land and kingdom as in want and chaos, and so succumbs to Mephistopheles' scheme of unearthing nonexistent treasures, is only reflecting its own view and its own creation.[20] In the world of the masquerade there is plenty. There is Peace, Hope, Prudence, Generosity, and Gratitude, though also the Fates and the Furies, all allegorically presented. Above all there is potential, in the form of Plutus, the god of wealth, who is played by Faust. He is accompanied, in balance, by Avarice, played by Mephistopheles.

The education of the Emperor can now begin. But it has been transformed, as has the drama as a whole, from dramatic discourse to poetry on stage.

The Emperor's sin is the abuse of plenty. In the real world his coffers are regularly replenished through rightful tribute and rent. Onto his table come 'deer, wild boar, / Stags, hares, fowls, turkey, duck and geese,' though it is regarded as a shame that there is a temporary shortage of wine.[21] In the masquerade this wealth in both its natural and just resources is fantasized in the 'glowingly rich ore' that the gnomes of the mountains have discovered and, unsure of the purpose to which it should be put, have come to their god Pan, who is played by the Emperor, to seek advice about. In the past they have mined

20 In speaking of the state of affairs to be imagined in Act I, Goethe does not mention poverty and want but only 'unheard-of wantonness left unpunished and unchecked' (to Eckermann, 1 October 1827).
21 Lines 4856–65.

gold and ore so that 'men thereby may pimp and steal, / Nor to the proud who murder plan / Wholesale [i.e., war], shall fail the iron hand.'[22] Now they turn to the masked Emperor in whose hands, as the Deputation of Gnomes believes, 'every treasure redounds to the common good.'[23]

Again, this is satire. In the hands of this monarch every treasure has every chance of being squandered. Yet the importance of the motif lies not in exposing the feckless character of the Emperor, whose weakness we know. Of course he will fail the test and mistake for reality the glittering false treasure that Mephistopheles has conjured. Approaching too close to the sparkling illusion, he burns his beard and reveals himself for the immature youth that he is: 'Who can that beardless wonder be?'[24] But now the failure has taken place in a context that tests not only character but the larger idea of kingship and the economy of power. A mock historic moment has occurred: 'O Majesty, with reason never / Will thy omnipotence be crowned?'[25]

Nor is the moment made to occur in a vacuum. A whole sequence in which the uses of power and plenty are elaborately adumbrated precedes the moment of their symbolic abuse. In an exchange between Plutus and the Boy Charioteer, who represent respectively wealth and poetry (the latter 'the son' in whom the former is 'well pleased'[26]), the gifts from nature of the one are played off against the gifts to the spirit of the other, neither of which are appreciated in this unguided world. Goethe goes so far as to have a tiny flame appear over individual heads in the mass of people and linger momentarily only here and there,

22 Doch bringen wir das Gold zu Tag,
   Damit man stehlen und kuppeln mag,
   Nicht Eisen fehle dem stolzen Mann,
   Der allgemeinen Mord ersann. (ll. 5856–9)
23 Jeder Schatz in deinen Händen
   Kommt der ganzen Welt zugut. (ll. 5912–13)
24 My translation of 'Wer mag das glatte Kinn wohl sein?' (l. 5932). Behind the
   magic conflagration lay the historical fact of Charles VI of France who at a masked
   ball found his beard afire and is said to have been driven mad by the experience.
   The motif reminds us, when we know this fact, how deeply rooted in reality are
   the fantasy and playfulness of Faust II.
25 O Hoheit, Hoheit, wirst du nie
   Vernünftig wie allmächtig wirken? (ll. 5960–1)
26 'Mein lieber Sohn, an dir hab' ich Gefallen' (l. 5629).
   The biblical allusion is to Luke 2, 3.

while the images of material wealth that are scattered before the crowd
are greedily seized. If the gifts of the spirit languish in this world, the
gifts of the temporal world corrupt. The poet in the figure of the Boy
Charioteer is banished to solitude. 'There where on thy genius thou
canst wait ... there thine own world create ... Here is not thy sphere.'[27]

When the education of the Emperor fails, with it fail the ideal of
unity in the soul and experience of Western man, which was the task
that history had set for the Christian world in the Renaissance, and
also the hope that was built on its premises: the two souls in man
might be reconciled. But in the kingdom before us the forces both of
spirit and of nature have been not only neglected but proscribed. 'Nature and spirit ... These words doom atheists to fire,'[28] the Chancellor
had said in the opening scene at court. But the point here is not to
explore the theme of kingship, which is soon submerged and surfaces
again only in Act IV. There the squandered energies of the present, as
if avenging themselves, will erupt in the destructive act of war. The
point is simply to note the presence of the theme amid the accumulating
mass of themes and motifs that the poetic freedom of the masquerade
has provided the opportunity to present and that will now emerge as
the dominant mode of expression in *Faust*. The background has been
made foreground in our minds in an evolutionist imitation of reality.
If by all logic, as we said, the masquerade scene seems too long, it is
only by a logic that recognizes the dramatic but not the thematic movement in the work. To have created and symbolically destroyed in a
single sequence a world of behavior and a system of values upon the
ruins of which a new order will attempt to rise at the end of the play,
and to have done so in a form and manner that not only fit the occasion
in the drama but established the mode for its further development,
was in fact economical and a stroke of formal genius.

For there would now be no turning back. Before the end of Act I
there will be another play within the play, again in keeping with the
pre-Lenten festivities, when the specters of Paris and Helen are magically brought to the court. While the Classical Walpurgis Night se-

27 Dorthin, wo Schönes, Gutes nur gefällt,
   Zur Einsamkeit! – Da schaffe deine Welt.   (ll. 5695–6)
   The lines are reminiscent of *Torquato Tasso*.
28 Natur und Geist – so spricht man nicht zu Christen.
   Deshalb verbrennt man Atheisten.   (ll. 4897–8)

quence that follows in Act II may be seen as a dream of the Faust who is asleep in the opening scene, it is precisely in the dreamlike freedom of association and movement that it resembles the action of the masquerade which, though conscious and indeed patterned on a traditional artistic form, reflects the same processes of the imagining or dreaming, not the organizing human mind.[29] The acts themselves are joined by the same free passage from world to world as are the elements and actions in the individual scenes and their unexpected and unexplained transitions accounted for by the presence of magic. Both have a common denominator in mind, in imagination, in magic, i.e., in poetry. Even Act IV, which in returning after a long wait to the imperial court might be expected to resume the action in a poetically more 'real' setting, in fact employs allegorical figures to prosecute its war, and magic to end it. It is as though after all the fantasy that Goethe expended and had had to expend in order to penetrate beyond the surface of the dramatic reality to the larger realms in which it had a deeper existence, he could not readily bring the action back to earth. *Faust II* remains surprisingly consistent, and appears disjointed only when we persist in looking for its unity not in the movement of themes but in the actions of characters, which the work in its entirety rather discourages us from doing. Only in Act V, as we said, where the luminous dramatic figure of the blinded Faust, like Lear on the heath, gathers himself up to die, does the whole seem finally re-anchored in the fate of an individual. But it is what we have experienced with Faust, at his side, and not merely through him, that lends significance to the moment. No more than he looks directly into the sun, do we now look often into his soul, as we did in Part I.

The symbolism of the masquerade issues in action. Meaning seems to be the cause of event in the play and not the reverse, event the cause of meaning. Of course, this inversion is only possible in a drama where magic, or imaginative poetry, not the poetry that imitates cause and effect, is the motive force. The specter of Helen precedes her reality in the play; it does not follow, as might a memory or a ghost. But it is

---

29 Katharina Mommsen sees the masquerade as the model for an understanding of the form the Helen episode as a whole will take (*Natur- und Fabelreich in Faust II* [Berlin, 1968], p. 99).

also true that the perspective in *Faust II* envisions deeper cause at such a great remove in history and in time that it might appear as idea and not as event, though the purpose in the work is to bring all occurrences, real and in the mind, to bear on the moment. *Faust II* is unique as a drama not least of all because, with magic at its disposal, it need not indulge the device of *post hoc, ergo propter hoch*,[30] the causal relation through temporal sequence that makes realism possible in the theatre. It deploys events in a manner in which they may be thought about, not in which they occur.

Here the action that results from the fantasy of the masquerade is the creation of paper money. In fact, the action is made literally to occur amid the confusion, the Emperor as the god Pan having unknowingly signed a promissory note during the masquerade, and the note having gone through the presses overnight and been reproduced and distributed throughout the land. The religion of money is further satirized in the remark, 'In this sign [i.e., his *sign*ature] all will be blessed.'[31] This is a deliberate anachronism, for paper money was not widely used until later in history; here it is intended to suggest the *assignats* issued during the French Revolution with disastrous financial results. But it is the symbolic meaning of the moment that is more important. The living in the present against a promise of the future, which the printed money represents, is the economic institutionalization of a practice already socially established in the custom of Carnival and, although it is not mentioned in Act I, morally sanctioned at the time in the sale of Indulgences against punishment in an afterlife. 'Who owns this note a thousand crowns doth own. / To him assured ... there lies, / Beneath the Emperor's land, a boundless prize.'[32] There is humor in the fact that here money can be said literally to be the invention of the Devil, since Mephistopheles orchestrates the action. And there is historical insight, if not accuracy, in making this emperor in his irresponsibility and ineffectuality the witness to its birth. Yet the symbol at its root is not an indictment of capitalism, as much as it may

---

30 'After this, therefore because of this.'
31 'In diesem Zeichen wird nun jeder selig' (l. 6082).
32 Zu wissen sei es jedem, der's begehrt:
   Der Zettel hier ist tausend Kronen wert.
   Ihm liegt gesichert, als gewisses Pfand,
   Unzahl vergrabnen Guts im Kaiserland. (ll. 6057–60)

appear so to us in an age of buying on credit, nor an implicit condemnation of the Church, as much as Goethe otherwise in *Faust* and elsewhere criticized its practices.

The sin here is a sin against time. As there is an economy of power introduced in Act I, and an economy of knowledge in the human perception of the universe reflected in the opening monologue, so there is an economy of time. The world that Goethe conceived in *Faust* is bound not by fixed laws, which in their constancy forever repeat the same challenge to man and assign benefit or loss according to success or failure, but by dynamic forces which, honored or abused, alter for better or for worse the nature of the challenge in a future world. Faust is saved not because he has not sinned, but because he has sinned in the deepest spirit of his time in attempting to join the two souls in his breast, which are also the two souls of his age, and to realize on earth a perfection that before had been promised only in heaven. His gravest sin in Part II, as if in a final, terrible aberration before he finds the true way, is the destruction he causes in order to remove a simple incongruity, an esthetic imperfection, in the plan he has devised for his great project at the end of the play.[33] The Emperor, however, simply defaults. Given the power to effect the balance between the temporal and the ideal that his times in their evolving course have defined as his mission, he has not only overseen the disuse of the one and abuse of the other. In the process, he has left to Faust, i.e., the Faust that Goethe creates in a later age, a world where his sins and aberrations, through frustration, are more likely to occur. The Holy Roman Empire comes to an end with a whimper in 1804. In Act IV we learn that the benefits from the lands that Faust would reclaim from the sea have already been tithed and taxed in advance by an ever hungrier church, with the Emperor's acquiescence. This is the Emperor who after first objecting to a court council having been called at Carnival time finally consents, not in remembering his duty but in the recognition that, 'If it has happened, so let it have been done': *Geschehen ist's, so sei's getan*.[34] The remark is time*less*, in the usual, and here in our special, sense.

Where does this leave Faust and Mephistopheles? For if the greater

---

33 The apparent superficiality of this desire is what shames him, I believe. 'Und wie ich's sage, schäm' ich mich' (l. 11238). See below, p. 168.

34 Line 4771.

part of the act, with its focus on the character and the education of the Emperor, serves as exposition for the broadest thematic developments in the play, still it can be said that the drama suffers at its expense. We might expect of a great drama that it further character in furthering theme and vice versa. In his original plan Goethe had in fact assigned Faust a more prominent role, as we know from a sketch of the action from 1816. He was not only to be more directly engaged with the Emperor but also allowed space to 'fall into his earlier abstruse speculations and demands upon himself,'[35] the characteristic by which we best know him.

Yet the question that can be asked most pointedly is not in terms of dramatic action but in moral terms. Why does Faust stand by idly as the Emperor leads his kingdom toward ruin, a consequence Faust in the earlier plan would surely have sought to prevent? There he was to impress upon the Emperor the 'higher demands and higher means of overcoming material adversity';[36] here he indulges the inanity and foolishness of the court in order to realize his own ambitions, though these are not stated. To say that in his role as Plutus he recovers something of the original design may be true, and important in illustrating the creative transformation that so often occurred between the thought and the deed in the composition of *Faust*, but it hardly bears on the moral issue. A warning hidden in allegory, though it may be a model for the mode of indirection that the work seeks to establish, will not substitute for open statement in the case of this unheeding Emperor who can even see in the conflagration that occurs upon his failing the test in the masquerade only a fiery homage to his person: 'I seemed, surrounded by my courtly train, / Over thousand salamanders ... to reign.'[37] Mephistopheles encourages him in his illusion; Faust does not say a word.

Yet it is precisely this passivity that might be dramatically important. What seems a dramaturgical lapse could in fact be intended as a tragic flaw. Only when one assumes that the masquerade is merely a colorful diversion[38] and not a part of a grand exposition of developing themes,

35 Beutler, Paralipomena, p. 558.
36 Ibid.
37 Von meinem Hof erkannt' ich ein und andern,
    Ich schien ein Fürst von tausend Salamandern. (ll. 6001–2)
38 Rickert expresses perhaps the strongest opinion in this regard: '... hier liegen Teile

does Faust's inaction appear dramaturgically awkward rather than dramatically significant. But if it is correct to say that the empty and illusory activities of Act I are the cause by default of the undermining of the deeds that Faust undertakes in Act IV, then he and not the Emperor alone is made responsible for this outcome. In his inaction he creates his nemesis. He too sins against time. Moreover, in his present inattention he only repeats the behavior by which we also know him well. He unintentionally caused the death of Gretchen's mother, only confusedly the death of her brother, and in his most atrocious crime at the end of the play he will have a submissive, not an active role. If we imagine the symbolic test in the masquerade as being staged cynically by Mephistopheles in order to humiliate the Emperor, and naively by Faust in order to educate him, we have before us again the same strange and sometimes ugly team as it lived and breathed in Part I and through its combination of connivance and passivity created tragedy. That Faust should be made to fail in his noblest endeavor through his own fault, while he is seen in the larger scheme of things as saved in the fact of his striving, would lend to the action the same split

---

der Dichtung vor, die bei dem Versuch, das ganze als dramatische Einheit zu verstehen, *ausgeschaltet* werden müssen' (*Goethe's Faust*, p. 299). Klett, in *Der Streit*, shows an almost uniform dismissal of the importance of the masquerade in her section 'Kaiserhof.' Gundolf sees in Act I Goethe's 'distaste for the historical' (*Goethe*, p. 764). Emrich sees the same ahistorical instinct in the late Goethe but finds deep symbolic meaning in the fantasy of the masquerade (*Die Symbolik*, pp. 116–30). At least since Lukács, Marxist and socialist interpreters, to the contrary, have placed great importance on the historical reality reflected in the scenes at the imperial court. Cf. Georg Lukács, 'Faust Studies,' in *Goethe and His Age*, trans. R. Anchor (New York, 1968). Lohmeyer (*Faust*) and Mommsen (*Natur- und Fabelreich*) place importance as well on the form of these scenes as guide to an understanding of the whole. With his concept of 'Daseinskreise,' Max Kommerell, of course, gives equal importance to all the 'worlds' created in the play ('Faust zweiter Teil,' in *Geist und Buchstabe der Dichtung* [Frankfurt 1939]). For Heinz Schlaffer, *Faust zweiter Teil: Die Allegorie des 19. Jahrhunderts* (Stuttgart, 1981) these early scenes are all important as a 'Kritik der politischen Ökonomie' (pp. 49–62). Schlaffer sees in the socioeconomic context of Goethe's home city of Frankfurt a model for the underlying, fundamental 'allegory' he believes to have found in *Faust II*: 'exakt vom Sozialen, Politisch-Geschichtlichen, Psychologischen und Künsterlichen nimmt die symbolischen Denkform ihren Ausgang ...' (p. 22). This is the familiar assumption, which also derives from Marx: It is not the consciousness of men that determines their being, but on the contrary, their social being that determines their consciousness (Preface to *A Contribution to the Critique of Political Economy* [1859]).

perspective in it resolution that has accompanied its development
throughout. Background and foreground, God and Caesar, would be
given equal due. It might lessen our uneasiness about Faust's re-
demption to know (though he would not) that even had he lived to
realize his final ambition, its results would already have been forfeited
in a world he had failed to save in time.

CHAPTER FIVE

Act I: Helen
Anticipated

A unity, but a wholly unfamiliar kind of unity, gradually emerges in *Faust II*. It is as if the usual modes of introducing the past and fore-shadowing the future on which the dramatic moment so heavily de-pends were not only interrupted so as to allow frames of reality to enter from other worlds, but replaced. There is less talk and more show of events and eventualities. Of course, Goethe had to use words in *Faust*, but even in the very form that the words took, in the meters and rhythms and rhymes, as we said, worlds of different times and places could often be evoked. The mere printed design of a page from Act III or Act IV as it stretches out to the margin tells us visually that we are in another realm.[1] Spoken on stage, we would *hear* the differ-ence.

These are the surface indications of that movement or instinct in the play to see behind and beneath reality, to motivate from a distance or depth so far removed at times as to seem unconnected to the action. Goethe himself had remarked, 'Every work of art, because it must isolate, motivates from proximate cause, not from remote or remotest cause.'[2] Yet it is precisely from remote cause that he motivates in *Faust II*. And this depth or distance is not bridged by words for the most part, not 'devoured' in speech, but made present.

Thus, a trip to the Mothers is devised in Act I. It is part of the

---

1 This is particularly striking on first encounter with Act III and in the last scene of Act IV.

2 'Jedes Kunstwerk motiviert nur durch *causas proximas*, nicht durch *remotas* oder *re-motissimas*, weil es sich isolieren muß. Das Motivieren, das ins Detail geht, haben die Engländer aufgebracht' (to Riemer, September 1810, n.d.).

exposition, a vision from the farthest reaches of the universe where all
things have their beginning, the imagined and the real, and in which
all is unified. The point is virtually made that the Mothers themselves
are a thought that proceeds from their own realm. For they are the
almighty distributors of the images of life that are dispensed to the
world to be either born as reality or conceived by the 'magus,' the
poet, in thought:

> beings of matchless might,
> [You] dispense life's pictures to day's pavilion or to the vault
>   of night.
> Life in its gentle course doth some arrest,
> Of others the bold magus goes in quest;
> In rich profusion, fearless, he displays,
> The marvels upon which each longs to gaze.[3]

If the Mothers is an idea in *Faust*, *Faust* itself must be considered an
idea of the Mothers made real and present through the poetry and
magic. Goethe had in fact originally written 'poet' for magus' in this
passage.

If *Faust* itself is ultimately a product that has come into being from
the remote realm of the Mothers, then its position in relation to its
own meaning is altered. We said that as a cultural artifact it took its
place in the very development it was attempting to re-create and so
produced, like all cultural phenomena, in being produced. This remains
true. But when the drama now looks behind the phenomena of culture
and history that appear to be its subject matter and uncovers a source
in which both have their origin, the poetry begins to present itself no
longer as a re-creation of the real world, however imaginative and
symbolic, but as an alternative to it. What has become *Faust* might
have become reality, the drama says in effect at this point and seems

---

3 Und ihr verteilt es, allgewaltige Mächte,
  Zum Zelt des Tages, zum Gewölb der Nächte.
  Die einen faßt des Lebens holder Lauf,
  Die andern sucht der kühne Magier auf;
  In reicher Spende läßt er, voll Vertrauen,
  Was jeder wünscht, das Wunderwürdige schauen. (ll. 6433–8)
  On the Mothers, Klett, *Der Streit*, pp. 30–4; Arens, *Kommentar*, pp. 273f; further
  Harold Jantz, *The Mothers in Faust* (Baltimore, 1969).

to act in this assumption and confidence. It creates freely, ignoring the laws that govern objective reality and making real what exists in the mind, which is the task of both magic and poetry.

The wonder is that in gaining this freedom through a philosophy or vision or myth that raises art in its origins to the level of reality, Goethe did not indulge the advantage and create in *Faust II* purely from fantasy. But there are two souls in *Faust II*, esthetically speaking as well. The division in the hero's breast which has its equivalent in the divided forces embedded in his times has an equivalent also in the war we have noted between the foreground and the background in the poem, its dramatic and thematic developments. These are likewise at odds in being impelled separately toward different goals, the material and the ideal, the sensual and the spiritual, the immediate and the visionary beyond. But no more than the conflicts in these other spheres are ultimately resolved in the play, but only passed on to a new age, rethought and immeasurably broadened, does the work itself end its artistic struggle in coming to a conclusion. It accomplishes what was accomplishable in its time and so itself passes on a vision in the esthetic sphere that is informed by its own dilemma.[4] The time of classical expression and completion had passed and was not recoverable in an evolving world. The classical unit that forms Act III is in conflict with the whole, and that is its meaning, as we will see.

Goethe was aware of the conflict that might arise between the opening scenes of the drama and the *Helena*, already conceived and in part written two decades earlier, which was to be the centerpiece of the work. Schiller had warned of a 'barbarization of form' that would be necessary to carry out a second part to *Faust*.[5] Goethe himself as he worked on the first two acts wanted 'very much to complete [them] in such a way that the *Helena* as third act would follow quite naturally and, properly anticipated, no longer seem phantasmagorically inserted

4 In 'Ancient versus Modern' Goethe draws this analogy: 'Since the suffering we have endured and the actions we have performed leave an indelible imprint on our face, it is not surprising if every work or achievement which may result from our struggling bears the same imprint' (Gearey, ed., *Goethe's Essays*, p. 91).
5 'Das Barbarische der Behandlung, das Ihnen durch den Geist des Ganzen aufgelegt wird ...' (13 September 1800). It is in this letter that Schiller speaks of the *Faustrecht* that Goethe must exert in writing *Faust*.

but a part of a logical-esthetic sequence.'[6] By 'logical' I believe was meant the continuity of themes hidden in the background that would gradually emerge as the action progressed; by 'esthetic' the variety of poetic forms and structures that were developing in their own right but might serve as well to contrast with the *Helena* which represented the highest norm. These 'lesser' forms were not, however, now to be regarded as simply preparatory to a standard once set and forever to be emulated. *Faust* itself does not continue after Act III in a classical vein, for it has then left the world of Helen and returned to its own world, with its own form or forms of expression, themselves striving toward a new ideal. Like Mephistopheles who has no power over matters in the pagan spiritual world, the modern artist has no power over his artistic properties and sensibilities, which he cannot simply appropriate. They are the product of a time, as *Faust* in its moral and formal relativity is a product of its age in the broadest sense.

But how to motivate the appearance of Helen so that it will initiate the theme of beauty, which is the last main theme of the exposition, as the monologue in Pleasant Landscape had initiated the theme of knowledge and the masquerade that of morality in relation to history and to time? For if ideal beauty was itself to be seen as the product of time, its representation in the play could not logically be introduced as a phenomenon that has suddenly come full-blown into being; hence, the trip to the Mothers.

We forget as we puzzle over the meaning of the Mothers that their initial function in the play was as a ruse. Faust is right: a simple act of magic might have brought Helen to life.[7] There is nothing in the drama to this point to suggest otherwise. Of course, Goethe creates a diversion: A Christian devil has no sway over spirits in the pagan realm – a 'serious joke' that continues to fascinate. But the play is not about this division of powers in an unseen world, but here in particular about beauty, not beauty in an absolute sense, to be sure, but like good and evil in the drama, in its evolution. It is this grand theme, now introduced through the spiritual appearance of Helen, and not the striving of Faust or the exigencies of plot, that accounts for both the nature and the progression of the subsequent action. Act II, which is made seem-

6 My translation of 'in aesthetisch-vernunftgemäßer Folge' (in a letter to Zelter, 24 January 1828).
7 'Mit wenig Murmeln, weiß ich, ist's getan' (l. 6207).

ingly disjunctively to follow upon the exposition in Act I, in fact cuts a layer deeper into the background to reveal a prehistory, a preformation, of the development that culminates in the creation of ideal beauty in physical being and in art. For when we meet Helen in Act III it is as the real Helen in her own setting and time, which itself now has a background, and not the Helen that is the unreal being of Act I. We meet her not only as the representation of ideal beauty but also in a setting that represents an artistic ideal as well, namely, in the noble form of classical Greek tragedy. *Faust II* is as much about the evolution of Western art as it is about the evolution of Western man. The wonder, again, is that these two themes could be joined in a single work.

There was also the matter of the drama. If the trip to the Mothers is a ruse, it is not simply a plot factor. It prompts Faust to action, to be sure, who has long been idle in the foreground. It also elicits from him the kind of response that Mephistopheles can only wish and Goethe the dramatist welcome: 'In this nothingness I will find the All!'[8] Moreover, this realm of 'formation, transformation, / Of eternal mind, eternal recreation,'[9] though we do not see it and, indeed, it does not exist in time and space, anticipates the realm that issues from it in the Classical Walpurgis Night, where we see the images of animals and man that have come into being but not quite entered history. It is here that Homunculus will seek a body. Faust will seek an embodied Helen in the same realm.

But now he pursues a phantom, and that is what is dramatically significant. Background and foreground are importantly joined in the final scene of Act I. In reaching out for the phantom or mere illusion of Helen, Faust repeats, dramatically and thematically, the Emperor's action and error in grasping for the glittering treasure at the end of the masquerade. The one scene ends in a conflagration, the other in an explosion, and both are plays within a play, since Helen and Paris appear as in a pantomime. However, no more than the Emperor learns from his experience, but deepens the folly by acquiescing in the creation of the paper money, does Faust emerge chastised. He pursues Helen through the whole of the following act, as if seeking, like the Emperor,

8 'In diesem Nichts hoff' ich das All zu finden' (l. 6256).
9 'Gestaltung, Umgestaltung, / Des ewigen Sinnes ewige Unterhaltung' (ll. 6287–8).

to uncover the material that will give substance to the illusion that has been issued in its place. When we recall that it was Faust who in the guise of Plutus had tempted and tested the Emperor, the irony increases. For it is the Emperor who has now unknowingly (the Emperor knows nothing, it seems) tested Faust by having demanded the appearance of Helen in the first place. In the legend, Faust or Mephistopheles initiates the action and in the sketch of 1816 Goethe had planned the motivation in the same way. We sense the activity of mind that occurred between plan and execution as revolving around motifs that would join the thematics and dramatics in the play.

The irony in the failure of both the Emperor and Faust to pass their symbolic tests[10] is dramatic irony as well. This is the Faust who in the opening monologue had turned his back to the sun and here he grasps at an illusion as hungrily as he had there at first reached to the light. His action is Faustian, but now doubly wrong. This is the Emperor whom Goethe had portrayed 'as a prince who has every quality of character to cause him to lose his kingdom, which he then proceeds to do.'[11] Now the fate of both is, if not determined, at least joined. For the pursuit of Helen will not end in a meaningful resolution but in her unexplained disappearance forever at the close of Act III. Not that the drama, or the irony, lies in the abrupt reversal, which is the staple of the Faustian fate, but in the turn that Faust will take, as beauty as well as knowledge elude him, toward the active life, where he then reencounters the world that the Emperor has been creating since Act I and which will now destroy his efforts.

It is perhaps useless to speculate on what might have been had Faust not met Helen, in whatever form of being. But it is important to remember that had the urge to the active life had its onset with the first step in the 'great world' Faust could not have stood idly by as the matters of this world, at least in the social and political sense, were being determined. In this perspective, his inaction in Act I is a dramatic moment: it proves to be his nemesis. In the same perspective, but thematically speaking, his action when it does occur proves a test not of his character but of the philosophy he had just adopted in order to

10 On the Emperor's and Faust's responsibility in the neglect of time see Deirdre Vincent, *The Eternity of Being: On the Experience of Time in Goethe's Faust* (Bonn, 1987), pp. 129–31.
11 To Eckermann, 1 October 1827.

approach a new world or, rather, newly approach the world. The acceptance of life as colorful reflection has led to the acceptance of beauty as a substitute for truth. Beauty and truth are not joined in Act I but exposed in a conflict that will later have to be resolved.

CHAPTER SIX

Act II: The Search
for Body and
the Search for Beauty

Almost line for line in the form it was written more than two decades earlier the Helen fragment was taken over and made to serve its original purpose in a drama that had now been reconceived. The *Helena* became a stepping stone and a stumbling block. The barbarism that Schiller said would result from the joining of the classical and the modern spirits was a barbarism that reflected on the latter, not the former. The barbarity would have arisen from the sacrifice of beauty to truth, a price Goethe was not willing to pay at the height of his classical period when he began the *Helena*. He all but abandoned the project at the time. But the very problem, we know, proved to be the eventual solution. The conflict of styles reflected a conflict of worlds. Rather than distort the truth, this esthetic barbarism only emphasized the differences in reality between worlds born separate in time and not to be joined by a poetic stroke of the pen. These became the worlds of Part II.

With the *Helena* in place, Part II had to come to meet it. Yet in order to go forward, by its evolutionist nature the action had to go back in time. The thematic and the dramatic were again at odds after they would appear to have come so imaginatively together at the end of the previous act. The play could not move immediately into the real world of Helen, or the world of the real Helen, except by magic, and what is created by magic cannot be real. But poetry might serve. Not the fact, but an imaginary reconstruction, of the physical and the social, the biological and the spiritual forces that produced that person and that world might be offered, not as reality, since in art we are not in the realm of the real, but as a valid substitute for reality which magic is not.[1] That is the substance of Act II. When Helen does appear in her own context in the following act her entrance remains as unexplained as her later sudden disappearance. She appears and disappears not by magic or by dispensation of the Mothers, both of which dramatic agents were now at Goethe's disposal in the play, but by poetry. We accept her existence not because it has been explained but because it has been anticipated by a poetic and fantastic display of the kind of events, divergences, and metamorphoses in nature that might have preceded it.[2] Like the masquerade in Act I, which was equally unreal, and anticipated and creatively motivated Act II itself, the Classical Walpurgis Night motivates the appearance and substantiates the existence of Helen in Act III. For, done well, anticipation in the realm of art is the equivalent of motivation. Neither can be said to *cause* in any real sense, since both have their base in an admittedly unreal world. This is the motivation that must be sought in *Faust II*. There is no consistent and continuous motivation from character as there might be in another play.

It is important to note how Goethe himself reacted to the dilemma of joining what was not to be joined in time and yet had to be joined in the mind. Until the very end he hesitated. The various plans and notations for Act II, altered again and again, show a Helen brought to life through a magic ring that lends her substance, or through the intervention of Persephone and the Thessalian sibyl, or, in one instance, with Faust, like Orpheus, descending into the underworld and pleading successfully for her return. At one point Manto[3] was to play a mediating role in a 'Prologue to Act II' which never materialized. This after the actual publication of 'Helen: An Interlude to *Faust*,' in the announcement of which Goethe had wisely stated: '[How] our companions in magic succeed after various hindrances in bringing the actual Helen personally out of Hades and back into life may remain

---

1 Poetry may be said to be more 'real' than magic in that it reveals process and not simply an inexplicable creation from nothing.
2 Helen might be 'created' or 'motivated' in the play by Faust's dream of Leda and the swan at the beginning of Act II, but as Kommerell notes, 'Das ist kein ursächliches Verhältnis, sondern es wird ein geistiger Bezug gestiftet zwischen dem leidenschaftlichen Gedanken Faust ... und der vollendeten Erfüllung des Wunsches ...' (*Geist und Buchstabe*, p. 32).
3 In Goethe, Manto is the daughter of the healing god Aesculapius, as per line 7450, not the daughter of Tiresias.

for the moment unsaid.'[4] There is, however, nothing resembling such an action in the final version. The appearance of Helen, the 'actual' Helen, is anticipated but never caused. She is caused by poetry.

Goethe had cut the Gordian knot. The conflict between the classical and the modern spirits in *Faust* was in fact only the symptom of a deeper conflict which was now confronted. *Faust II* had broken with the past not only in joining traditions out of time but in defying the principle of imitation as such and replacing it with an associative principle. A revolution had occurred almost imperceptibly and yet was written all over the surface of *Faust II* when it was completed. I doubt that a decision was deliberately made. For it was not with enthusiasm or in a spirit of experimentation that Goethe had undertaken the continuation and completion of the work. It was from a sense of responsibility to his theme. A remark he made in a letter toward the end of his life illustrates this fact in a paradoxical way. It was not esthetic or philosophical theory that had sustained him in his struggle with *Faust* but, as he says in the letter to Wilhelm von Humboldt, 1 December 1831, a pair of lines from the play itself:

> If you profess yourself poets,
> Show your command of poetry.[5]

It was this supreme, surely unsurpassed, command of poetry in all its forms that allowed Goethe at this highest stage of his development to meet the demands his theme would make, allowed the theme to make the demands another poet might have turned from. When the demands caused a breaking of form at the deepest level, it was only after the greatest resistance. The sketches of the action and the paralipomena reflect to the very end a desire somehow to resolve the problem within at least the broadest scope of the tradition. A respect for the evolution of art as well is evidenced here. When the break finally came, with the philosophical and dramaturgical ungrounding of Helen, and with the reader or audience now accounting in the mind for what the poet had not accounted for in the play, Goethe might

---

4 In the final, greatly shortened version of the 'Ankündigung' to the *Helena* which appeared in *Kunst und Altertum*, 1827 (Beutler, Paralipomena, pp. 573–4).
5 My translation of 'Gebt ihr euch einmal für Poeten / So kommandiert die Poesie' (ll. 220–1).

even have felt that he had failed. Yet this new association, this 'supplying,' was the connection with the future. In its struggle with tradition, *Faust II* had not broken down but broken out. By that time it
had done more than honor to the tradition in its own variegated form.

Yet this artistically important moment could not have occurred without a moral purpose. For all that the struggle with Part II took place
in the realm of form, its result, the true break with the past, would
not have come had its consequences not been acceptable, indeed de-
sirable, in another way. What had resulted from the abandonment of
causal unity as first principle was not only a reality reflected as if in
the mind but also a new mental setting or climate in which moral acts
and decisions would be made and understood to be made. If *Faust II*
had been written for and through its hero alone, a conventionally
conceived dramatic world might have served. Dialogue or dream sequences might have been interspersed to expand its limits to the reaches
they in fact attain in the product as it stands. We have had, after all,
a trip to the Mothers in dialogue, and a dream sequence is about to
unfold in Act II. But the drama was written for another consciousness
as well, for the supplemental mind. We experience the play not through
Faust, as we do in Part I, but as a world or set of worlds in which he
plays a part, but which in the last analysis are there for us and would
almost be the same without him. We cannot in the same way think of
Denmark in Shakespeare without Hamlet. There was no reason for
Goethe not to close the causal gaps in the play through magic, or some
other device he had at hand, if it was not to activate this observing
mind. He might have created for Faust and for us a world philosophically and dramatically sufficient unto itself, for all its fantasy. But that
was not the point. The point was to involve us in a continuity open
enough and incomplete to allow for completion. When Faust dies we
continue with the world. As the work falls artistically, we fall morally
with it, into the future.[6]

We should not imagine because Goethe chose through dramatic disjunction to effect what is essentially a change in the realm of mind

---

6 Bennett writes: 'the work compels us to continue living in the atmosphere of the
   tragic. And that we continue living at all, therefore, takes on the quality of a
   moral achievement' (*Goethe's Theory of Poetry*, p. 37).

that *Faust II* now became abstract. He was a concretizer. 'Ich bin ein Plastiker,' he said to the art historian S. Boisserée at the time when he had turned to the completion of the work as his main task.[7] When *Faust II* leaves the real world it is only as the context demands. Even in Act I, where the trip to the Mothers evokes such images as 'fleeing what is / For the reaches of realms unbound,'[8] the action soon returns to the particular. The final scene renders reality, as Gundolf put it, 'as if Goethe were Voltaire.'[9]

These two instincts or demands of the drama are not only balanced through contrast and by that palpable imagination that informs the poem throughout. There is also the tension between the dramatic and the thematic, which while threatening, on the one hand, to retard the action seems, on the other, to give rise to the greatest imaginative creations. The Mothers is one such creation. Another is Homunculus, who will now dominate Act II and play the part in the foreground that the Emperor played in the previous act. But where the Emperor carried the theme of historical evolution, if only by default, Homunculus bears the theme of evolution as such.

His search for a body that will house his spirit is at once the eternal urge of the vital force or forces of life to realize themselves in matter; of anticipation to become reality; of thought to find expression in action. In his nature he is Becoming itself and thus in the play all that attaches to him suggests this idea of which he is the symbol. Creatures that might otherwise seem mere colorful imaginary figures in a backdrop, such as the pygmies and dactyls, the sphinxes and lamiae, the centaurs and one-eyed monsters that populate the Classical Walpurgis Night, begin to suggest origins in the light of his own desire to originate. Not that we are to see in this display a scientific, if poetic, reflection of the human descent into being. Least of all is a Darwinian progression implied. Rather the figures call up for us a world behind the mythology in which they have their existence and which itself is originating and developing, biologically, physically, and in terms of mind. It is a world, like the world of history in Act I, that has not as yet been devoured

7 From 19 May 1827. The first reference to *Faust II* as his 'Hauptgeschäft' occurs in a diary note for 18 May 1827.
8 My translation of 'Entfliehe dem Enstandnen / In der Gebilde losgebundne Reiche!' (ll. 6276–7).
9 Gundolf, *Goethe*, p. 762.

by the mind, which is only in the process of grasping it. Hence the philosophers, mentors, and sibyl appear among the sphinxes and pygmies. Our own supplying modern mind, to be sure, cannot help but see in the Walpurgis Night patterns that will later emerge with Darwin. He stands immovably between us and Goethe. Yet we stand between Darwin and a future yet to be defined. It is not, in other words, the transition to particulars that concerns Goethe in Act II and of which Homunculus is the symbol, but the taking and giving of form in nature and in thought that is the soul of evolution.

The pairing of the search for body with the search for beauty, of the Homunculus theme with the Helen theme, at least when so described, comes to represent as well the principle of art in its urge to embody thought, and Homunculus, then, the spirit of poetry. In that way he joins those figures more often so identified, the Boy Charioteer, Lynceus, and Euphorion. Since Faust in his search for beauty is reaching out for the loftiest ideal, while Homunculus clamors for the life of the earth, together they now appear to represent the two souls in Faust, in mankind, and in the poem as a whole. The alternating passage of Faust and Homunculus from background to foreground as they pursue their separate goals reflects the struggle of the drama itself to locate the action in character or in theme, which, since theme is thought and character body in dramatic art, is the struggle in the play as well. That Goethe did not always succeed in making thematics and dramatics one in *Faust II* is not only an indication of the difficulty of the task he had set himself but also a measure of the integrity of the solution. For a simpler solution existed had he chosen it. He might have strung out a series of experiences for Faust without regard to time and place but only as to the effect on his person, much as Ibsen does later in *Peer Gynt*,[10] and have allowed him to come to a conclusion about life after his long experience. Faust would have appropriated the world. But in Goethe's view, the world appropriates the person as the person attempts to appropriate the world. It is for that reason that the worlds in Part II are made to maintain their independence and are not devoured by the hero or by the play.

---

10 In the play, 'The action takes place in the Gudbrand Valley and the surrounding mountain-tops, partly on the coast of Morocco, partly in the Sahara Desert, in the Cairo Lunatic Asylum, at sea, etc.' The 'etc.' best makes my point.

The legend also played a part in determining the content and the form
of Act II. One of the surprising features of *Faust* is the way in which,
for all its modernization and reinterpretation of the theme, it continues
to touch base in the legendary material, as if gaining through the contact with its origins not only strength, like Antaeus, but direction. One
can almost see at times how a motif or detail of little importance in
the legend takes on in the creative process such great significance for
the new interpretation as to seem invented solely for that purpose and
not to be derived.

I am thinking again of Homunculus, but not as representative of the
homunculi that were allegedly created by the alchemists at the time
of the historical Faust (he will be discussed later in that vein) so much
as in his role as bearer of the action at this point in the play. He explores
the deepest past as he seeks out the formative powers of life. With
him we enter the bowels of history. Just as the Faust legend in its
sixteenth-century instinctive mode of thought often included a trip
through the heavens to the ethereal region where it believed the ultimate source of things to exist,[11] *Faust II* in its evolutionist mode seems
just as instinctively to have included a trip in the opposite direction,
through earthly time to the origins in nature. Nothing illustrates more
clearly the position in the universe of man in the legend and in Goethe
than these flights of imagination from separate eras, the one content
with unfathomable mysteries and glorying in the order of the cosmos,
the other seeking the causes of life in nature, which it too will celebrate
in the end. We have come not simply from a theological and metaphysical to a scientific view of life. The contrast rather is between an
outlook on the world that could and would find its 'innermost workings' in an unknown design beyond and one which seeks them on and
in the earth. Above the former stands the Sign of the Macrocosm, above
the latter the Sign of the Earth Spirit which Faust chose in Part I in its
place.

Not that, after Goethe, either the Faust dramas[12] or the drama in

11 See P.M. Palmer and R.P. More, *The Sources of the Faust Tradition: From Simon
   Magus to Lessing* (New York, 1965), ch. 18, for the English trans. of the *Historie*
   (London, 1592); also H.G. Haile trans., *The History of Doctor Johann Faustus* (Ur-
   bana, 1965).
12 Lenau will hardly have had time to absorb *Faust II* when he completed his own
   Faust, in 1838. Grabbe's *Don Juan und Faust* (1829) pre-dates Part II and depicts a

general now conceived of man as *of* the earth, a biological and historical
being, and formed their plots and action in frames that would reflect
that fact of existence. Man remained in the drama essentially the same
social being he had been in the tradition that had determined the nature
of theater from its classical beginnings.[13] It was not that the new concept of man in an evolving world was rejected as such, but rather that
its implications for the form of drama were as unsettling as we know
them to be from observing Goethe as he pursued the matter to its end,
and thus prohibitive. In the drama of the nineteenth century a compromise was generally struck, surely unconsciously. Those aspects of
determinism and historicism that could reasonably be reduced to the
stage, to a moment in time from which all moments of history in their
essence might be extrapolated, such as the sense of environment and
the power of heredity, were retained and at times molded into modern
classical forms that might rival the ancients. Again we think of Ibsen.
Yet the same view that provided a scientific and naturalistic sense of
the deeper context of human actions also precluded, and again surely
unconsciously, that perspective on the whole of experience which is
contained in the universe of language. The metaphorical, allusive, and
virtually unbound nature of the elevated language that creates the
unseen world in traditional drama had no place in the modern experiment, which was further constrained by the now even greater demands
of imitation in the new realistic or naturalistic mode. One often hears
the demise of tragedy attributed to the limited character of modern
subjects and subject matter. But it is also true that the full potential of
language, had it not generally been denied to modern drama in its
beginnings,[14] might likewise have developed as an instrument to un-

---

hero reminiscent of Faust in Part I. Heine's *Faust: Ein Tanzpoem* (1847) is erotic
and in that sense of the earth, but not philosophically conceived. Valéry's hero in
Mon Faust (1946) is intellectualized.

13 This is the point that Brecht makes in his notes to *Mahagonny* (1930). Brecht and
Goethe may seem strange bedfellows, especially the Goethe of *Faust II*, but the
concept of epic theater relates to that of cubistic drama. Both grew out of the need
to express a radical new vision, the former deriving from Marxism, the latter from
an evolutionist concept of life, themselves not unrelated philosophically and in
their historical origins.

14 By 'modern' drama I mean here the drama that began in the eighteenth century
as middle-class drama and evolved into realism and naturalism in the nineteenth

cover the nobler, because more distant and infinitely attached, reality that underlies simpler things as well.

Goethe, of course, still had at his disposal all the advantages of poetic drama and the genius to exploit them. Yet his task was to uncover the deeper context not only of a single, static, or constant world but of a broader cultural development amid historical diversity, as if in an excavation of a collective unconscious mind.[15] This latter demand caused the break with the dramatic form as such.

---

century. In any elaboration of this point, one would have to mention Strindberg, whose *A Dream Play* is reminiscent of *Faust II* in form, and the verse plays of importance in the twentieth century by Claudel and T.S. Eliot, as well as the whole movement of Expressionism in drama, all of which form exceptions to my generalization. But it is true that the use of prose in drama was determined by the nature of the subject matter and the subject matter chosen to fit the prose.

15 On archetypes and *Urbilder* in Goethe and in *Faust II*, see Gottfried Diener, *Fausts Weg zu Helena* (Stuttgart, 1961), pp. 14–18 and passim. The bibliography contains full reference to relevant works of C.G. Jung.

CHAPTER SEVEN

Act II: Homunculus
and the Classical
Walpurgis Night

Goethe was never comfortable with *Faust*. Not only his remarks about its strange and even monstrous qualities are evidence of the fact. These reflect the discrepancy between the changes in his own development and his attachment to the theme over a lifetime. But almost from the beginning there was reluctance and hesitation. Only *Urfaust* seems to have been written with ease and dispatch. Thus, the casual remark in a letter to the Duke of Weimar, 16 February 1788, which was written even before the publication of *Faust: Ein Fragment* (1790), 'I have in front of me the hill *Tasso* and the mountain *Faustus*.'

One might have imagined, therefore, that the prospect of finally composing a part of the work that would seem by its nature to lie on the other side of the mountain, that is in the open ground that had been created by the decision to break with the dramatic past, would have presented a welcome change. Yet Act II, which represents this passing over from imitation to the associative or symbolic mode, also gave Goethe pause. He must announce the successful completion of the first part of the act 'quite modestly,' he says in a letter to Zelter, 26 July 1828, 'because if it were not there, I wouldn't write it.'

The remark is the more surprising because the beginning of Act II was the first opportunity that Goethe had in the second part of the play, or rather took, to return the theme to its moorings in the legend and in Part I from which it always threatened to stray. The opening scenes reintroduce not only Wagner and the laboratory in which Faust once conducted his alchemical experiments but also the student whom Mephistopheles had interviewed in what would seem now ages ago in *Urfaust* and here interviews again. An important sense of continuity and the passage of time is reestablished. Since Faust in effect will be removed from the scene once more, in that he will be caused to sleep and see in a dream the image of Helen who is the spiritual mistress of the pursuant action, the birth of Homunculus, that serious joke par excellence that is now introduced, serves ingeniously as diversion. Homunculus is born in thought in a test tube and Helen engendered in a dream in the mind of Faust, side by side. Science and art set out, the one in search of reality, the other of beauty. Theme and setting and action could hardly be more at one, and yet Goethe was still uneasy.

Yet what we might see, and celebrate, as a significant breakthrough in the drama and in the history of dramatic art Goethe will have seen as necessity. His struggle with *Faust II* did not appear to him as it might to us the harbinger of a development that would culminate almost a century later in the modern movement of symbolism. It was not with confidence or satisfaction that he described *Faust II* as 'highly symbolic.'[1] For he was demanding of himself, of the reader, and of the dramatic form, the creation through symbols and associations of a context itself, and that a newly conceived context, not one established or presupposed but existing in the mind of the author and being created in the mind of the audience or the reader. It was imitation by association. At this point the disjunctive dramatic frames of the play no longer appear, as they might have before, the contrivance of a learned poet to reflect an erudite vision but rather the inevitably disruptive result in art of the attempt to express a truly new perception of reality. The attempts in the literature of more recent times to re-create the working of a human psychology more deeply understood remind us of Goethe in his attempt to state a similarly persistent but as yet not wholly defined new sense of life in an inherited form. Neither attempt is a description of what is but a re-creation of what is coming into being; neither is a definition, but a part of the defining process. That Goethe made the attempt in the drama and not in another form caused the more disruption, on the one hand, but, on the other, seems to project the problem even further into the future.

---

1 'Dies Gedicht ist hochsymbolisch intentioniert' (to Felix Mendelsohn-Bartholdy in a conversation of 21 May/3 June 1830). 'Alles was geschieht ist Symbol' (to the philologist Karl Ernst Schubarth, 2 April 1818).

Homunculus, we said, represents the idea of evolution, the coming into being. He also occurs, as it were, at the point where the drama itself comes into its essential being. Act I, technically at least, remained bound to objective reality by creating plays within the play when it wished to escape the limits of sequential cause and effect. Magic may have been involved, but the dramatic frame was respected. In Act II, what was in any case a pretext is abandoned and the action allowed to pursue its imaginative and imaginary course, with Homunculus, himself a product of the imagination, in the lead. The phantasmagoric substance of this course, the Classical Walpurgis Night, is neither a play within a play nor a dream, as some interpreters in their attempt to rescue *Faust II* for the literary tradition have claimed.[2] For if Faust dreams his pursuit of Helen in the Walpurgis Night and, for that matter, his life with her which comprises the whole of Act III, who dreams Homunculus? If the action is a play within a play, who are the audience if not us alone, which is the working frame of the drama as a whole? Nothing will have changed conceptually.

Not that the matter, again, is a dramaturgical or literary question alone. The issue, as we noted, is also moral. The state of mind created by the action in a drama forms the reality that constitutes the arena of decision. When that reality extends to the farthest reaches of history, as it does in *Faust II*, and in a manner that is associative rather than causal or motivative, not only is the broadest context for action and decision created, but the broadest freedom. The state of mind that will bring Faust ultimately to the renunciation of magic and to 'wisdom's final say' we know to have been caused by this broadest and freest expansion of reality, not because we know him to have experienced it but because we assume that all that has passed before *us* from the beginning will inform *his* actions in the end. This is true of all drama, with the difference that here the action is not wholly devoured by the hero alone. He need not dream what occurs in order for us to possess it, nor we imagine what is not caused in the play as existing in the mind of others. When no one is 'creating' in *Faust II*, we become the creators. That is the new freedom the drama affords us. While Goethe could not have foreseen the extent to which the emerging historicism and scientific determinism of his own age would soon lead to an almost

2 Atkins, *Faust*, p. 181, speaks of a 'double dream.'

overwhelmingly restrictive sense of the human position in the larger
order of nature, it is precisely this creative open-mindedness in the
structure of the poem that renders its moral atmosphere free. In its
moral as well as its esthetic implications *Faust II* appears again to leap
over the nineteenth century and seem more in place in our own time.

We know almost exactly how Act II took shape. The detailed scheme
of action that Goethe set down in 1826[3] and which became over the
next few years the scenes we know as Laboratory and Classical Walpurgis Night is a revealing document. The difference between the action as planned and its eventual poetic representation is striking. The
planned antecedents to the Helen act showed similar discrepancies
from the final version, but these were eventually resolved, as we saw,
by an act of creative neglect: Goethe simply abandoned the principle
of dramatic causation. But the differences here reflect neither simple
change nor complete rejection. Rather it is as if in the death of the
plan a poetic product was reborn on a higher level. If in the development of the Helen theme we saw a launching or springing into a
new form, in Homunculus we see an organic growing into the future,
in the work no less than in the imaginary character himself. All the
elements and motifs that would eventually find expression in Act II
are there in the scheme in their initial form. But the scheme reveals a
Goethe leaning backwards; in the actual composition he leans forward.

The return to persons, places, and things from Part I, which the
scheme outlines and the opening scenes of Act II develop, already
suggests a looking to the past for guidance. Hence the appearance of
Wagner from out of the past, as the scheme required. But what is further
projected is the point, and the projection goes little beyond satire.[4] In
the plan Wagner has created a homunculus in a glass tube and is
'glorying'[5] in his invention. But this homunculus immediately shatters
his retort and emerges as a lively, perfectly formed little creature. There
is no suggestion of his future evolving. The formula for his creation is
only mystically suggested, but he gives evidence of his unique capac-

3 See Beutler, Paralipomena, pp. 564–73.
4 The most extreme view of the satirical content of these scenes is Otto Hoeffler's
   Homunculus (Vienna, 1923) in which A.W. Schlegel is seen as a creature of Wagner whom Goethe is satirizing as a type.
5 'Beutler, Paralipomena, 'hoch glorierend' (p. 566).

ities, notably of a world almanac preserved within him which enables him to say what has occurred on earth under the same constellation of stars and planets at any precise moment since Adam's birth. The present moment he determines as the night before the famous battle between Caesar and Pompey in Thessaly, so that the Classical Walpurgis Night, more or less as we know it in detail and sequence, might begin. Its purpose is not further made clear in the scheme.

But it is obvious that Goethe initially intended Homunculus to function as a recording device of history no less than as the object of satire. On their trip to celebrate the Walpurgis Night, in which Wagner in the plan also takes part, Homunculus records an 'incessant buzzing of geographical-historical facts'[6] relating to the lands and nations they traverse on their way from the German north back in time to the classical Thessalian battlefield at Pharsalas. In this capacity he resembles the Faust of the plan who was to descend to the underworld in pursuit of Helen and there likewise encounter 'limitless incidents'[7] – of a historical and mythological nature and import, we must assume.

However, satire soon has the upper hand in the projected version. We find Homunculus settled in the right breast pocket of Wagner's coat and in the left another vial, should the occasion present itself to gather elements for a female homunculus, *ein chemisch Weiblein*.[8] We are even presented with Homunculus scooping up from the mold of the battlefield phosphorous atoms streaming blue and purple light which are then scattered to the winds, as Pompeian and Caesarian forces, now joined, vie to capture these components of their individuality in the hope of restoring themselves to life. But the ingredients of their Roman greatness have already been absorbed, they are told, in 'millions' of cultural effects in later history.[9] Resurrection and immortality have as well been naturalized.

What distinguishes the projected scheme of action from its creative counterpart are not the details. Rather it is the way in which these details, though retained, are made to serve the new scheme of thought that has taken form from the decision to have Homunculus conceived

6 'Ein grenzloses Geschwirre geographisch-historischer Notizen' (p. 567).
7 'hier gibt es zu grenzenlosen Inzidenzien Gelegenheit' (p. 572).
8 Beutler, Paralipomena, p. 569.
9 'durch Millionen Bildungsfolgen aufgenommen und verarbeitet worden' (p. 569).

as a spirit and begin a journey in search of physical being. We now have the life and birth, in that order, of Homunculus. The images of fantastic creatures, 'evolving as if out of themselves,'[10] which served in the plan simply as phantasmagoric backdrop to the pursuit that was to end in the freeing of Helen from the underworld, now with the transfer of the burden of the action to Homunculus serve as physical reminders of the passage to human life he must traverse before he can 'come properly into being.'[11] He traverses the passage, in fact, in reverse, proceeding from the highest level, which is symbolized in the faculty of speech with which he is 'born,' back through ever lower and incomplete forms, to the deepest primal environment of the sea. These same images that would have served in the plan as the transitional, hybrid, monstrous, and ungainly forebears of the physical ideal that Helen represents, and as the disorderly stumbling of nature toward the supremely ordered beauty that is hers and that of ancient classical art, now become the reflections of a protean creative force that underlies all things and is accepted in its own right. All four elements that in the view of ancient philosophy comprised the whole of creation are celebrated as Homunculus enters the sea. 'Highly honored evermore, / Be the elemental four!'[12] It is the same joining of conflicting forces that Goethe seems himself to have accepted in art when he completed *Faust* in the way he did. The monster art was not easily to be tamed again, as had once the ancient Greeks.

The point at which Goethe decided to lean forward and allow his drama to take its course into the future[13] cannot be determined, for there is no documentary evidence, but it can be surmised. It must have come in the composing and not in the planning. The idea, at once poetic and philosophical, that provided the base and anchor for the widest range of action, namely the Mothers, is not present in the plan. '[So] very much depends on luck, almost on the very mood and power

10 'sich gleichsam aus sich selbst entwickelnd' (p. 568).
11 My translation of 'im besten Sinn entstehn' (l. 7831).
12 Hochgefeiert seid allhier,
   Element' ihr alle vier! (ll. 8486–7)
13 He had little hope his drama would be appreciated in his own time. To Wilhelm von Humboldt, in the last letter he write before his death, 17 March 1832: 'The times are really so absurd and confused that I'm convinced that the long and earnest effort I have made with this strange creation will be ill rewarded and at first lie shattered like a wreck and be covered over with the debris of the hour.'

of the moment,' Goethe said to Eckermann about the process of writing, after the latter had ventured the remark that with a detailed plan already there for *Faust* only quick execution was needed.[14] But it was hardly luck, or rather it was the kind of luck that attaches to creativity, that produced the Mothers. This single poetic idea, like the vision from eternity in the Prologue in Heaven, but now resident in the fecund center of the universe and not in a beyond, not only serves as the source of all things real and imagined in *Faust II*, and thus of both Helen and Homunculus as they appear and will appear in different forms, but as the productive source. For the Mothers create, they do not predetermine. No poetic idea could come closer to the evolutionary concept of the workings of nature, and yet this idea emerged, as it were, at the last minute. In the letter quoted above where Goethe speaks of his hesitations with Act II, he mentions the fact that with the completion of the first scenes he had only to 'close Act I, which is complete almost to the last detail.' One wonders whether that detail, nowhere present in any of the sketches and plans for *Faust*, was not after all the motif of the Mothers. The Mothers, then, would have been conceived in the 'mood and power of the moment' and not through the processes of thought. Other facts speak for this assumption.[15] If so, we would have in that moment not only the creation by an author of an image that was clamoring for expression in his work but also the birth in and through poetry of an idea that was simultaneously finding its way into the science and philosophy of the time. It is as if with the idea of the Mothers Goethe had found the reason why his imagination had led him to conceive the fantastic festival of the Classical Walpurgis Night. Everything leads back to the Mothers. It is where we begin in thought in *Faust II*. It is a beginning deeper than with the God who appears in Part I.

14 15 January 1827.
15 There is no mention in earlier plans of Mephistopheles's resistance to calling Helen back to life through magic. In the plan in question there is hesitation, but the ruse takes the form of an argument about the Benedictine calendar which supposedly would not recognize this night as the Classical Walpurgis Night. The obstinancy is then moved to Act I where it occasions the motif of the Mothers.

CHAPTER EIGHT

Act II: The Classical Walpurgis Night

The distancing of cause did not entail the ignoring of continuity, either in the science of the age or in Goethe's poem. Remoteness did not mean inscrutability, as it had in the Christian and Judaic idea of God or the ancient concept of fate, both of which, like the Mothers, might function as *causus remotas* in drama or in thought. It was the insistence on continuity that gave rise in science to the sense of expanded distance and time, since the attempt to fill the gaps historically and conceptually, which was required in the new but not in the older mode of thought, led to a pushing back and a pushing out in order to accommodate the facts that the research into nature increasingly revealed. Goethe had much the same task in *Faust II*. Of course, he could not in a drama, or perhaps in any creative literary form, include as action all the antecedents of a human fate. Nor did he choose to let the one stand for all, which again would have been an absolutist, or classical, or traditionalist approach to the matter. But he could, and did through the device of form, create the images and allusions that together would fill the gap between the present and a receding past, if not with logical, then with imaginative causal thought. Thus the Classical Walpurgis Night.

Even before this fantasy begins, all is evolving in Act II. Not only Homunculus comes into being, and with that act symbolizes the very phenomenon, as if we were present at the birth of mankind, but also Wagner reemerges, extended now to his extreme, and producing at the height of his powers his magnum opus, a human spirit. The satirical element of the plan has been rendered almost sublime. Mephistopheles, it is true, has a hand somehow in the creation and yet the creature itself, in its freedom, energy, and intellectuality, is no longer the object of ridicule. The new Homunculus does honor to Wagner and, behind him, to the tradition of rationalism and the beginnings of science in alchemy, which relates to the former in its principle of abstracting from nature. Both are wrong, but in a right way. 'Him I love who desires the impossible,'[1] Manto says, and Wagner has accomplished at least part of the impossible. In that he resembles Faust. The difference is that he is satisfied with the accomplishment.

In the passage from plan to execution even Homunculus becomes touched by a certain pathetic irony that emerges with his change in function and meaning, as if the satire in the plan that was now suppressed would have its revenge. Homunculus is an idea that must become reality and so in his idea stage enjoys all the freedom of possibility and suffers none of the constraints imposed by actual birth. Freedom above all is what radiates from him. In that sense he represents the artistic creative act in its luminosity of conception and inevitable graying in the approach to eventual being. When Homunculus is born he will bring with him, we know, not only the mortal casing that will have evolved with his spirit from its ocean origins to the stage of man, but also the conditionings of culture and the ravages of history, whatever the form they may take in his time. Here he seems eternal – which is perhaps why he can address Mephistopheles as 'cousin.'[2] There is a deep irony, however, in his clamoring for birth when all we have been given to see of human existence thus far in the drama has been dismal in the main. Proteus warns satirically: 'Once you have become a man, / Then surely you are finished.'[3]

But since he appears at the very moment when the action has again suffered a reversal, with Faust at the beginning of Act II reclining 'paralyzed'[4] from the events of the preceding act, Homunculus seems to hover over the scene like Ariel, a spirit of affirmation and rebirth. Together they remind us of the rejuvenation and revitalization which

1 My translation of 'Den lieb, ich, der Unmögliches begehrt' (l. 7488).
2 'Herr Vetter' (l. 6885). On the relation of Faust to Homunculus see Ronald Gray, *Goethe, the Alchemist* (Cambridge, 1952), pp. 217ff.; further, Klett, *Der Streit* pp. 34–7; Diener, *Fausts Weg*, pp. 275–81.
3 My translation of 'Denn bist du erst ein Mensch geworden, / Dann ist es völlig aus mit dir' (ll. 8331–2).
4 Line 8568.

not only the hero and the action but the work itself when paralyzed in its composition has so often undergone. *Faust II* may not be, as Jung has suggested, a poetic representation of an alchemical design,[5] but it contains within it so many expressions in different ways of death, rebirth, and ascent that surely that principle was at work in the drama in some insistent fashion. The Homunculus who dies with the plan is clearly reborn in a poetic environment that raises not only him but all that he touches to a higher level.

The historian is concerned with evolution, the evolutionist with history. Nothing in *Faust II* illustrates more clearly the acute awareness of the past, and of the importance of the past in forming the future, than the motif that Goethe now introduces quite unexpectedly. The student from Part I, whom we may well have forgotten, revisits his university and speaks with his old academic adviser, Mephistopheles. The motif is not in the plan, but appears to substitute for the satire that was lost in the ennoblement of Homunculus. This present satire is a lesson in history and evolution. The Student who reemerges from Part I (in terms of composition, some fifty years before) has not simply developed but has progressed in a vacuum. The vacuum has been created precisely by a lack of awareness and knowledge of the past. 'The world was not, till I it did create,'[6] he tells Mephistopheles, who if anyone knows how untrue that is. 'While half the world we 'neath our sway have brought, / What have you done? Slept, nodded, dreamed, and thought, / Plan after plan rejected. Nothing won.' 'If one is over thirty / He's as good as done.'[7] There is enough truth in this statement, not to make it valid, but to uncover the seriousness of the premise that would give rise to such logic. In a world viewed not simply as repeating in its history the familiar patterns and errors of the past, but as devoid of all beginning and meaning until it is first experienced, the passing of generations can only be regarded as replacement, not as regenera-

---

5 Jung meant as well a pattern in the human unconscious mind. See C.G. Jung, *Psychologie und Alchemie* (Zurich, 1944); also Diener, *Faust Weg*, pp. 247–53; Gray, *Goethe, the Alchemist*, pp. 217–18.
6 'Die Welt, sie war nicht, eh' ich sie erschuf' (l. 6794).
7 Indessen wir die halbe Welt gewonnen,
  Was habt ihr denn getan? genickt, gesonnen,
  Geträumt, gewogen, Plan und immer Plan ...
  Hat einer dreißig Jahr vorüber,
  So ist er schon so gut wie tot. (ll. 6782–8)

tion. 'It were best if you would kill yourselves in a timely fashion,' the student says, referring to his elders.[8]

Beyond the natural aggressiveness and arrogance of youth, Goethe is here satirizing specifically the subjective philosophy of Fichte that had captured the mind of much of the younger generation in his time. Yet Fichte had simply romanticized the absolutism of the previous age by identifying its source not in reason but in the supreme ego. His thought can be seen as an offspring of the *Sturm und Drang*, with which it shared the tendency to cataclysm. But the cataclysmic was what Goethe would reject as the primal force in nature, as the Classical Walpurgis Night itself will show. Yet the destruction of the old to make room for the new was no more easily denied in the social order[9] than in nature. The geological formations that had been formed by violent eruption were as much in evidence as the changes in history that had been gained through revolution. A philosophy built on nature had to accept its violent ways. Before the play ends there will in fact take place the egregious destruction of an old couple to make place for Faust's grand project of the future. The Student may be mocked, the violence rejected, the *Sturm und Drang* repressed, but if one goes out from life and nature, as Goethe does in *Faust*, they are not to be denied.

History, like evolution, is rendered poetically in *Faust II*. The passage from the present to the remote, imaginary past in which the Classical Walpurgis Night takes place is not made abstractly. The geographical-historical account that seems to have been intended in the plan, with Homunculus as recorder, is abandoned, but the transition point in time and place, that is the setting of the festivities on the eve of the decisive battle between Pompey and Caesar in 48 BC, is retained. These Pharsalian fields are the cultural and historical Brenner Pass of the mind. Through this battle, through these fields, passed and were formed, the makings of European history. It was only right that they should be traversed again in the mind on the way to what came before, like the sand through the narrow neck of the hour-glass reversed.

8 'Am besten wär's, euch zeitig totzuschlagen' (l. 6789).
9 There is a clear anticipation of Social Darwinism in the line, 'Falleth the weak, the able presses on' (l. 6781). This brave new man has the sun *before* him, 'Brightness before me, darkness in the rear' – 'Das Helle vor mir, Finsternis im Rücken' (l. 6806).

The mood on an eve of battle is magically evoked in the classical verse form fitting to the subject:

> O'erwhitened seems to me,
> With waves of dusky tents, the valley, far and wide,
> Night phantom of that dire and appalling night.[10]

And the outcome is known: 'Knows the world who here prevailed.'[11] But it is the far-reaching result of this battle that relates it to the world from which Faust and Mephistopheles have emerged. Pharsalus established the monarchial over the republican form of rule.[12] The Emperor of Act I is the successor to the Caesar who envisioned in the individual the rule of order he believed dissipated when left in the hands of the many. He is his empty image. The power invested in this Caesar (the German for 'Emperor' is *Kaiser* and a transcription of Caesar) is itself dissipated. In the end Faust will envision an ideal social order grounded in active freedom and ruled by individuals of greatness. The vision is unrealized, but it remains the stated ideal.[13]

One might have expected as conduit from the modern into the ancient world a setting or moment associated with the birth of Christ. We date our calendar from that time. Yet it is clear on second thought that neither Christian philosophy nor morality, except in a negative sense, has any important role to play in Part II until the very end, where amid imagery and assonances of mystical religiosity distinctly Christian intimations of forgiveness, salvation, mercy, and love are heard. But Christian thought in both its story of creation and its concept of nature was directly opposed to the idea of evolution, a priori as well as in practice in Goethe's time. The pagan world was closer to life and to nature in their deeper beginnings. It not only reflected mutation and transformation in its myths and its images of monsters but seemed

---

10   Überbleicht erscheint mir schon
     Von grauer Zelten Woge weit das Tal dahin,
     Als Nachgesicht der sorg- und grauenvollsten Nacht.   (ll. 7009–11)
11 'Weiß die Welt doch, wem's gelang' (l. 7024).
12 Some see the decisive change as occurring later with Augustus.
13 This might also account for the high esteem in which he held Napoleon to the
     very end. See below, ch. 13, pp. 154–5.

itself to partake in the process of the evolution of mind in so imagining them. The generative force of evolution that produced changes in nature at the same time produced change in the human mind that was created to deal with this evolving world.[14]

Not that the conduit into the pagan world leads into a realm politically, historically, or philosophically conceived. Only the entrance to the Classical Walpurgis Night has historical or political significance. The world within is pre-historical. The reappearance on this night of figures and creatures from different eras of reality and myth renders the scene eerily timeless and, yet, marks the great passages of time like the strata of geological formations. Though all come together, each remains in its place. The Sphinxes, who are ageless, do not 'reach up to' Helen in time,[15] as they tell Faust, and so cannot help him in his pursuit. If the drama as a whole creates the sense of continuity and the passage of time by juxtaposing distinct worlds in its individual acts, the Walpurgis Night in one setting creates the same impression within a single realm. What seems a dream is in fact a consciously structured, multilayered vision of an evolving world of animate and inanimate nature. Foreground gives way almost wholly to background. Faust, Mephistopheles, and Homunculus, though they do not lose their purpose, lose their importance for a time against this broadest and deepest backdrop in the play.

The task for Goethe in the Classical Walpurgis Night was to select from among the myriad fantastic creations of the ancient mind those that would provide 'the necessary visual impression.'[16] But to what purpose they would be necessary is not immediately clear. No more than the other worlds in *Faust II* is this imaginary realm made to conform solely to the needs of the play, that is, its dramatic needs. Like the masquerade sequence, it acts as if it had a life of its own.

---

14 Goethe in 'Stages of Man's Mind': 'While the primitive masses look about with fear and amazement in search of the barest necessities, a more advanced spirit gazes at the great phenomena of the world, perceives what occurs there, and gives utterance to what exists with profound awareness as if it came into being before his very eyes' (trans. from 'Geistesepochen' [1817], in Gearey, ed., *Goethe's Essays*, p. 203).

15 'Wir reichen nicht hinauf zu ihren Tagen' (l. 7197).

16 To Eckermann, 24 January 1830: 'bildlich den gehörigen Eindruck machen.'

After the illusion of the battlefield is dispelled, the creator of the illusion, the ancient classical witch Erichtho, dispatched, and Faust and Homunculus dispersed to seek their own ends, the action begins with a seemingly idle confusion and play with words. Mephistopheles addresses a griffin, *Greif*, as an old man, *Greis*, which leads to a mock etymological discussion. A sphinx offers a riddle. Ants, 'of the colossal kind,'[17] appear and complain of the one-eyed arimasps who have stolen from them the gold it is their duty to guard. There is banter about the proper title for the Devil, which Mephistopheles, after looking round to see if any Britons, 'who otherwise travel so much,'[18] are present, selects as Old Iniquity from their ancient plays. Mephistopheles and a Sphinx exchange insults in regard to their respective characters and physical traits. Sirens appear and attempt to lure Mephistopheles away from 'these hideous wonders,'[19] or, as Erichtho described the scene, 'this ghastly fête.'[20]

Little of substance but much of importance emerges from this recreation of the images that populated the early ancient Greek imagination. Nature teems in them, monstrously but therefore more clearly. The mixture of bird and beast, of man and animal, in seemingly endless variation and distortion of size suggests an animal kingdom never seen but nonetheless as vivid in our minds as the unknown creatures that a responsible modern science attempts to depict. A past is recaptured in the present in terms of its own knowledge, imagination, and purposes. The purpose in *Faust II* was poetic, and while its mode was fantasy, it was historic fantasy rooted in a past and behind it we are to imagine some form of fact.

What we are to make of these first impressions beyond their suggestion of animal and man perceived by the developing mind becomes clear only with the return of Faust to the scene. What we see as monstrous, he sees as the inchoate beginnings of greatness. In these hybrid and disproportionate forms he finds and anticipates, finds *through* anticipation, a later beauty. 'How strange! ... In the repugnance, what

17 After l. 7103: 'von der kolossalen Art'
18 'Sind Briten hier? Sie reisen sonst so viel ...' (l. 7118).
19 Ach was wollt ihr euch verwöhnen
   In dem Häßlich-Wunderbaren! (ll. 7156–7)
20 'Schauderfest' (l. 7005).

strength! It augurs well.'[21] Faust in his passion and pursuit would of course see beauty everywhere, as Mephistopheles is first to observe. He might 'even welcome monstrosities.'[22] Yet this disposition is not simply engendered in the moment. It is inherent in Goethe. From the beginning in both his esthetic and his work, in theory and in practice, there was the demand for the embodiment of truth, whatever its form. 'Art is long creative before it is beautiful,' he had stated in his early essay, 'On German Architecture,' written about the same time (1772) as *Urfaust*. For all its attempts in the intervening years to become whole in its thought and form, *Faust* remained creative, a work in search of beauty and order, not in possession of them. Its hero pursued a similar course. For form and morality are related. Try as he may to attain the perfection of experience that is moral beauty, Faust fails and must accept in his final reckoning with life the necessity of imperfection, which in the moral realm is sin or error or evil. The drama has set itself the formidable task of making even the monstrous actions and moral failings of Faust themselves seem in the evolving order of things to 'augur well.'

In the Classical Walpurgis Night we are on the threshold of beauty and order. Act II presents the antecedents to Helen. Its wild imaginings anticipate, they augur, a later time when they will emerge in art in perfect proportions and the realities behind them produce after eons the model of human physical perfection.[23] The Walpurgis Night is the *Sturm und Drang* of the classical world. That world of seemingly eternal perfection had as well its formative years. And just as the *Sturm und Drang* of a later day eventually produced a classical Schiller and Goethe only to compel them to change in order to meet the new demands of a developing world and mind,[24] so the ideal that Faust is seeking, once realized, must be passed beyond. The drama does not end with Helen,

---

21 My translation of
   Wie wunderbar! ...
   Im Widerwärtigen große tüchtige Züge.
   Ich ahne schon ein günstiges Geschick. (ll. 7182–4)
22 Denn wo man die Geliebte sucht,
   Sind Ungeheuer selbst willkommen. (ll. 7193–4)
23 Goethe believed, as we noted earlier, that man existed at the top of the scale of creation.
24 See above, ch. 1.

as might a play conceived within a frame of absolute values in which
the attainment of the ideal is a final end. The ideal in Goethe is progressive. It exists in time. Faust must realize the ideal within time,
which is the logical and tragic contradiction in the play, time being the
element that renders the ideal less than eternal and so less than ideal.
The moment will not linger, whether fair or not.

Faust, we know, will not attain the ideal. It would be his damnation.
Yet the ideal in Part II is not merely stated or posited, and stated or
posited in such a way as to forebode its failure of realization. The ideal
in this world of time and places gains its significance and character
not simply by its existence but equally by the way it comes into being.
In an evolving world, what is is explained by what has been. Amid
the confusion of the Walpurgis Night, the stages in the ascent to Helen
are dramatically marked. Not only is she anticipated and, as it were,
progenerated in the dream of Leda and the swan in the previous scene,
but now in the ritual of the Walpurgis Night Faust sees her conception
reenacted. The language in which the scene is described is itself an
ascent to classic beauty. Zeus the swan approaches:

> Most wonderful! Swans now draw near.
> Forth from the bays their course they steer,
> Oaring with majestic grace ...
> Head and beak they move apace!
> But one seems before the rest
> Joyfully the wave to breast,
> Sailing swift without a peer.[25]

There is no deliberate intent to gradate the poetry in these scenes from
the more primitive to the nobler forms. The creatures of the Walpurgis

---

25 Wundersam! auch Schwäne kommen
  Aus der Buchten hergeschwommen,
  Majestätisch rein bewegt.
  Ruhig schwebend, zart gesellig,
  Wie sich Haupt und Schnabel regt ...
  Einer aber scheint vor allen
  Brüstend kühn sich zu gefallen
  Segelnd rasch durch alle fort ...   (ll. 7295–304)
  On the nature, forms, and varieties of the poetry in the drama, see Kurt May,
  Faust, Zweiter Teil (Berlin, 1936).

Night speak the verse appropriate to their nature or being, not because it has been created for them but because it is the verse of the Faust world, which like its hero is itself seeking definition and resolution. Sphinxes, griffins, lamiae, and sirens are as hybrid in nature as the Faust verse and, like the verse, in their unformed state have the freedom and potential for development.[26] Nor are these figures themselves graded in the progression of the ritual. Its character is wholly fantastic and its actions based on the premise of the recurring of these specters all at once on a single night in a display of the wonders of nature primitively conceived. Goethe said that one must imagine the separate actions of Faust, Mephistopheles, and Homunculus as occurring at the same time.[27] Rather it is the choice that each makes in pursuing his ends that determines what comes to the fore, much as in the mind, but not as in nature where all is blended.

Faust seeks out Chiron. Chiron 'reaches up' to Helen in time and so can guide Faust as the Sphinxes cannot. The centaur is hybrid, but ennobled in both his parts. In place of the ungainly and ugly features that the creatures of the Walpurgis Night thus far present, he displays the fine body of a steed and a human torso. He exists on a higher physical plane. He also represents a great stride in culture. He is the tutor and mentor of demigods, among whom are the heroes and heroines who stand for the highest virtues and human accomplishments from noble action through wisdom to the pursuit of beauty, this last symbolized by Orpheus.[28] In contrast to the Sphinxes, whom 'war and peace and inundations'[29] all fail to perturb, and who remain the observers and not the promoters of human endeavor, Chiron is in constant motion. His wondrous figure itself suggests a compelling animal force which his human part might control only with difficulty. Helen has

26 To S. Boisserée, in a conversation, 3 August 1815: 'Everything is metamorphosis ... the more perfect, the less the potential for transformation from one form to another.' That our own forms of poetry could still be at a relatively primitive or formative stage is not a thought that is often entertained – or that mankind is still in a state of youth (to K.F.A. Conta, 16 March 1809).
27 Beutler, Paralipomena, p. 570.
28 There is even the suggestion of a hierarchy of cultural values in the progression of his heroes from martial prowess to the finer arts, though Heracles remains the 'indescribably' (ll. 7393–4) greatest among them.
29 Überschwemmung, Krieg und Frieden –
Und verziehen kein Gesicht. (ll. 7247–8)

ridden on his back and occupied a position which Faust now assumes with erotic awareness as he mounts the centaur. That such a figure of wisdom and counsel, otherwise so common in high epic and drama, should appear at all, however, is surprising. It reminds us that Faust has no friends.

As much as Chiron recalls in his speech, and himself symbolizes, the advent of a heroic age, and through the recollection inspires Faust to great accomplishment, he has otherwise no influence on him. The instinct of wisdom is to temper and Faust will not be held back. The very principle of moderation, appropriate in an age overwhelmed by action, is not suited to the world or state of mind from which Faust has emerged and where action is a rare virtue. The Lord had in mind modern, not early Greek, humanity when he spoke in the Prologue in Heaven of the tendency in man to seek 'unconditional rest.'[30] Chiron can only direct Faust to Manto, prophetess and daughter of the famed physician of myth, Aesculapius, in the hope that she will cure him of his passion for Helen. Manto responds quite oppositely. It is here that she says, 'Him I love who desires the impossible.' For the feminine element in Goethe is not the tempering but the inspiring element. The Eternal Feminine 'draws us on,' as the Chorus Mysticus will state. Although in the reclusive quiet of her temple Manto seems remote from the world of action: 'I wait, time encircles me,'[31] it is she and not Chiron who accompanies Faust into the underworld to recover Helen.

What the knowledge of anatomy did for the painting of the Renaissance, the knowledge of science did for the poetry in *Faust II*. When Goethe passes to the next phase of the Classical Walpurgis Night he creates a new poetic backdrop to match the new action in the foreground. The first phase, or panel, since we may think of the Walpurgis Night as a triptych, with the action, as Goethe said, occurring all at once and the separate missions of Faust, Mephistopheles, and Homunculus taken up in order, has as its setting the biological kingdom. The second explores the making of the physical world. It is here that

30 'Er liebt sich bald die unbedingte Ruh' (l. 341).
31 'Ich harre, mich umkreist die Zeit' (l. 7481). Manto's similarity to Makarie, the modern sybil of the *Wanderjahre*, has often been noted. On Makarie see, e.g., Schrimpf, *Das Weltbild*, pp. 313–22.

the knowledge of geology and geomorphology plays its part. The accomplishment was quite extraordinary. It was not that Goethe the scientist expressed his knowledge of physical nature in a poetic way. Erasmus Darwin had done as much and Lucretius long before him. Rather he conceived poetically what he had received scientifically; created for a poetic, not a didactic, purpose a vision of the physical world not as sensation or impression, but as fact. Lyric poetry by his time had abandoned the use of the physical world as artificial landscape and entered into an intimate relationship with nature. He himself had written some of the greatest nature poetry in that sense. Yet always in this poetry nature was seen as there for man and not man as a product of nature. This natural fallacy helped to produce what we now may think of as poetry as such, so much has its lyrical and rhapsodic qualities, its musicality, come to dominate the physicality of the world it presents. Goethe went behind sensation in *Faust II* to the making of physical nature, its coming into being. Where an earlier age might have seen God or an unfathomable universal design behind what the eye could not perceive, he saw physical occurrences and physical laws. He saw them poetically. We have already noted the phenomenon of the rainbow and its significance. But the going behind to what the mind knows but does not see is the mode of creation of the work as a whole. The past is brought to bear on the present not only historically but physically. In it nature does not serve, but encompasses and accounts for, man.

In creating now the physical backdrop to the primitive figures that had come to the fore, Goethe invents a new god, Seismos. He invents him because he might well be present in the Walpurgis Night, as were potentially all the ancient titans and demigods who played a part in the development of Western thought.[32] The invention of the magical night was itself a stroke of genius. For it was not simply a means of representing symbolically a range of ideas and experiences, it was the only means of bringing together in dramatic form a perception of reality that included in its glance the past in the present, the inner workings in the outer forms. Again, paradoxically, it was the mythical and mag-

---

32 Goethe personifies what was traditionally simply a power or characteristic of Poseidon.

ical that served best to express the scientific observation in art. Seismos, indeed, through the workings of intellectual history, no longer suggests to us simply myth, but science, and yet poetry. Seismology and the god both come to mind at the mention of the name. Yet when Goethe made use of the god to symbolize and act out the creation of physical features in an earthly background, he was thinking poetically. The science of seismology had not yet been born in his time. In the same way that he evoked 'the collected monstrosities of the ancient world' and allowed them 'to develop out of themselves'[33] in order to suggest a progression in the biological kingdom, which we now call evolution, he caused a god to move the earth, knowing equally well the physical explanation for the phenomenon. The point was not to state poetically what was better known scientifically; the point was to make into an experience what otherwise remained only an idea. It was as if once the idea were formulated scientifically and had become fixed and defined, it could no longer, or less easily, be conceived poetically. But *Faust II* came into being *with* Darwin and *with* Lyell, not before or after them.[34]

Goethe has us experience the formation of the earth poetically by presenting an earthquake which he has occur and describing it from afar. This teichoscopy, or 'view from the wall,' which the Greeks used to preserve dramatic unity as they described an action that occurs offstage, he employs to make present what is real and yet unseen.

> Now uprears itself a dome ...
> Arms wild-stretching, back low-bending,
> Atlas-like, amid the surf
> Shale he raises, grass and turf,
> Pebbles, gravel, loam, and sand
> Tranquil cradle of our strand:

33 From Beutler, Paralipomena, p. 568: 'die sämtlichen Ungestüme des Altertums ...,
   sich gleichsam aus sich selbst entwickelnd.'
34 The first volume of Lyell's *Principles of Geology* appeared in 1830. Goethe's reading, or knowledge, of Lyell, if any, came after the plan for the Walpurgis Night of 1826. Yet Alexander Humboldt, who was close to Goethe, had met Lyell earlier in Paris, after the latter had delivered the famous paper on which his later *Principles* was based. Bielschowsky sees an anticipation of Lyell in Goethe (*Goethe: Sein Leben und seine Werke* [Munich, 1906], vol. 2, p. 443). H.B. Nisbet, *Goethe and the Scientific Tradition* (London, 1972), makes no mention of Lyell.

Crosswise he a track [has] wrest
From the valley's tranquil vest.[35]

In the original plan it was intended only that an earthquake occur and that the god who had been banished beneath Etna, Entceladus, appear and celebrate the occurrence.[36] In introducing the god who 'creates' the earthquake, Goethe joins his science with his poetry and we see a mountain formed before us.

The earth that Seismos has created through violence stands, he claims, to the glory of man:

Had I not shaken and upthrown,
How had the world been now so fair?
Into the pure ethereal blue,
Their crests how should the mountains raise,
Had I not heaved them forth to view,
To charm the painter's raptured gaze?[37]

This last line is not incidental. At issue in the Classical Walpurgis Night is the emergence of beauty and order from the chaos of creativity, in art as well as in nature. Helen will so emerge, or seem to have emerged, in Act III after the wild celebration of creation in Act II. Out of the chaos will come order, in the play as well as in nature. But as the action moves toward the ideal, it seems to have the need always to return to

---

35 Nun erhebt sich ein Gewölbe
   Wundersam ...
   Er, mit Streben, Drägen, Drücken,
   Arme straff, gekrümmt den Rücken,
   Wie ein Atlas an Gebärde,
   Hebt er Boden, Rasen, Erde,
   Kies und Grieβ und Sand und Letten,
   Unsres Ufers stille Betten.
   So zerreiβt er eine Strecke
   Quer des Tales ruhige Decke.   (ll. 7530–43)
36 Beutler, Paralipomena, p. 569.
37 Und hätt' ich nicht geschüttelt und gerüttelt,
   Wie wäre diese Welt so schön? –
   Wie ständen eure Berge droben
   In prächtig-reinem Ätherblau,
   Hätt' ich sie nicht hervorgeschoben
   Zu malerisch-entzückter Schau?   (ll. 7552–7)

its origins, which are rooted, as here, in disorder. The anticipation of Helen seems to produce in Goethe and in the play the urge to reassert the freedom that resides in chaos. Act II is the 'antecedent' to the *Helena*, as Goethe put it, in that way also.

Yet the movement from vital chaos to order, which is the scientific no less than the esthetic movement, is not the most important moment that is captured in the arising of a mountain before our eyes, or mind's eye. Rather it is the crucial recognition of the nature of creation, in art as in physical matter, which is in time and in process. This applies to the creations of God or of man. The Sphinx observes:

> What here has struggled into birth,
> Had we ourselves not witnessed how
> It tore itself from out the earth,
> *Primeval* we would deem it.[38]

Like the moment of Carnival in Act I, which illuminated a political, moral, and social view of life, this geomorphic moment throws into perspective the new understanding that views all things as emerging 'from out the earth' through eons and not as made each in immutable form. The art that was once seen as immortal and timeless is now viewed as wrested from its time, like the seemingly timeless mountains. Only the Sphinxes, like the Mothers, seem untouched and remain unmoved. 'Yet not for this shall any sphinx retreat; / Untroubled we retain our sacred rest.'[39] Not surprisingly, Mephistopheles wishes always to return to them as to a base for his own unmoved and immutable nature, though in appearances he changes. 'A mountain, hardly worth the name, / Yet high enough to keep me from my Sphinxes.'[40]

Knowledge is experience. No more than Goethe in creating Seismos

---

38 Uralt, müßte man gestehen,
   Sei das hier Emporgebürgte,
   Hätten wir nicht selbst gesehen,
   Wie sich's aus dem Boden würgte. (ll. 7574–7)
   My italics. I have altered the last line slightly from Swanwick.
39 Ein Sphinx wird sich daran nicht kehren:
   Wir lassen uns im heiligen Sitz nicht stören. (ll. 7580–81)
40 My translation of
   Ein Berg, zwar kaum ein Berg zu nennen,
   Von meinen Sphinxen mich jedoch zu trennen
   Schon hoch genug ... (ll. 7688–90)

allowed himself the indulgence of abstraction but caused his mountain to arise on the shoulders of a god, does he describe the effects of the action in an intellectualized way. The god himself does not act with vision or from higher purpose, for all that he takes full credit for the beauty and grandeur that are the end result of his periodic eruptions: 'That I have wrought, myself alone.'[41] He incorporates the will to power and little more. Seismos knows not what he does, but does what he knows and justifies it. The mountain he has raised, and on which he now invites plants and animals as 'happy dwellers'[42] to grow and so complete the beauty of his creation, in fact attracts ants, dactyls, and pygmies who scurry to find the gold released in the new fissures of the earth, though it will also have released the iron that may be forged into chains. The ants and dactyls, the lower orders to the pygmies, have failed before they have begun:

> Deliverance in vain!
> The iron we bring,
> They forge the chain.[43]

This action ends with the Cranes of Ibycus, the avenging spirits, shrieking hatred overhead at the pygmies who have killed the herons, their brothers, to procure the colorful plumes that grace their helmets in war. The political overtones are apparent.[44] All this the mountain has occasioned before it becomes beautiful. The backgrounds diminish and subvert the foregrounds time and again.

Yet the intent and instinct of the work is not destructive. Goethe did not wish to destroy in order to create again from nothing. For him the negative was not the negation of the positive, but part of it, as

41 Line 7550.
42 Und fordre laut, zu neuem Leben,
Mir fröhliche Bewohner auf. (ll. 7572–3)
43 Wer wird uns retten:
Wir schaffen's Eisen,
Sie schmieden Ketten. (ll. 7654–6)
44 Its relation to political events of the day is described most recently by John R. Williams, 'Die Rache der Kraniche, Goethe, *Faust II* und die Julirevolution' (*Zeitschrift für deutsche Philologie*, vol. 103 [1984], pp. 105–27). Arens, *Kommentar*, pp. 481–3, surveys the differing allegorical interpretations of the conflict between the cranes and the pygmies.

error is a part of truth, evil a part of the good. If there was as much of Mephistopheles as Faust in his own nature, the result was not a conflicted mind but a comprehensive grasp of reality. His two philosophers, Thales and Anaxagoras, whom he now introduces on the occasion of the newly arisen mountain to speculate on the origin of earth formations that was the heated geological question of the time, likewise possess no exclusive grasp of the truth. They partake in their natures of the beliefs they express. Anaxagoras, fiery by temperament, is the proponent of violent upheaval as the former of the earth, and has the new mountain before him as proof. Thales, of a conciliatory nature, is the champion of slow process, the ways of water and not of fire, and represents the Neptunist against the Vulcanism of his opponent. Yet the character observation is not in the spirit of satire but of that comprehensive view in the drama which can combine playfulness with seriousness and finds an underside to all things it touches, not in order to expose them but to see them round.

At this stage in his development Faust would instinctively have sided with Anaxagoras had he been present to witness the argument, Goethe at his stage with Thales. The latter position, however, was the more radical, strange as that might seem. The question was so heated in the first place because the view of the Neptunists, which pictured a process of formation that was conceivable only over vast periods of time, contradicted the standard view derived from the Bible of a Creation once and for all. Fossils found beneath layers of formations that bespoke millions of years were attributed to animal remains from the Deluge – a violent upheaval of water, to be sure, but a vulcanistic principle.

All this is background of the broadest nature. Yet it has its dramatic point. The appearance of Thales and Anaxagoras is justified not by the light they cast on a contemporary controversy but by the context their argument provides for the action of Homonculus, who like Faust and Mephistopheles has been launched into this fantastic night with a purpose. Against a backdrop of teeming nature that engenders life and living beauty, Faust has descended into the underworld in search of his ideal, from which he will reemerge in Act III in its possession. Mephistopheles, in a context formed by the actions of both his companions, is transformed and likewise only appears again in the world of Helen. Homunculus stands alone and must decide on the basis of this strange argument he hears what form his life, literally, is to take.

His concern in the matter is of a keenness that can only be produced by such vested interest and it gives rise to the priceless line, after Anaxagoras has presented his forceful opinion, 'And what says my good Thales?'[45] Amid the serious joking Homunculus must choose. He opts for the slow processes, unlike Faust who in his impatience cannot wait for a new form of beauty or of the ideal to arise from the history and processes of his own age. He returns to the sea in order to come properly into being, and we await his second coming.

The Neptunist-Vulcanist controversy has less to do with *Faust II* in terms of content than in terms of form. Whatever the position Goethe ultimately held on the question,[46] and whatever thoughts other than geological he might have had in mind in introducing the motif into the Classical Walpurgis Night, such as the relative merit of evolution or revolution after the events of 1789, the controversy has its meaning in the play, whichever side one takes. The drama itself is not predicated on the attainment of certainty or conscious knowledge as the antecedent to action. It is not veiled over with the cast of thought, for all that it is in essence a philosophical poem. It attempts to capture truth through action and not through thought, much as in its transitional and incompatible position as a work of art in its own time it attempted to capture beauty on the wing and not in repose.

So too with Mephistopheles' transformations. What begins as a romp in an element and among personages seemingly compatible with his nature develops into a variation on a theme. Mephistopheles also must change. Metamorphosis is at once the theme and the dramatic purpose of the Classical Walpurgis Night. But unlike Faust and Homunculus, change is what Mephistopheles fears most. He must be lured into *becoming*, which is inimical to his immortal nature and so natural to man. Yet everything he encounters in this eerie element is not what it seems – with a mountain that has arisen 'in a single night'[47] and attractive Lamiae who when he embraces them transform themselves

---

45 My translation of 'Was sagt mein Thales?' (l. 7881).
46 For Goethe's position as it is reflected in *Faust*, see the differing views of Lohmeyer, *Faust*, pp. 253–9, and Mommsen, *Natur- und Fabelreich*, pp. 190–206, and the concise discussion in Barry Laine, 'By Water and Fire' (*Germanic Review*, vol. 50 [1975], pp. 99–110).
47 Line 7859.

or burst: 'I fear, those rosy cheeks behind, / Some metamorphoses to find.'[48] The humorous use of the scientific term speaks to the seriousness with which the concept is otherwise employed throughout.

The one thing that can tempt Mephistopheles and lure him away from his sphinxes, who like him are immune to the mutations of time, is a degree of ugliness that will impress even him who has existed from the beginning of time. This he finds in the phorkyads, ancient witches who share among themselves a single eye and tooth, which they exchange. They are the daughters of Chaos, as he is the son, and like the Mothers, reside apart, 'immersed in solitude and night profound.'[49] Mephistopheles borrows the eye from the three sisters, turns in profile, bares a single tooth, and resembles them exactly.

> *Meph.* I, the wondrous son of Chaos!
> *Phorkyads.* Daughters of Chaos we, indubitably![50]

Mephistopheles has made his own descent into the underworld or, better, has descended into his own underworld, and will reappear in the following act transformed into Phorkyas.

With this transformation the second sequence in the Walpurgis Night ends. The first showed Faust in his pursuit of beauty against a background of biological change, the second the Devil in his antics and eventual capture against the deeper and broader transformations of the physical world. Homunculus will now begin his transformation into a human being: 'Away to Proteus! Ask that being strange / The secret of existence and of change.'[51]

His catabasis, or descent, is thus played against an accumulated background that includes all the forces and elements of nature that will go into his making and, when he reemerges, will sustain his being. The final scene of Act II is an ode to creation, and like the finale of

---

48 Und hinter solcher Wänglein Rosen
   Fürcht' ich doch auch Metamorphosen.   (ll. 7758–9)
49 Line 8000.
50 'Des Chaos viel geliebter Sohn!' – 'Des Chaos Töchter sind wir unbestritten' (ll. 8027–8).
51 Hinweg zu Proteus! Fragt den Wundermann:
   Wie man entstehn und sich verwandlen kann.   (ll. 8152–3)

Beethoven's Ninth Symphony seems to leave its setting and enter a mode that does not so much transcend as underlie all that has gone before. What began as interruption, or seemingly so, now serves as continuity. The pursuit of beauty, which appeared to be the main motivation to action at the outset, has gathered to itself so many of the ingredients and associations that constitute and accompany the pursuit of life itself that by the end of the act the latter has consumed the former. *Faust* the quest has become *Faust* the accumulation, as does all life, if not all art.

This development was not foreseen. The 1826 sketch of the antecedents to the *Helena* makes no mention of a final celebration of the forces of life by the Aegean Sea, since no apotheosis or further development for Homunculus was planned. The idea of metamorphosis and transformation came in the writing. It was the same with Mephistopheles, who had been created as Phorkyas in the *Helena*, and had now to evolve into him/her – the figure is conceived as hermaphroditic. Phorkyas, like the *Helena* as a whole, was written *toward*. But the movement toward is the movement of transformation, of evolution, of the creative act. It is also the historical moment of *Faust II* when we see the drama as a work of transition and not of culmination, and its existential moment, as it were, when we think of the sixty years of thought and composition *toward* its completion. For Goethe, the completed *Faust* was never there, it was always going to be, until the very end. One cannot help thinking that this state of becoming in the unseen form of the work not only accompanied but gave rise to the images, aspects, and, ultimately, philosophy of transformation and evolution that are projected in its action. 'Everything transitory is only a metaphor,' and metaphor is poetic metamorphosis.

There is an excitement of sounds, images, and activity in the finale of Act II that might well have been experienced in the creating as frenzy. Goethe spoke of a kind of state that might be called insanity in which he composed parts of *Faust II*.[52] Of the some 450 lines of the scene, more than 300 may be designated song, some in chorus. If drama in fact had its birth in music and ritual, in the Walpurgis Night it is reborn. Not that there is in birth a madness. Yet the confluence of forces that

---

52 To Wilhelm von Humboldt, 1 December 1831: '... was Aristotles und andere Prosaisten einer Art von Wahnsinn zuschreiben würden.'

marks all creativity would seem to produce a freedom from self and from conscious purpose that is a 'kind of insanity.' Confluent, and finally conjoining, in the scene by the Aegean Sea were not only the cumulative images and themes of metamorphosing nature that were the substance of the act as a whole, not only the celebration of the origins of life itself that was to be its finale, but all this in the form of dramatic action. Homunculus, who has now stepped again into the foreground, is being born, or reborn, and we are to witness his birth. Since this fate was not originally planned for him but came into being, or so we may assume, in the execution as a product of art, we may see in it and in him the idea of metamorphosis itself metamorphosing in the composition of the work. That Goethe might have experienced the creation of these passages relating to Homunculus as coming from a source deeper than thought is reasonable, given what was brought together in this single figure and action. The fact remains that he did not know what to do with Homunculus when he first conceived him, and now the purpose had become clear.

All must be comprehended in the urge, intent, and forces of nature that cause Homunculus's birth. Though he will be made with humor, he will not be made lightly. Time will go into his making, as it will not for Faust in his realization of Helen, so that eventually she simply disappears. All elements will inform his birth. The new assemblage of gods and mythical creatures that now appears not only suggests the healing and changing and staying powers of the sea, with snake charmers on sea bulls and sea rams accompanying the shell on which Galatea crosses the waves, but in recalling the creatures we have met through the Night suggests teeming life on the water as well as on land. Nereus, the sea god, is present, as is Proteus, the symbol of diversity and change. The Cabiri, the oldest and most revered of the gods, are in attendance, brought forward as idols in a procession, though it is hard to tell whether they are being honored or mocked.[53] These gods possess above all the instinct for development, 'still desiring / What can never be reached.'[54] Like the masquerade in the previous act, the scene sug-

---

53 It is generally assumed that Goethe is mocking the efforts of Schelling and the classical scholar Georg Friedrich Creuzer to identify and describe these Urgods. Schelling's 'On the Gods of Samothrace' had appeared in 1815.
54 Sehnsuchtsvolle Hungerleider
   Nach dem Unerreichlichen. (ll. 8204–5)

gests life itself, but in its biological and primitive stages, not in its social order. When Homunculus enters the sea there is a thematic climax in the play. The dramatic climax must still be accorded the meeting of Faust and Helen, whom Galatea in her beauty in her own right anticipates.

Climax is the appropriate word also in its sexual sense. Homunculus's birth is the most serious of the very serious jokes in *Faust II*. Goethe makes the event symbolically explicit. The vial in which his essence is contained, 'throbbing from the pulses of love,' amid 'symptoms of forceful desire,' 'glows,' 'flashes,' and finally 'spills its contents'[55] as it dashes itself against the shell of Galatea, itself in shape and color suggestive of the female sexual organ.

Commentators and translators often diffuse this explicitness in the description, perhaps from a misguided sense that the profundity of the poem is compromised by its instinct for the natural. There is more talk of Eros than of orgasm in most discussions of the passage. In that spirit Homunculus,'s action can even be described as a sacrifice of self, as if his, and human, existence were the product of a spiritual and not a physical act.[56] Yet the natural in its immediacy and palpability, and not merely in its abstraction as *Naturphilosophie*, is the principle on which *Faust* is built. In it religion is naturalized, morality made one with the laws of nature. 'The spirit of the real is the truly ideal,'[57] Goethe once said in a remark that well describes the work. It describes as well the quality present in Raphael which I believe attracted Goethe and his age to the painter. His *Triumph of Galatea* probably served the poet as a visual model for his poetic imaginings in the present scene.

For Homunculus to come into being through this most common and universal act of nature not only comports with, and indeed epitomizes,

---

55 Homunculus ist es, von Proteus verführt ...
　Es sind die Symptome des herrischen Sehnens,
　Mir ahnet das Ächzen beängsteten Dröhnens;
　Er wird sich zerschellen am glänzenden Thron;
　Jetzt flammt es, nun blitzt es, ergießet sich schon. (ll. 8469–73)
56 For example: 'Through self-destruction he wins the way to existence on a higher plane' (Alexander Gillies, *Goethe's Faust* [Oxford, 1957], p. 145). Barker Fairley is the exception: '[Homunculus] thus enjoys in a state of innocence ... the erotic climax that Mephistopheles had been vainly seeking all night in a state of sin' (*Six Essays on Faust* [Oxford, 1953], p. 82).
57 'Der Geist des Wirklichen ist das wahre Ideelle' (to Riemer, no date, 1828).

the deeper truth that the poem is seeking, but is a triumphant serious joke. Eros in the higher sense is not denied. 'Prime source of creation let Eros be crowned'[58] immediately precedes the paean to all the forces of nature that closes the act. But this Eros is not Platonic, as it would not be in the work of a poet who stressed the oneness of body and mind.

Goethe assumed a purpose in creation, especially in regard to man, whom he saw, as we noted earlier, as its crowning achievement. But he did not accept the teleological view which was generally held in the eighteenth century. 'The question of purpose, the *Why*, is in no way scientific. One gets somewhat farther with the question *How*,' he said to Eckermann, 19 February 1831. His Homunculus, which reverses the Frankenstein myth that pictures a body in search of a mind, reflects as well a reversal in the approach of science to nature in the nineteenth century which Goethe shared. Mary Wollstonecraft's *Frankenstein*, to be sure, appeared at the beginning of that century, in 1818, but it reflected the earlier view that mind alone identified the human being. Homunculus brings us solidly back to earth.

58 'So herrsche denn Eros, der alles begonnen' (l. 8479).

CHAPTER NINE

Act III:
Helen Alone

The Helen fragment he had written almost three decades earlier Goethe took over virtually intact into *Faust* and continued from where he had left off. One might wonder why the relatively insubstantial piece was not simply abandoned after so many years so that the project might begin wholly anew. Yet the same urge to return to beginnings that we find in the substance and thought of *Faust*, we find also in its composition. The *Helena* of 1800 had faltered, but not for lack of ability or will. Its some 300 lines show that Goethe had 'mastered the Greek sensibility.'[1] Initially the will to continue was not only there but expressed itself in the greater desire to create a tragedy in its own right from these beginnings. 'I feel no small urge to build a proper tragedy on this foundation,' he wrote to Schiller at the time. '[I] would not like to have it turn into a mere parody.'[2]

Yet the mastery itself was the problem. To use an exaggerated expression, Goethe had attained a perfection that is death. He had long since emerged from his *Sturm und Drang* literary beginnings and through a progression of works had reached what seemed an ideal. *Iphigenia* and *Torquato Tasso*, completed more than a decade before, are the epitome of Weimar classicism. But what followed the epitome? What can follow an epitome? In order now to progress with the *Helena*, he would have to create or uncover a broader vision in which it would find new purpose as thought and as art. That he was at an end in this

---

1 Barker Fairley, *A Study of Goethe* (Oxford, 1947), p. 163. See also Humphrey Trevelyan, *Goethe and the Greeks* (Cambridge, England, 1941).
2 From 13 September 1800: 'in eine Fratze verwandeln.'

regard is clearly indicated by the number of uncompleted manuscripts and aborted literary plans of the time that are classical in form and subject matter.[3]

Faust provided the new context and purpose, not the Faust that had already been conceived and written but the part that was about to come into being as Faust II. The schema of 1800, the year of the Helena, reflects precisely the situation:

> Conflict between form and the formless.
> Preference for formless content over empty form ...
> These contradictions, instead of reconciling them,
>   are to be made more disparate.[4]

This is the 'barbarous' conflict that Schiller immediately sensed but which for Goethe would now take place within the frame of 'all of nature,' as the scheme states,[5] and thus be resolved not in the realm of art, or at least not first there, but in the realm of experience. 'A Spirit as Genius of the World and of Action,'[6] which we might well regard as associated with the Earth Spirit of Part I, was also to appear. There is almost defiance in the stressing of the prospective contradiction rather than prospective artistic harmony in the plan.

Yet it was out of conflict that Faust II arose. Goethe might have ignored its radical demands and completed his drama as it had begun, free in form, broad and imaginative and symbolic, and yet in its essential perception of reality conforming to the world as it had always been seen in the tradition. The Helena forced his hand. If he was to have his Helena and have his Faust, his true Faust, he would need to return to a new 'barbarism' and a new beginning. The Helena inspired, or forced, not the content of Faust II, since the Helen motif was already present in the legend, but its structure. That structure was predicated,

---

3 The epic Achilleis, the dramas Elpenor, Nausikaa, Die Befreiung des Prometheus, and in a lighter vein, Proserpina.
4 Streit zwischen Form und Formlosen.
   Vorzug dem formlosen Gehalt vor der leeren Form ...
   Diese Widersprüche, statt sie zu vereinigen, disparater zu machen.
   (Beutler, Paralipomena, p. 541)
5 'Einwirken und Einfühlung in die ganze Natur.'
6 'Erscheinung des Geists als Welt – und Taten-Genius.' I use here the English rendering of Cyrus Hamlin, ed., Goethe's 'Faust' (New York, 1976).

to repeat, on the creation of independent but interrelated worlds that would reflect reality as registered in the prism of a knowing eye. Goethe the poet could have written a *Helena* complete in itself and perfect in the sense mentioned above; Goethe the scientist, or better, Goethe in the consciousness of science, had to create a 'barbarous construct' that would include that perfection and by its very inclusion create through contrast the apparent barbarism.

We must think of Helen in her own right. Goethe had no intention of devouring her in his larger plan. He not only retained his fragment intact but added an additional 300 lines before any mention or anticipation of the appearance of Faust who was to save her from an impending fate. Interpreters have tended to ignore this patently undramatic, or antidramatic, persistence. The tendency has been to elevate Helen to a primal moving force or symbol and regard the incidents and actions in the play that are not moved or motivated by this force as secondary or irrelevant. Rickert in his important attempt to establish the dramatic unity of the work regards the whole of the first scene at court in which we saw the creation of a basic world in *Faust II* as 'of no importance for the dramatic development of the poem, as imaginative as it might be.'[7] There is a unity in *Faust II* but it is an allusive, not a dramatic, unity, as are works of art in their essence allusive because they are unreal. The effort to reduce all the action in the work to motivational relations proves not only tenuous but distracting. If we follow the action solely from Faust's point of view, Helen seems always to be turning her back on us. Their encounter itself must be a disappointment if we have been told that all the forces in the action and not only those in Faust's mind have been leading up to it. There are other worlds in the play and states of mind and Helen simply, though importantly, occupies one of them.

But it is not for the sake of the inner structure in *Faust II* alone that we must keep these worlds separate and equal and contradictory, or at least contrasted. The decision to continue *Faust* in the face of the contradictions it presented esthetically, and to make those contradictions more disparate while yet not foreseeing clearly a resolving end, was a moral act in the evolutionist spirit of the work itself. That the act occurred in 1800 with the creation of the Helen fragment is the

7 Rickert, *Goethe's Faust*, p. 297.

more striking, since it may be seen as marking precisely the division between a new and the older, eighteenth-century view that understood creativity, morality, and science as means to a clearly envisioned end. The potential greatness of *Faust II* when it began lay not in the clarity of its vision but in its uncertainty, which lent it the openness to expand.

From yonder strand I come, where first we disembarked,
Still giddy from the roll of ocean's billowy surge ...

These opening lines from the fragment which in the final version will follow the choral songs of the Walpurgis Night finale and open Act III, and in which Schiller heard the 'lofty noble spirit of ancient tragedy,'[8] are distinctive. We attend to them without their meaning. They are as attractively strange to us as will be the rhyme to Helen in the speech of Faust when they meet. They are distinctive, not foreign. The cultural context in which we ourselves hear them provides easy reference from the layers of experience and history that comprise our own world. They sound ancient and classical. They bring with them a mode of experience or state of mind that differs from the always anticipating and concluding, separating and resolving, rhymed verse that is so familiar to the modern mind.

We cannot say what Goethe thought and felt in writing these lines, but we know what the classical Greek world meant to him at the time. It represented an ideal that contrasted with his own experience of life. To him that world was at one with itself, while his own world knew no such peace. He had tried in Italy to recapture the mind of the past among the remains of its monuments, yet the mood would not persist. – 'Why are we moderns so distracted, why challenged by demands we can neither meet nor fulfill?' For the condition was as much cultural as personal. It was not he, or Faust, who sought the seemingly impossible, it was a state of being. There existed outside his world, he had discovered, other states of being that had produced the perfect and the ideal without apparent conflict and struggle. The classical Greek experience represented for him such a state and thus an ideal.

8 They are the iambic trimeter of Greek tragedy:
  Vom Strande komm' ich, wo wir erst gelandet sind
  Noch immer trunken von des Gewoges regsamen Geschaukel ...   (ll. 8489–90)

But the ideal had now become historical and was no longer absolute. As he understood the Greek world, he also understood the circumstances that had created it and recognized that the same circumstances did not obtain in the modern setting. The essays on art that he wrote on his return from Italy are not composed under the banner of the Greek ideal, as is often assumed. The essay on Winckelmann, for example, points out the limitations of the art historian who believes he has found in the Greek model a form of beauty from which all other forms of beauty should and could derive. In the essay 'Ancient versus Modern,' he suggests that the Greeks themselves could be called mannerists in their late development in art. In 'Literary Sanculottism,' which defends contemporary writers against the charge that they have not produced prose works that could be called classical, he asks 'What is a classic?' and in reply lists a set of required circumstances, social, political, and cultural, which together suggest that such a work *happens* to a writer as much as he produces it.

The Helen fragment was created in this moment when Goethe, having mastered the Greek sensibility and its mode of expression, at the same time recognized that mode not as *the* form of beauty but as *a* form. The ideal had not been outlived so much as put in its place. It seems to have been put in its place, as such things often are, first emotionally and then with reason. The number of abandoned projects of the time in the classical vein, the *Helena* initially among them, suggests a combined desire and disinclination to continue in a pursuit that had already found its proper goal, its European goal, in *Tasso* and *Iphigenia* and in the hexameters of *Hermann and Dorothea*.

There is in the Helen fragment, though not in its form, a profound emptiness and the sense of a world lost. The form maintains the clear, intense, and noble bearing that reflects a world perceived as whole, and yet it is a world that is past and holds no future, much like the verse form in which it was being created. Goethe might have chosen any Helen to call back to life but he imagined the figure as the tragic heroine after Troy, condemned by Menelaus, who when the fragment begins has sent her forward to their ancestral home to prepare for the sacrifice to the gods which she will be. Not knowing her fate, she is both obedient and apprehensive – like the author who has undertaken to create her in a context that can only barbarize her being, as will the act that Menelaus has planned. The feeling of the writing and that in the writing are not unalike. In exerting his *Faustrecht*, Goethe will wrest his drama from a fixed form and embark on a new mode of creating. At the time, however, this new mode is not a vision but merely an attempt to proceed. It stops after 300 lines. Only later, when the processes of nature, life, and history have been newly seen and understood, does Goethe seem consciously and deliberately to employ a new process of dramatic art to reflect them and find a new place for Helen in the larger new scheme.

The emptiness or unexpressed sadness in the fragment cannot be said to stem simply from the mood or moment in which it was written. The wholeness that existed in the Greek world existed in the negative as well as the positive. What Helen recounts for us in her opening speech is a bleak reality unadorned by sentiment. 'For the Greeks, actuality had the unique significance that the imagination and emotions have for us,' Goethe wrote in the essay on Winckelmann.[9] Helen is resigned to her fate as a fact and not as an emotional state. If she suspects what Menelaus has planned, she cannot know it, and she spends her words not in speculation, which is the mental expression of emotional uncertainty, but in the simple relating of events. She cannot disobey her husband and therefore cannot change her fate. But she is not afraid: 'No vulgar fear beseems the daughter of high Zeus.'[10] Her almost indifference as she recounts her instructions from Menelaus, who during the sea journey 'looked seldom on me, spoke no comfortable word,'[11] is the measure not of her depth of character but of the way in which she sees all things, as fact.

> As many tripods take, as needful thou may deem
> And vessels manifold, which he at hand requires
> Who duly would perform the sacrificial rite,
> The caldrons, and the bowls and shallow altar plates.
> Let purest water, too, from sacred font be there,
> In lofty pitchers ...
> Finally, a knife of sharpest edge, let it not fail at last.[12]

---

9 Gearey, ed., *Goethe's Essays*, p. 101.
10 'Der Tochter Zeus' geziemet nicht gemeine Furcht' (in the final version, l. 8647).
11 From l. 8536: 'auch sprach er kein erquicklich Wort.'
12 Dann nimm so manchen Dreifuß, als du nötig glaubst,
　　Und mancherlei Gefäße, die der Opfer sich

Moreover, Menelaus speaks these words 'as if by the god inspired.'[13] When the gods speak, all passion is stilled and everything simply is.

It is sometimes said that Helen does not respond as we might expect because she is a spirit.[14] Indeed, she simply vanishes when her purpose in the play has been served. Yet Mephistopheles is also a spirit and very real. It is we as 'moderns' who expect emotion to intervene to lend significance to event. In having Helen act as she does, Goethe was attempting to convey, I believe, a special sense of being. Like light, the Greek mind attached itself to objects. The names and actions, the details of the physical world that Helen evokes as she retells the 'tale that, expanding, has to fable grown'[15] *are* her emotions, as only objects can be for one who sees and needs not think to feel. Seeing is all in this Greek world we have now entered, as feeling was all in *Urfaust*. Later Goethe will lend Faust the tower watchman Lynceus to describe the world around him with eyes that have learned to see as Helen sees.

The vision here in the fragment is dark and unrelieved. Almost without interruption Helen recalls her experience, mentioning in passing the events and names that carry all the weight of meaning, the horror and the glory, from her past. What her present fate will be, she does not know: 'Conquered I am, but whether captive know I not.'[16] In the final version the chill is partly removed from the telling by the interjections of the Chorus who express sentiments and hopes. For the Chorus may show emotion where the hero or heroine, the demigods, may not. Unlike Helen, her Trojan women vent feelings. But it is Helen, with her objective eye, who describes the ugliness that is Phorkyas:

> There saw I, by the light of dimly smoldering fire,
> Crouched on the ground, a crone, close-veiled, of stature
>   huge ...

Zur Hand verlangt, vollziehend heiligen Festgebrauch.
Die Kessel, auch die Schalen, wie das flache Rund;
Das reinste Wasser aus der heiligen Quelle sei
In hohen Krügen ...
Ein wohlgeschliffnes Messer fehle nicht zuletzt. (ll. 8570–7)
13 'Wie vom Gott bewegt' (l. 8540).
14 See Klett, *Der Streit*, pp. 41ff.
15 'Von dem die Sage wachsend sich zum Märchen spann' (l. 8515).
16 'Erobert bin ich; ob gefangen, weiß ich nicht!' (l. 8530).

When, on a sudden, starts the wonder from the floor.
Barring with lordly mien my passage, she herself
In haggard height displays, with hollow eye, blood-grimed,
An aspect weird and strange, confounding eye and thought.
Yet speak I to the winds ...
There see herself! The light she ventures to confront![17]

At this point the invective argument between Phorkyas and the Chorus begins and, in the final version, it continues insistently until a means of rescue for Helen presents itself in the person of Faust.

The argument in its persistence and ugliness is surprising. We might have expected to find in this much anticipated world of order and beauty which Helen represents a less contentious atmosphere. But the world that Goethe was presenting was not ideal, merely whole. Its very wholeness produced out of the beauty at its center its opposite in the ugliness that Phorkyas/Mephistopheles represents. The contrast is observed in the play itself: 'Dare thou, Horror, / Thus beside Beauty ... to unveil thee?'[18] For Mephistopheles in any guise continues to function in his role as chameleon in reverse and take on the colors that distinguish him from his environment. If he is evil in a world whose ideal is the good, he is ugliness in a world where beauty is the ideal, as he is always the negative of the positive force. Already in the fragment Helen stands for order, and in the final version she explicitly and continually seeks appeasement. 'Not wrathful, but in grief, I step between you now ...'[19] Phorkyas/Mephistopheles stands for contention, which is the moral counterpart of physical ugliness. He is the opposite of the queen of order, beauty, and peace, for all the contention among men that beauty might have caused.

We can see why Goethe at one point entitled his fragment 'Helen in the Middle Ages: A Satyr Drama.'[20] Not only does the scurrilous exchange that begins now and extends into the final version lend a gro-

---

17 Lines 8675–93.
18 Wagest du Scheusal
   Neben der Schönheit
   Dich vor dem Kennerblick
   Phöbus' zu zeigen?   (ll. 8736–9)
19 'Nicht zürnend, aber traurend schreit' ich zwischen euch' (l. 8826).
20 Beutler, Paralipomena, p. 531.

tesque aspect to the proceedings, but the piece when it is completed will stand precisely in the relation to the whole *Faust* that the satyr drama stands in relation to the model Greek tragedy. These plays, though they were later discontinued, offered a parody of the earnest subjects that were presented at the Dionysian festivals and were staged along with the tragedies. Goethe later wrote an essay on 'Greek Tetralogies' (1823), and in it approved of the practice.

To be sure, he was not writing a parody in the *Helena*. He was attempting to capture, or recapture, a whole world and state of mind. But he seems to have been aware in first entitling the piece 'A Satyr Drama' that he had been put in a position by his approach to his developing *Faust* where he would have to proceed in the manner which we call today parodistic, that is, in imitation of the classical or traditional for new or modern purposes. He surely did not know in 1800 how the fragment would develop, as witness the variety of forms and titles it took in prospective versions. But he was conscious of the 'barbarous' esthetic act he was about to commit in joining the classical and the modern forms in a single work. He may have wished to ease his conscience by reminding himself of the barbaric way in which the Greeks themselves had handled their noble themes in their satyr plays.

CHAPTER TEN

Act III: Helen
in Faust

The Faust theme itself virtually forced the author to expand his vision. But how was such an expanded world not to be devoured in some scheme of thought or form of art, but simply to be received? No theory, or system of thought, but poetic urge and instinct had guided Goethe from the beginning in *Faust*. Not that the work was thereby diminished in weight of meaning, if we believe with Goethe in the equal but separate powers of art and thought in pronouncing on the nature of reality. But no form had presented itself from the tradition in drama which could have served to delimit and define the unlimited and progressive scope of the subject matter. No form had presented itself, as has been mentioned now a number of times, because no such conditions of thought had obtained that would make its existence necessary. For form is the expression of a model or manner of thought, though at first it is its unconscious expression.

Goethe's position in relation to the new evolutionist sense of history and nature was just such an initial and participatory position. Others, such as Schelling and Hegel, who were equally possessed of that sense, attempted to direct, and subject, the abundant matter of history and nature to a higher design and purpose. They sought, like the astrologer in Act I, 'to earn the things below through what is above.' But for Goethe, like Herder and Kant, 'Nothing in God's kingdom is only a means, everything is means and end at once.'[1] His concept of the symbol as meaning and yet as the thing itself is an insight of the same order. What resulted in his art from this rejection of abstract idealism

---

1 *Auch eine Philosophie*, Abschnitt 2 (1774).

in his thought was the instinct or tendency we have already seen to make the things and persons of his poetry always themselves and not subject to theme or to one another. There is a makeshift quality in *Faust II*, a *basteln* in its making. It is a *bricolage*, as the French term has it.[2] We have seen historical milieus maintain their independence against the poem, Mephistopheles pursue ends that would seem to have little to do with his avowed purposes, Faust wander in and out of the action in Part II, and persons introduced, like Wagner and the Student, never to be heard from again. All are becoming together, all evolving, even the Devil in his different guises.

Yet this creative freedom, this non-systematization, for all that it requires us to systematize, to 'supply' meaning, can itself produce from its essence and at its pinnacle the total sense of its intent and inner vision in a single person or symbol, a Homunculus, for example, or the Mothers. Goethe counts in large measure on our consciousness to give sense to the signs, persons, things, and motifs he juxtaposes in the separate acts and within the acts themselves. But that consciousness or state of mind is the model of thought in the evolutionist view, which also does not see or experience cause and effect in actual and natural progression but measures it after the fact. It is after the fact as well that we see, and only can see, the past in the present, a milieu in a verse form, a world of meaning in a single figure such as Helen. We bring to *Faust II* a historical consciousness and return with an evolutionist vision.

I am repeating much that was said or at least implied in earlier chapters. But the decision that Goethe made after so much hesitation, trepidation, and distraction to take up the *Helena* and finally to finish his *Faust* was not, I believe, wholly a personal decision. The responsibility he felt to continue cannot have been experienced as a responsibility to himself alone. This author who was so concerned in his work with the phenomenon of development and change must have sensed in his struggle with *Faust* the evolutionary process that his art was

---

2 As applied to evolution and to the development of myth. Cf. Claude Lévi-Strauss, *The Savage Mind* (Chicago, 1966), p. 16. Goethe to Schiller, 1 July 1797: 'I would only need a quite month and [*Faust*], like a family of sponges, would grow out of the earth to the amazement and horror of all and sundry.' See Helmut Schanze, 'Szene, Schemen, Schwammfamilie: Goethes Arbeitsweise und die Frage der Struktureinheit von *Faust I und II*' (*Euphorion* 78 [1984], pp. 383–400).

undergoing as he attempted to reflect the new thought of his times and that he should not impede the process. He seems sometimes not to have known at all how to proceed and only in the execution to have found his way. Helen herself was 'formed and re-formed over almost incalculable years [and] remains now solidified in a moment of time.'[3] We can almost sense the forces of a new art exerting themselves in these years and finally becoming solidified in *Faust II* as we have it. If we had to pick a moment when the influence of these forces triumphed in Goethe, it would not be 1800 when the plan for the second part was made, but 1826 when the *Helena* was resumed. For it was not in the plan but in the execution – 'In the beginning was the deed' – that the unconscious genius of *Faust II* expressed itself.

Because Goethe did not always know clearly how to proceed, or sometimes altered his intent, does not mean that he wrote wholly from instinct. On the contrary, he complained about the necessity in *Faust II* of having to produce with conscious effort what should be left to the natural laws of creative intuition.[4] The *Helena*, once re-begun, took a quite deliberate course. The purpose was to make the potentially conflicting esthetic and artistic elements in Part II even more 'disparate,' and to that end Goethe now created in what would become the middle of his dramatic action a Greek tragedy.

The fragment had already shown that intent in its verse form and with the introduction of a Chorus. Now the narrative exposition, which earlier went almost uninterrupted and seemed to take on an epic rather than a dramatic character, is balanced by the interjections of the Chorus. The familiar dithyramb joins the iambic trimeter:

> Much have I lived through ...
> Manifold horrors have my eyes witnessed:
> Warfare's dire anguish,
> Ilion's night,
> When it fell.[5]

---

3 To the scholar and 'Naturphilosoph' C.G. Nees von Esenbeck, 24 May 1827.
4 To Alexander von Humboldt, 17 March 1832.
5 Vieles erlebt' ich, obgleich die Locke
  Judenglich wallet mir um die Schläfe!
  Schreckliches hab' ich vieles gesehen,

When the Chorus confronts Phorkyas, it is in the retortive exchange of single lines that is so distinctive a feature of classical drama. If they, as Trojan women, are to her 'conquered merchandise,' she is to them the 'produce of Father Erebus, of Mother Night.' The stichomythy continues:

> *Phor.* Harpies, so I suspect, did rear thee up in filth.
> *Chor.* For corpses dost thou hunger, loathsome corpse thyself!
> *Phor.* Within thy shameless mouth the teeth of vampires gleam.
> *Chor.* Thine I should stop were I to tell you who thou art.[6]

When Phorkyas reviews with Helen the events of her life that have brought her to this point, it is in an exchange of recurring two lines which ends in a set of three. One can sense from the printed page the state of mind that is deliberately creating this imitation of an action in the Aristotelian sense. In the moment when the action approaches the discovery of the truth, the peripeteia of which Aristotle also speaks, single lines are halved between Helen and Phorkyas, made into four parts in the instant of discovery.[7] But it was not for the page that Goethe had written the *Helena. Faust II* was not created *for* the stage but it was created with the stage in mind. Goethe speaks often enough in passing of the effect of his material on the stage. We also cannot discount his wish that the drama be set to music.[8] At the close of the present sequence of action he has the following stage direction: 'Helen and the Chorus stand astounded and terrified, *in a striking, well-arranged group.*'[9]

The content of this model ancient tragedy is not merely incidental to its form. Its dramatic purpose, of course, was to create a dire situation from which Faust might rescue Helen and gain her favor. Immediately

---

Kriegrischen Jammer, Ilios' Nacht,
Als er fiel.   (ll. 8697–8701)
6 Lines 8819–24.
7 Lines 8923–5.
8 For example, to Eckermann, 25 January 1827. *Faust II* could not be *read* to accompanying music.
9 My italics; after l. 8929.

Menelaus' intent is known and the altar prepared for the sacrifice of Helen, Mephistopheles/Phorkyas speaks of liberation. Yet this seemingly trivial solution has a dramatic undercurrent. If we have learned at all from Helen in her frighteningly mechanical obedience, which seems an almost willful acquiescence in fate, we have grasped the emotional component in the vision which sees reality unmediated. For Helen to join Faust, as much as that may be necessary for the dramatic and thematic development of the play, and as much as we may see the option as one she cannot under any circumstance refuse, is a decision of weight. Life has bandied her about. Her recalling of her experience in the exchange with Phorkyas, which includes her own and those misadventures in which only her spirit or phantom took part, amounts to a litany of pain. She faints at the end of this recital of her past, not knowing, in a quite symbolist modern manner, whether she is now a phantom or real: 'A dream it was – even the very words so declare. / I faint, and to myself a phantom I become.'[10] But she stands, she does not swoon, when the knowledge comes that she will be sacrificed. For her death is a fate no worse than life. 'Let these be afraid. Pain I feel, not fear.'[11]

The theme of the tragedy is resignation. This *Entsagung* (and the German word should be used for its special meaning in Goethe) is not the resignation of defeat. Rather it is an inspired or elevated pragmatism that in its denial of the hope that forces from outside the laws of nature can affect the affairs of man, focuses the mind on the things of this world alone, but with a certain sense of loss. The Greek concept of an ineluctable fate had the same orienting influence. Helen is close to Goethe in spirit, at least to the older Goethe after Italy. When she chooses to join Faust it is not in expectation, she is simply resigned.

Yet resignation is in no way the answer in *Faust*. For all that *Entsagung* persists in his thought, and for all that it is inexpressibly written in the tragic black eyes of the famous portrait of 1826–7, it is not the philosophy by which Goethe resolved the questions of a lifetime he had set down in his play. 'Or the Resigned,' to be sure, is the subtitle of the *Wanderjahre*, which was completed at much the same time as

10 Es war ein Traum, so sagen ja die Worte selbst.
   Ich schwinde hin und werde selbst mir ein Idol. (ll. 8880–1)
11 'Laß diese bangen! Schmerz empfind' ich, keine Furcht' (l. 8962).

Faust II, in 1829. But if the characters of the novel are resigned, it is only those who have chosen to remain in their own world. There is an alternative, America, which the younger choose. America is the virgin land that need not be reclaimed from the sea in order to build a new world upon it.

Faust is anything but resigned in the end.[12] But resignation at that point has not been gone beyond as a philosophy so much as, again, put in its place in the larger scheme. Just as the classical model in art, this classical model of thought will serve its purpose in the drama as it had served its purpose in historical time, and in the end will cause a new beginning. Faust learns in the world of Helen, and with Helen, to live vitally in the moment. Life is a duty, not a gift: *Dasein ist Pflicht*. Yet Faust will not remain captured *in* the moment, for that imperative obtained in and for another time, but he and the drama will have put behind them the living *for* the moment, which he himself could never do but which the world he lives in knows too well.

The clash between the classical and the Faustian world, long antici-pated, occurs at the end of the model tragedy. We must assume that Menelaus in no way instructed Phorkyas to sacrifice Helen, or even knew of the existence of the ogre, and that Mephistopheles has or-chestrated the crisis.[13] It is not the less real for Helen. But the unreality that brings Faust and Helen together, which is the historical unreality, must bring with it in the logic of the poem the outward signs that separate their worlds and thus conflict esthetically. They will speak differently, as we are made aware in the scene to come when Helen asks Faust to teach her to rhyme. He will come from a different realm. The first concern of Phorkyas/Mephistopheles after she has ensured that Helen will make the right choice is to describe that realm and its history. It is here that the ancient and the modern clash as the two

---

12 Yet *Entsagung* remains otherwise a dominant thought in Goethe. See Schrimpf, *Das Weltbild*, ch. 4, 'Faust und Wilhelm Meister.' Schrimpf makes what I believe is a most important point in emphasizing the differences in the *Weltbild* reflected in *Faust II* and that in the *Wanderjahre*. The tendency has always been to find simi-larities in the interest of upholding a unified picture of Goethe. Also, Arthur Hen-kel, *Entsagung* (Tübingen, 1954).

13 Euripides has Menelaus reconciled with Helen in the only extent *Helen* tragedy, though legends abound with other versions of her fate after Troy.

realms are made more disparate in the description and yet joined in the dramatic action.

The seam is transparent and for that the more revealing. In order to create the existence of a people to the north of whom Faust might be the lord and leader, Phorkyas describes a series of events following the Trojan War in which through the exhaustion and inattention of the Greeks a barbaric tribe was able to settle in the region and plunder land and people at will. The anachronism spans some three thousand years, if we think of the tribe that Phorkyas places in the Peloponnesus as descendants of the Franks. We may think of any or all of the celebrated invasions from the north, for clearly the purpose in this distorting of time is to deal in those large historical masses which are the subject matter of *Faust II* and to see in the one event in time a repetition or an anticipation of another. Faust's conquest of Helen is again an invasion from the north.

More striking is the manner of this appropriation within the play itself. Faust is not brought to Helen's world, nor she to his, either of which solution would have been convenient in terms of dramaturgy. Magic would provide the means. Instead, the fortress that Faust commands from afar and which Phorkyas has just described comes to envelop Helen and the Trojan women. 'Say yes ... and with that fortress I'll encompass thee.'[14] It is Mephistopheles who creates this sensation of enclosing walls emerging from a mist which he has made to dispel the present scene and introduce the enclosure of the fortress where Faust will now appear. The motif is theatrically impressive.[15] But the concept of a later cultural realm enveloping the events of art and history that issue from an earlier time is the prism in general in which *Faust II* captures its reality.[16] Notice that it is not thought, but the conditions that produce thought and are reflected in art and in history that are absorbed. Phorkyas in describing this alien and barbaric people of

14 From ll. 9048–9: 'sagt mit Ernst vernehmlich Ja! / Sogleich umgeb' ich dich mit jener Burg.'
15 This would also afford finally an opportunity to use the 'settings and machines' long ago promised in the Prelude in the Theater: 'Drum schonest mir an diesem Tag / Prospekte nicht und nicht Maschinen' (l. 233–4).
16 Of course we know from ll. 9113–15 and 9144 that Mephistopheles has in fact moved the group to the castle, not vice versa. Why it is more practicable to move the former to the latter represents a vestige of logic from the real world employed in the world of magic.

whom Faust is the master, speaks not at all of their beliefs but of the expression of their beliefs in their surroundings. It is almost a treatise on architecture that she indulges in as she describes the fortress:

> Upright and level, all is fixed by square and rule.
> Gaze on it from without; upward it strives toward heaven,
> So straight, so well-adjusted, mirror smooth like steel.
> To clamber there, indeed, your very thought slides down.[17]

Mephistopheles, who in his immortality appears to know the architecture of both the ancient and the modern world, is behind these remarks. Nor is the latter slighted in the comparison as we might expect. We are reminded explicitly that the building forms that surround Helen in her early world are little more than 'one unwieldy stone, on stone unwieldy [hurled].'[18] Nothing in the play, no single quotable line and no motif, suggests as well the essence of its movement in the mind than the actualization of the processes of history and education in the enfolding of Helen in the architecture of a later time.

There is no denying that Helen is surpassingly beautiful and no way of conveying her surpassing beauty. As Chiron said of the attempts to portray the model of male perfection, Hercules, 'Stone strives in vain to tell his worth, / Tortured is marble too in vain.'[19] An approximation of perfect beauty can be created on stage by various means, but Faust is not a man of approximations, and it is to him now as they meet that she must appear beautiful beyond description.

Goethe seems to have been aware of the problem, for he went almost to an opposite extreme in resolving it. No astonishment or praise, and not the least sign of passion, comes from Faust in this first encounter. This is not the Faust of earlier scenes, and we can only think as he

---

17   dort
   Ist alles senk- und waagerecht und regelhaft.
   Von außen schaut sie! himmelan sie strebt empor,
   So strarr, so wohl in Fugen, spiegelglatt wie Stahl.
   Zu klettern hier – ja selbst der Gedanke gleitet ab. (ll. 9022–5)
18 From ll. 9020–1: 'rohen Stein sogleich / Auf rohe Steine stürzend.'
19 Vergebens mühen sich die Lieder,
   Vergebens quälen sie den Stein. (ll. 7393–4)

descends a stair to meet Helen 'slowly and with dignity'[20] that what he sees before him is the cause of the transformation in his behavior. Nowhere in the play is he less the aggressor. Not having seen it, we cannot say how one is to act in the presence of perfect beauty, but the flight to restraint is certainly a more plausible reaction than the un-leashing of emotion, which may be tolerable in anticipation but not in the face of reality. Like Helen in the face of fate, Faust reacts almost mechanically. Moreover, he is now the medieval lord, or rather the lord, the representative man, in a medieval setting, and his actions reflect his surroundings. His behavior is as stylized as the expressions of thought and emotions in the poetry and art of his time. His actions are almost gauche – partly, we might want to assume, because of the very fact of the overwhelming beauty in his presence and partly be-cause as the leader of a barbarous tribe he cannot be expected to know how to act. He places Helen in the position of deciding in her first moments at court on the punishment for the tower watchman who, blinded by her beauty, had taken her approach as a 'rising of the sun in the south'[21] and failed to report her arrival. The failure of the watch-man, of course, produces an explanation which in proportion to its ability to exculpate must make the more convincing the effects of the beauty that caused it. For that reason we hear from Lynceus, not Faust, a lyrical evocation of that beauty, and in rhyme, which historically in its beginnings must be placed in the medieval period.

The point is not that Goethe has succeeded. These first moments of the meeting between Faust and Helen might be unintentionally awk-ward. They would be unthinkable in a classical French tragedy. But the very purpose of classicism was to capture in the historical moment that which is supposed universal and eternal. In a world regarded as evolving, the moment in its essence reflects a reality that gains its significance from its position in time. Individual action is not measured against character or will but against its surroundings. Far from em-bracing the determinism and historicism that are the logical outcome of this view, however, Goethe recaptured through his juxtaposing of separate historical moments or spheres of existence in time the activity

20 After l. 9181: 'kommt langsam würdig herunter.'
21 Harrend auf des Morgens Wonne,
   Östlich spähend ihren Lauf,
   Ging auf einmal mir die Sonne
   Wunderbar im Süden auf. (ll. 9222–5)

and freedom of mind that is the truer equivalent of the state of human consciousness, and thus the moral state, than is the more mechanistic reflection of reality that is normally found in drama.[22] Yet this freedom that is gained for the observer is not always granted to the observed. Time and again, as we have seen, Goethe allows background to dominate foreground, thematics to interrupt dramatics. The deflection of the impact on Faust from the confrontation with ideal beauty does not suggest perhaps this tyranny of background over foreground, but the principle is the same. One often hears about the avoidance of tragedy in Goethe.[23] But it is rather the avoidance of the dramatic that is characteristic of *Faust II*. It results from the instinct in his late works to see reality, as we said, in the round, not dramatically focused.

He succeeds with the next moments of the action. It is here that Helen, struck by the melodious repetition of sound in the speech that Lynceus makes in his defense, asks that she too be taught to rhyme. What was earlier lost dramatically is now recovered in ineffable charm. There is an overwhelming cultural flattery implied in the desire of the symbol of classical beauty and art to assimilate a native custom of speech. We who have anticipated the creation and advent of the noblest form of artistic expression, and found its reflection in the model tragedy that opens Act III, now find the essence of our own poetic tradition honored, as if for the first time. If the meeting between the new and the ancient world did not initially express itself through its protagonists in as dramatic a fashion as we might have expected, thematically it is triumphant. The union between Faust and Helen represents not simply union but assimilation, which is the aspect and essence of rhyme. Helen not only offers Faust her hand, but with that word she completes the bond and the rhyme she is learning to command:

Faust. What confirms [the happiness] we demand?
Helen.   This – my hand.[24]

---

22 I use mechanistic in its philosophical sense of ineluctable cause and effect. The Greek idea of fate might in that sense be considered mechanistic.
23 For example, Erich Heller in 'Goethe and the Avoidance of Tragedy,' *The Disinherited Mind* (Cambridge, 1952).
24 Schatz ist sie, Hochgewinn, Besitz und Pfand;
    Bestätigung, wer gibt sie?
                Meine Hand.   (ll. 9383–4)

Theme and action are again one. The motif of assimilation, which is
the grand theme of the evolution of European culture that has its poetic
beginning in the present union, comes to dominate the scene. It may
even account for the dispassionate behavior of Faust at the outset.
Reason would comport better than passion with the weight of the
moment. Faust's modern romantic protestations as he warms to his
new conquest indeed seem out of place:

> Filled with amaze, O queen, I see at once
> The unerring smiter, here the smitten one ...[25]

As much reason as rhyme emerges from the lesson in versification.
The paradigms that Goethe chooses are conveyors of meaning. The
imperative of living in the moment is first expressed here. Faust: 'The
spirit looks not forward nor behind, / In the present only' – Helen:
'Our fortune we find.'[26] The rhymed couplets that Faust and Helen
exchange stress the immediacy and importunity of human existence.
Helen would cry out in the moment, 'Here am I, am here,'[27] though
it is Faust more than she who has lived too much in anticipation. Not
since the Easter scene before the city gates in Part I has the sense of
human presence in and before the world emerged so clearly. There it
was said of man in nature, 'Here I am human, here I dare be!'[28] Here
of man in time: 'Here am I, am here!'

This is what Faust learns through his union with Helen. What he
forgets is that the moment itself is constituted in time. The *Helena* was
the first world or historical moment that Goethe imagined and set down
in Part II, but he must have been conscious of the other worlds and
moments he was about to create that would stand in contrast to it. Yet
these contrasts are not explicit in the play. The play juxtaposes, it does
not account for, differences and change. Yet we can judge from the
vision of a new kingdom which Faust now presents to Helen as the

---

25 Erstaunt, o Königin, seh' ich zugleich
   Die sicher Treffende, hier den Getroffnen ...   (ll. 9258–9)
26 Nun schaut der Geist nicht vorwärts, nicht zurück,
   Die Gegenwart allein –
                           ist unser Glück.   (ll. 9381–2)
27 'Und sage nur zu gern: Da bin ich! da!' (l. 9412).
28 'Hier bin ich Mensch, hier darf ich's sein' (l. 940).

realm over which she shall reign that the present is still not the world in which he lives. His moment is in any event unreal since it has been created by magic outside of time. Moreover, if it is true that rhyme is in essence a joining of the past with the future, and not a creation of a living present, then his moment is vitiated by the manner in which he has learned to live in it. 'The spirit looks not forward nor behind, / The present only –' should not, theoretically, be completed in rhyme. If rhyme brings about the union of Faust and Helen symbolically, it is through her assimilation into his world and not, as he had sought and as we might have expected, his assimilation into hers.

His first action in the new moment makes that clear. After Mephistopheles has concocted the threat of an attack from Menelaus and the prospect again of a 'sharpened axe ready on the altar,'[29] Faust dispatches his generals to repel the enemy, with Goths, Saxons, Franks, Normans, Germans all playing their part in an achronological composite picture of the disposition of powers in the Dark and Middle Ages. Yet in victory, peace shall prevail: 'Then shall each one, at home abiding, / Powers and strength make known.'[30] Faust lays before Helen an imagined new world, as if he has taken back the Holy Roman Empire in which in reality he has his existence and put in its place a finer and nobler progression of history. In as beautiful and visionary a poetic passage as appears in *Faust*, Goethe sees land stretching from Greece, whose ranges 'blend with Europe's mountains, widely branching,' to the farthest reaches where 'meadow, gorge, and valley all are green' and where one asks in beholding its inhabitants, 'If gods they be, or men, so fair are they.'[31] It is an empire that Helen shall rule from Greece, presumably with a justice and grace that would match her beauty. It is not at all a land of fact, but an imagined arcadian empire that puts to shame the Holy Roman Empire that is the reality at the base of *Faust II*.[32]

29 Line 9434.
30 Dann wird ein jeder häuslich wohnen,
    Nach außen richten Kraft und Blitz ... (ll. 9474–5)
31 'Ob es Götter, ob es Menschen sind.' See ll. 9522–57.
32 Already in *Urfaust* were the lines, 'Das liebe heil'ge Röm'sche Reiche / Wie hält's nur noch zusammen? (ll. 2090–1).

Thus happy fate has me, has thee, attended.
Behind us henceforth let the past be thrown![33]

Faust does not err in placing before Helen a utopian world. His final
vision in the last act will also be of an ideal future. He will not come
to live in the moment but always toward the moment. He will establish
his existence, as it were, in rhyme, which joins the past to a future and
thereby expresses the modern state of mind, itself the natural progression out of a historical tradition that also had envisioned a future
ideal, but in a life beyond, not within time. His error rather is in thinking that the past can simply be 'put behind.' That is an absolutist, not
an evolutionist, concept. In Act IV, the past in the form of a corrupt
established order will undermine his ideal plan for the future. Faust
does not, like the Student, believe that the world did not exist before
he created it, but his ignoring of the past distorts or, better, inflates
his idea of the future. No more than he learned through the symbolic
vision of the rainbow to keep his back to the sun so that he might
better see to the future, but continued to pursue his goals with passion,
has he now learned through Helen to live in the present. He still
remains the Faust of old, indeed of Part I.

---

33 So ist es mir, so ist es dir gelungen;
   Vergangenheit sei hinter uns getan!   (ll. 9562–3)

CHAPTER ELEVEN

Act III: The Fruit
of the Union

A glance at the printed pages of the final scene of Act III already
suggests much about its poetic nature. There are five distinctly different
verse forms recognizable on their surface.[1] It is as though this finale
to the act, and it is a finale thematically as well, was to include all that
had come before separately, in sound no less than in content. It is an
operatic ending. Goethe speculated with Eckermann, on 21 February
1831, about the possibility of an able poet from the romantic school
collaborating with Rossini to transform the *Helena* into an opera proper,
and with opportunities for ballet and for 'costumes of the ages.'

   This was only after the fact, when he had seen what he had wrought.
But when we think of the *Helena* in its position in the completed drama,
we see that there was a tendency from the beginning toward a mul-
tifaceted form. Ballet and music would merely have added the final
touches. Act I with its extended masquerade scene might well have
been written as ballet, especially when one assumes that the purpose
of the latter is symbolic. The most relevant scene dramatically, the
appearance of Paris and Helen, is in fact pantomime. The Classical
Walpurgis Night is as much theater and spectacle as it is drama. The
whole second part of the Faust drama, which was undertaken in an
awareness and new perception of the relationship of things and events
in time, when reduced to art by a poet who refused to reduce his
perceptions to thought, demanded a form so unlimited that it verged
on other genres and other forms. The decision to employ a variety of

---

1 In addition to the *Faust* verse, there are iambic and trochaic measures and choral
   odes in different forms suggestive of an operatic libretto.

versification, which was born of a historical empathy or sensibility, produced in its wake a symphony of sound as it extracted in this manner the essence of contrasting cultural milieus. The decision led not to the barbarism that Goethe had anticipated, but to the reflecting of a complexity of consciousness that he himself regarded as characteristic of the modern mind. This final scene reveals the make-up of this complexity in content and form.

Faust II, Goethe said, was highly symbolic. Yet it is only in the final scene of the *Helena* that he totally abandons the dramatic conventions of time and place and represents his meanings in an avowedly imaginary manner. No carnival masquerade, no pantomime, no fantastic celebration in an eerie night explains or excuses the present occurrences, although together they may be said to introduce them. The actuality of Act I plus the fantasy of Act II prepares the way for symbolism. Euphorion, for example, the offspring of Helen and Faust who comes into the world, matures, and completes his fate all within the shortest moment, is not 'a human, but only an allegorical being. In him poetry is personified, which is bound to no time, no place and no person.'[2] The person to whom Euphorion becomes attached as sign or symbol, however, is Byron, the 'familiar figure'[3] who is recognizable in the body that plummets to the ground at the end of the scene. The fate of Euphorion is Byron's fate, which in turn is the fate of modern poetry, as if in admonition.

If Homunculus, another symbolic figure, is in search of a body, this embodiment of poetry is in search of a purpose. Euphorion represents unbounded aspiration and imagination without a direction. He resembles Homunculus in his antics. We see him in Phorkyas's description springing from his mother's lap to his father, from his father to the earth, which then propels him after a second or third leap to the height of a vaulted roof.[4] His next step, logically, is to break the arc and attempt to fly. Like Homunculus his being is reflected in his actions and, like his actions, is incommensurable. The sense of freedom we

---

2 To Eckermann, 20 December 1829.
3 After l. 9902: 'man glaubt in dem Toten eine bekannte Gestalt zu erblicken.' On the general topic, see, e.g., E.M. Butler, *Byron and Goethe* (London, 1956).
4 Lines 9599ff.

experience in finding in Homunculus intellect and consciousness un-weighted by body and matter is matched by the human sensation of flight, as in a dream. Both seem related to the sensation that poetry creates through thought and sound in its own inexplicable way.

Yet Euphorion has more often been seen as the embodiment of Romantic poetry, not poetry as such, mainly because of his identifi-cation with Byron. Against his undisciplined, albeit beautiful expression of self in body and sound (for he is a lovely youth and the 'purest melody'[5] comes from his lyre) is set the ordered, classical norm Goethe supposedly continued to advocate in the latter stages of his own de-velopment and Faust to have learned through the contact with Helen. Goethe himself in effect discounted the view: 'Byron is not antique [i.e., classical] and not romantic, but he is like the present day itself,' he said to Eckermann, 5 July 1827. Moreover, the drama in which both Byron and Euphorion have their being does not deal in abstract es-sences such as classic and romantic but with the expression or repre-sentation of these essences in time. Euphorion is born outside of time, or rather, in its willful, unnatural, and artificial creation through the union of Helen with Faust. He is neither constrained nor sustained by the natural laws and exigencies of time that form the context for human action. He thus attempts the humanly impossible, which is to fly.

The desire for the impossible in *Faust*, however, is a virtue. 'Him I love who desires the impossible.' But the impossible must have a pur-pose. What disturbed Goethe about the fate of Byron, who just a few years earlier had joined the Greek uprising against the Turks and met his death at Missolunghi, was that he had undertaken this noble act outside his element. It was as if a poet and a great talent, 'the greatest talent of the century' in Goethe's view, had been wasted in an idealistic endeavor better attempted by others. There was 'something impure' in the act; the decision had been taken not freely but from a 'misad-justment to the world.'[6] The fiery will to death that is reflected in Euphorion as he pictures the human adventure of war may be attrib-uted to Byron as well: 'Hence away! No delay! / There where glory may be sought ... And to die / Is the high / Command delivered to

---

5 After l. 9678: 'reinmelodisch.'
6 'Sein griechisches Unternehmen hat etwas Unreines gehabt' (to Fr. von Müller, conversation, 13 June 1824).

their trust.'[7] This at the point in the drama where *life* has just been declared a sacred duty and responsibility. *Dasein ist Pflicht* contrasts so strikingly with *Und der Tod / Ist Gebot* that again two worlds are juxtaposed.

The 'three thousand years' that elapse in Act III between the siege of Troy and the death of Byron at Missolunghi[8] brought great change not merely in the forms of verse but in the reactions to life that gave rise to these forms. Romantic poetry does not promote a desire for death, or classical art a will to live. The famous dictum that equates the romantic with sickness, the classical with health,[9] and for which Goethe is perhaps best known as a critic of literature, was not intended as criticism. The romantic is not in itself pernicious or destructive in his view but simply more tolerant of, more attracted to, the forces that can destroy, whereas the classical instinctively rejects them. Like good and evil in *Faust*, the romantic and the classical are two sides of a coin. What attracted Goethe to Byron, in other words, and determined the fate of Euphorion whose end had initially been otherwise imagined,[10] was not the will to criticize but to empathize.

Faust II was also not romantic and not classical, but 'like the present day' in which it was being written. Byron's death provided Goethe with a resolution to Act III, as he himself admitted,[11] but the fate of Byron/Euphorion was not conceived by way of making or proving a point. It was a representation of a problem and a struggle. The romantic and classical tendencies and elements that had come together in the *Helena*, and had to come together with the union of Helen and Faust, created a conflict that resulted in dilemma, not in a denial of one or the other force. *Faust II* continues, and could only continue, in anything but a classical vein and yet it is not romantic in its conclusion. Its 'final wisdom' takes both tendencies into account, the endlessness of aspiration and the need to live in relation to a real world. It is the description of a dynamics or dialetic in life and not a solution to its problems.

---

7 I quote these lines (9888–90) from the trans. by Charles Passage (Indianapolis, 1965) to suggest the operatic quality of the verse in the closing scene.

8 Goethe to the art historian S. Boisserée, 22 October 1826.

9 To *Eckermann*, 2 April 1829.

10 What his original intention had been, Goethe does not say – 'ich will es euch nicht verraten' (to Eckermann, 5 July 1827).

11 To Eckermann, 5 July 1827.

The romantic openness that creates such freedom creates at the same time an outlet for the destructive as well as the aspirational urges in man. Yet the classical in its restrictiveness may deny expression to real but undefined needs in the name of nobility and order. The openness and endlessness of the perspective that envisions a life beyond leads to a neglect of present imperatives, as in Act I, while a living in the moment may ignore aspiration, as when Helen will not even question her fate. It was not that Goethe, observing Byron from a knowing position, saw and sympathized with the dangers the younger poet faced but which he himself in his *Werther* period had experienced and escaped. It was rather that the classical methods of resolution and resignation he had employed to escape these early dangers no longer served him well. The 'failure' of *Faust II* in that sense is its greatness. The complete work had taken up its times into itself freely and comprehensively and did not attempt to make of them a classical whole, which few times are.

The play has again carried us away from the dramatic toward the thematic. Euphorion is a personification, not a person. Not only are his actions to be seen in a symbolic light, but the reactions to him of others must be similarly seen. Otherwise they would seem to speak out of character. 'Gently! ... gently! / Be not so daring!' Faust says to Euphorion in a wholly uncharacteristic admonition. He is now The Father in an opera. Helen is The Mother, no longer stoic, but plaintive: 'Think how it grieves us / When thou disdainest / Mine, thine, ... all / That has been won.'[12]

There is a rift here between the classical and the modern at a number of levels and Goethe is aware of the fact. He acknowledges it in the play itself indirectly. He has Phorkyas step forward as the Euphorion action begins and command the Chorus to attend now to the beautifully melodious music that emerges from within, and learn: Fable and myth will no longer serve. The old gods are dead. The new age makes the nobler demand that 'From the *heart* must flow ... What to touch the heart aspires.' The Chorus is reduced to tears by the music and, 'as if reborn,' resolves henceforth to renounce 'the splendor of the sun' and look within to 'find what the world denies.' The passage begins:

12 Lines 9717–18 and 9729–34.

To these tones, so sweetly flowing ...
They in us, new health bestowing,
Waken now the joy of tears.[13]

The classical chorus has been seduced into rhyme.

One practical purpose of this introductory exchange, of course, is to anticipate anomaly. Euphorion was not the son of Helen and Faust but of Helen and Achilles. If old myths and gods are put aside for the moment, however, and a new myth, which comes from the heart and from within, is allowed in their place, then he can be and mean what we will. Equally obvious is that the new myth is modern and romantic. It comes from the individual creating a world in his mind from what he feels. Yet this same romantic and modern inwardness stands in such clearly intended contrast to the attempt in Pleasant Landscape to find objective clarity in the reflected light of the sun that it is no less obvious that the new myth itself is being questioned, if not mocked, as it is being presented. It is after all Mephistopheles/Phorkyas who pronounces the noble demand of the new age as 'from the heart upspringing,'[14] who rejects tradition, and who succeeds only in moving the young women of the Chorus, whom he has already cursed as frivolous. He would have reason as the Devil to seduce the whole world into a romantic approach to life and to art if that were the wrong path for humanity. In speaking through the Astrologer in Act I he had promoted the 'earning from above of the things below.'

Yet as the specialized Devil in Faust he would also only effect good by his evil intent. On a practical level, the romanticism will allow for the operatic design that makes the symbolic and fantastic Euphorion sequence possible and yet warn against it. At the thematic level, classicism and romanticism, the ancient and the modern, are juxtaposed and acted out artistically, not complementing but reinterpreting each other. Philosophically, a resolution has been reached. What we would call today after Nietzsche the dionysian and the apollonian elements of art and of life have been recognized and given their due.

For the images, words, and symbolic actions that stand for the con-

---

13 Diesem Schmeichelton geneigt,
   Fühlen wir, also frisch genesen,
   Uns zur Tränenlust erweicht. (ll. 9687–90)
14 Denn es muß von Herzen gehen,
   Was auf Herzen wirken soll. (ll. 9685–6)

tending forces in *Faust*, again like good and evil, are not now presented as absolutes in opposition, though they are not joined. Helen and Faust have married, but Faust has not changed; nor has the drama in which he has his existence. The words that Goethe places in the mouth of Mephistopheles/Phorkyas to herald the new age of feeling are so close to the words and sentiments that Faust expresses at the very outset of the drama that we cannot think that Goethe has forgotten what he has written but must rather think that he has remembered and is consciously making a point. Faust had said, as far back as *Urfaust*, in a passage celebrated for its *Sturm und Drang* and early romantic sentiment, 'that which issues from the heart alone / Will bend the hearts of others to your own.'[15] At this point in the drama, and in his own development, Goethe again needed the freedom that the romantic and symbolic approach to art afforded, though he did not now need its sentiment.[16] He had once again to reject the demands of verisimilitude and the traditional literary picturing of the world, but for different reasons. For what he had come to see in his long preoccupation with *Faust* was a world with more aspects of reality in more relations than any single form or approach to art thus far had hoped to comprehend. Behind that world stood no absolute design to which it was to be related. Hence the need for myth and fable as guides, which themselves have their origins in the deepest unknown, rather than known, human feeling, and which speak to the heart.

Goethe's hesitant relinquishing of the past is not a sign of an inveterate conservative nature. It is more a reflection of an acute consciousness of the need for a directive from behind now that the 'view beyond,' as it is said at the end of the drama, had 'become blurred.'[17] He did not need Darwin to disabuse him of the belief that the world was created for man. His science had taught him the indifference of nature to human concerns. But when the last vestige of guidance in the form of inherited culture and transmitted history was also to be ignored or denied, as when the Student in Act II would make the past begin with him or Phorkyas now would 'Cast aside fable and myth,'[18]

---

15 Doch werdet Ihr nie Herz zu Herzen schaffen,
   Wenn es Euch nicht von Herzen geht. (In the final version, ll. 544–5)
16 On the romantic see, e.g., Stuart Atkins, 'The Evaluation of Romanticism in Goethe's *Faust*,' *Publications of the English Goethe Society*, n.s., vol. 54 (1955), pp. 9–38.
17 'Nach drüben ist die Aussicht uns verrannt' (l. 11442).
18 'Macht euch schnell von Fabeln frei' (l. 9680).

not only Goethe the thinker but the poet had to resist. The word fable
is important in this context. *Fabel* in the original means both myth and
plot, as in drama. Goethe and Schiller used the word regularly in this
latter sense in their correspondence, and it shows the original relationship of myth to creative literature. Thus, when Mephistopheles/
Phorkyas casts aside myth and fable, not only are the illusions and
superstitions of the past rejected but form itself is threatened. There is
nothing on which to hang experience. The apollonian principle is
thwarted. This would truly be a paramount Mephistophelean aim,
whose goal after all is to reduce the world to the chaos from which it
was created.

Euphorion is an admonition and an ideal, his story a cautionary tale
and an inspiration. In that he resembles Faust as well as Byron.

With the writing of Act III Goethe seems to have become clear in his
own mind how to proceed with *Faust*. The confusion he would in fact
encounter in preparing the 'antecedents' to the *Helena* is of little importance in comparison with the freedom he had gained in resolving
the conflict between the classical and the modern by making of the
enemies antagonistic but inseparable allies. The anticipated barbarism
had emerged as modernism.

Nothing shows this sense of freedom and this resolution more clearly
than the decision to end the *Helena* in the fashion that he does. After
he has Helen embraces Faust once more and inexplicably disappear or
dematerialize, he has the Chorus dissolve into nature, as Homunculus
had returned to the sea. The return to nature is already appropriate in
that nature represents the deepest roots of man in his formation, as
we learn from Act II, and so the source to which we might eternally
return. The classical view had seen immortality as gained only through
accomplishment. 'Who has no name achieved, nor at the noble aimed,
/ Belongs to the elements,'[19] the chorus leader, who herself will accompany Helen to Hades, says as she condemns the timid group of
Trojan women to nature and the elements. Goethe may not be glorying
these battered creatures from the Trojan War in his paean to vital

19 Wer keinen Namen sich erwarb noch Edles will,
   Gehört den Elementen an ... (ll. 9981–2)

nature, for little sympathy has been shown them thus far, but we cannot help feeling now in the finale to Act III that the drama is again exploring its deeper reaches and that those who declaim its words are dignified by them. This final great chorus is wholly unexpected and almost overwhelming.

The Chorus is divided into four parts, each identifying itself with a specific thing in nature, with trees, with cliffs, with streams, and with vineyards, and becoming these things itself. The language is so concentratedly poetic that in the midst of sounds and syllables it is difficult at times to say where sense ends and we seem to be experiencing meaning through music. Yet the Chorus maintains a measured classical meter. The modern element of sheer musicality (Euphorion had played 'purely melodic tones') has been introduced into the ancient mold, the romantic made to respect the classical form. The opening lines are particularly striking in this regard and must first be quoted in the original:

> Wir in dieser tausend Äste Flüsterzittern, Säuselschweben
> Reizen tändelnd, locken leise wurzelauf des Lebens Quellen
> Nach den Zweigen ...

> We amid the wavy trembling of these thousand rustling
>   branches
> Gently lure with dalliance charming from the root the vital
>   currents
> Up into the boughs ...[20]

And another part of the Chorus, identifying with mountain streams:

> Where these rocky walls are imaged in the smooth,
>   far-gleaming mirror,
> Moving in the gentle wavelets, soothingly we onward
>   glide ...[21]

---

20 Lines 9992–4. Kurt May: 'Der Reichtum der wechselnden Versrhythmen überragt bei weitem noch die unabsehbar ausgebreitete Fülle von Reim- und reimartigen Wirkungen' (Faust, p. 211).

21 Wir, an dieser Felsenwände weithinleuchtend glattem Spiegel
Schmiegen wir, in sanften Wellen uns bewegend, schmeichelnd an ...
(ll. 9999–10000)

Yet the sense prevails. The observation of the sap springing from the
roots and not the trunk of the tree to feed the growth of the branches
in unified design is an observation from knowledge and natural science,
not from poetry. Commentaries on *Faust* sometimes note the relation
of this passage to the *Metamorphosis of Plants*, the scientific treatise as
well as the poem that Goethe wrote under that title. It needed art to
reduce to poetry what was conceived and learned in another realm of
perception. But there was also passion involved. Not since the early
period in such poems as 'Ganymed' and 'Mahomet's Song,' which are
infused with pantheism, do we find Goethe in so seemingly intense,
almost crazed, a relationship with nature.[22] Helen has gone the classical, the Chorus goes the romantic way to death. Yet that characteristic
of his mature poetry in which the objective facts and not the mere
impressions of the physical world serve as inspiration is as much in
evidence as the musicality and rhythmic flow. This is especially true
of the vineyard sequence with its celebration and comprehension of
husbandry.

> Now with hoe, and now with mattock, earth upheaving,
>   pruning, binding,
> Prays [the vintager] to all celestials, chiefly to the Sun god
>   prays.
> ... at length have all celestials, has now Helios before them
>   all,
> Breathing, moistening, warming, glowing, filled the berries'
>   teeming horn.
> Where the vintager in silence labored, there is sudden life,
> Busy stir in every alley, rustles round from vine to vine,
> Baskets creak, and pitchers clatter, and the loaded vine
>   troughs groan,
> All towards the mighty winepress, to the presser's sturdy
>   dance.[23]

---

22 The paralipomena to Act III has the simple notation 'Pantheismus' as the last entry; Beutler, p. 587.
23 Lines 10015–27.

Art and passion went into this choral finale, but wisdom and cunning as well. The vineyard motif seemed not wholly appropriate from the outset. We could recognize the familiar spirits of air, earth, and water in the forms of rebirth in nature that the Chorus chooses and might have expected fire to complete the classical four elements as in the finale of Act II. Fire appears here as part of the equation, to be sure, but Helios merely represents a transition. Goethe is not celebrating the comprehensive workings of nature as he had at the end of the previous act but rather an aspect of that comprehensiveness which is the inevitable dissolving and returning to its original chaos of all that has been formed, accomplished, or has fulfilled its purpose. Bacchus (Dionysus) is introduced. He stands idly by and 'frets himself, the weakling, little for his faithful vassal,'[24] the vintager who has toiled and prayed to the sun. Only the indwelling spirits 'See what doubtful issue waits on his [the vintager's] loving care.'[25] Indeed the product of his labor produces the frenzied activities of the bacchanalian or dionysian celebration that now ensues and in which the 'goat-footed satyrs' and 'reeling nymphs goat-footed, too,' trample all before them.

> Naught is spared. All laws and order cloven hoofs are
>   treading down –
> All the senses whirl distracted, hideously the ear is stunned.[26]

In order to make room for the new wine, the old skins are quickly emptied.

If the *Helena* were about life and not about art, we might see in this drunken revelry that closes the action little more than the human abuse of a gift of nature. The cloven hooves of the satyrs might, and surely do, suggest the Devil and the demon wine. Social and moral disintegration would forebode. But the *Helena* is first about art and beauty and only through them about life. Coming at the end of an action that has established the principle of beauty through its own formal poetic

---

24 'Bacchus kümmert sich, der Weichling, wenig um den treuen Diener' (l. 10017).
25 From l. 10014: 'des liebevollsten Fleißes zweifelhaft Gelingen.'
26 Line 10030–5.

expression, has made love and expounded philosophy in rhyme, and has created in fantasy the personification of poetry itself, the final Chorus in calling up the potential disorder that underlies all creation calls up at the same time the potential for disorder in art, for the chaos out of which art springs. The Chorus convinces poetically, not dramatically. It does not propound the dionysian principle, but in its creative outburst it undermines again any confidence and security we have gained in the principle of ordered beauty we found established at the beginning of the act, saw challenged in the Euphorion sequence, and might expect now at the close to find reaffirmed. Instead, the phantasmagoric classical tragedy returns to and dissolves itself in the primal dionysian ritual in which it has its origins. Consciousness itself is threatened and the threat welcomed by the drunken mind. When the hellenic or Helen influence is not present, one might say, the untamed forces of nature prevail. Yet the wild array of content and sounds in the final Chorus is contained within measured classical meters to the end.

It is not the center that holds in *Faust II*, at least not in terms of drama, but rather the instinctive structures of a great mind that looks at the comprehensive contradictions in life and in art and does not blanch. When Goethe has Phorkyas as the curtain falls 'step to the proscenium, rise to a gigantic height, descend from her cothurns, lay aside mask and veil, and reveal herself as Mephistopheles,'[27] he is asking us to think as he does. For if we ask now what is the meaning of what we have just seen, we will be caught up totally in the incommensurability of the work and, as Goethe liked to believe, of all true art. He once commented a propos Cellini: 'The cast of Perseus is truly one of the high points, where throughout the piece natural talent, art, craftsmanship, passion and chance all work and relate together and thereby make of the artwork, as it were, a product of nature.'[28] *Faust II* as it evolved also became more and more like a product of nature, which is but does not mean.[29]

The last chorus of the *Helena* was longer than the others, Goethe wrote to Fr. von Müller, 26 July 1827, because 'symphonies like to end

27 After l. 10038.
28 To Schiller, 8 February 1797.
29 A poem should not mean
    But be. (Archibald MacLeish)

with all the instruments going.' Comprehensiveness had come to out-weigh all other concerns at this point. The work that had begun in its earliest period as a revolt against the traditional limits to art was search-ing now for boundaries to contain its scope.

CHAPTER TWELVE

Act IV: The Return
to the Real World

Schiller made an observation about *Wilhelm Meister* that has an unexpected application to *Faust*. He pointed out in a letter to Goethe, 8
July 1796, that the hero of the novel as he underwent his apprenticeship
toward the mastery of life should not be conscious of the rules of that
mastery as goal or he would thereby already have attained to them.[1]

After the Helen episode with all its implications for life and for art,
Faust is at just such a point where its hero might come to an awareness
of his purpose. Yet nothing in his words or actions at the beginning
of Act IV suggests approaching realization, as if the result of his collected experience was to become conscious only in the collection and
not in the particulars of life. Not that we must see Faust as untouched
by the world until the very end, though magic does throughout protect
him from reality. Rather we must assume that he is as yet only sub-
consciously aware of the significance of his experience and must remain
so. This in contrast to the Faust of Part I who in his confrontation with
the world was willing to place before us, and himself, a moving but
unclear and incomplete picture of the human condition. We might
imagine his maturer self not expressing thought and feeling from the
simple recognition of their very want of clarity and completeness. But
there is something more. *Faust II* demanded the presentation not only
of the hero's development but also of the development and past of an
evolving world in which he has his existence. He will be formed in
this *Bildungsdrama* to take his place in a world that itself is being

---

1 My translation of 'so hätte er [das Ziel] *eo ipso* auch erreicht.'

formed. Not only he, but we, are not to attain too early to a mastery of life, which in *Faust* is death.

That Faust is not made aware of the significance of his experience is not a measure of its importance to him. The importance is suggested through allusion. After he steps down from the cloud that has carried him from the classical and the arcadian lands of the previous act, it disperses and seems to take shape again in a form that resembles in turn Juno, Leda, and, finally, Helen. It then becomes a formless mass that settles in the East and there, like

ice hills far away,
Mirrors the deep significance of fleeting life.[2]

It is not that the Helen experience was fleeting, as the cloud image might suggest. Rather to it have become attached other experience and associations which only through it gain their meaning. Gretchen now appears in the vision, though apart. Since the symbolic as well as the dramatic figures in *Faust* do not exist absolutely but also as products of successive worlds or moments in time, the progression from Juno through Leda to Helen and Gretchen reflects not simply the development of an individual understanding or experience but also the evolution of the circumstances that create understanding and experience. Gretchen is now the measure of beauty – but only she can be in a world that has combined the moral and the esthetic inseparably and to which Faust has now returned. That she comes last in his thought, is the one who last takes form in his vision and goes unnamed, suggests that what we see clearly is for him only dawning. He must look also in the present in his search for beauty. He must shake off the classical meters, which his speech still retains as he enters Act IV, and readopt with the drama as a whole the manner that is 'like the present day.' Yet his anticipation is significant. The cloud that takes the shape of Gretchen does not dissolve, but floats upward 'And with it, of my being draws the best away.'[3]

The final thought of the Chorus Mysticus has in effect been stated in

---

2 From l. 10054: 'spiegelt blendend flücht'ger Tage großer Sinn.'
3 'Und zieht das Beste meines Innern mit sich fort' (l. 10066).

these lines: *Das Ewig-Weibliche zieht uns hinan.* But Act v had already
been completed when they were written, so that they represent an
artistic anticipation after the fact.

It might have been otherwise. The sketches of the action and some
of the paralipomena to Act IV indicate an initial urge or plan to state
the significance of the Helen episode dramatically rather than symbolically in dispersing and re-forming clouds that reflect only the processes of mind. One notation reads: 'Paralogos in the proscenium. Faust,
cloud: Helen, Gretchen.'[4] Paralogos implies an unexpected event, as
the confrontation of Helen and Gretchen would be. Sets of lines that
were likewise omitted show a Faust more consciously involved in recollection. We find him in despair. 'To despair is duty.' *Verzweiflung*
nur ist Pflicht.[5] 'Beauty has snatched me from barbarism, / The light,
noble spirit freed me from narrowness.'[6] He sounds here like the old
Faust, a creature Goethe could never quite suppress in himself. He is
even made in one particular pair of lines to rise above his dramatic
self and express a sentiment that in the symbolical *Faust II* is more
appropriately left to the reader or to the audience, to the supplying
mind. 'An earthly loss is to be deplored, / to a spiritual loss is left
despair alone.'[7] For the premise in the *Helena* was that the very cor-
poreality of beauty and not its mere ethereal spirit is what Faust had
sought and found and would therefore have lost. It is we who see the
spiritual loss in the once glory that was Greece, he who was to have
experienced its palpable and earthly reality in Helen. That is why he
continues to speak in classical meters when he first descends from the
cloud that has carried him from Greece. He is like the traveller to a
region where a dialect of his own language is spoken and who on
returning retains for awhile traces of that language is his own speech.

It is not that the reader has prerogatives; nor is the point to show
that Goethe even in the very last stages of composition did not always
create with a sure hand, with a clear knowledge of his direction. The
importance of the discrepancy between plan and execution is that it

4 Beutler, Paralipomena, p. 588.
5 Ibid., p. 611.
6 Der leichte, hohe, Geist riß mich aus dieser Enge,
   Die Schönheit aus der Barbarei. (p. 611)
7 Ein irdischer Verlust ist zu bejammern,
   Ein geistiger treibt zu Verzweiflung hin. (p. 611)

again reveals how the deeper forces of theme and instinctive vision, which were the product of the needs of an age, overcame the lesser needs of dramatic or dramaturgical purpose. As with the altered fate of Homunculus, which made a modern myth out of an intended satire, the vision that absorbs the actual appearance of Helen and Gretchen into the unconscious processes of thought makes of a dramatic occurrence, or potential dramatic occurrence, a model of the thinking mind. The juxtaposing of Juno, Leda, Helen, and Gretchen in reforming images in a cloud is the same juxtaposing of worlds or layers of reality as in the drama as a whole and is the model of its inner form, which itself reflects the new consciousness in the times. To see in the immediate world a past evolving into the present is the new view that lends 'the deep significance to fleeting life.'

Act IV has nothing to do with Gretchen beyond this important anticipation. Like the monologue at the beginning of Act I, the cloud vision creates a perspective in which we see all occurrences and events. It is a *way* of seeing. If Gretchen does not play a role in the action that follows, and in fact appears again only as a spiritual entity at the end of the play, the perspective in which she has just been glimpsed becomes the perspective in which we must see the action that now unfolds. While the monologue that opened Act I pictured the experience of life as colorful reflection, and might thus account for the movement in the drama through masquerade to fantasy, myth, and symbolism, the new monologue has immediate reality as its organizing principle. The things of the past, both real and imagined, emerge in our mind in the present and lend it meaning. Juno becomes Leda becomes Helen becomes Gretchen in a continuing metamorphosis. The *Urbild* becomes myth becomes legend becomes reality in the present, which soon becomes the past. The reflection that was once merely colorful for Faust has gained a form.

The world of power, war, and politics is the substance of Act IV.[8]

---

8 Emrich and others seem to regard the great profundity in Goethe, on one hand, and the imaginative and symbolic nature of *Faust II*, on the other, as reasons to assume an essential indifference to history in the play. 'Der wahre Grund des Scheincharakters des Ganzen liegt ... darin, daß Geschichte, Krieg, Ritter, Könige und Kaiser *nur uralt-neue Wiederholungen eines immer gleichen Kampfes* sind ... die Goethesche Position [ist] vollkommen klar: Der Krieg ist wie alle Geschichte – im

In it we see the late medieval world of the Holy Roman empire become the ancien régime become the restoration of power in Europe after Napoleon during the very last days in which *Faust* itself, that is, Act IV, was being completed. Faust's relation to this world is also less tenuous than it has been to the other worlds, or acts, in the drama. He has already been to the Emperor's court but it is only now that he truly arrives. He comes with a purpose. He will lay claim to the power that is his legendary due, as it were, power being the opposite magnetic pole to the pursuit of beauty in the legend and in the chapbooks. Goethe remains surprisingly close to the legend in his seemingly more and more abstracted interpretation of the theme, partly to gain artistic direction in an otherwise directionless undertaking, to be sure, but partly from his faith in the unconscious wisdom of legend and myth.

Act IV does not have the antecedents in the drama that the themes of beauty, nature, and knowledge have. It grows out of Act I, which in turn had no organic connection with the first part of the work. It is a lesser act in that sense, and yet a necessary one. It represents a return to the 'real' world, not a world free of magic and fantasy, but the world we cannot escape from. Without this return to a base in reality, with its stubborn evil and persistent violence, the vision of an ideal society in Act V would seem not only utopian but hardly urgent. It would come as a leap in the mind to the future after a disappointment in the past and seem more the personal need of the hero to set himself a new goal than the imperative of a historical moment. What Faust will now undertake is not born of altruistic motives or a sense of historic mission,

---

geschichtsskeptischen Sinn Goethes – ein unaufhörlicher Hader' (*Die Symbolik*, p. 383, my italics). But there is a historical reality or base in the play without which its final resolution becomes an ideal vision and nothing more, a vision which would itself then be an 'uralt-neue Wiederholung.' Act V must be read as dependent on Act IV for its meaning, as we shall see, and Act IV is the 'historical' act. The importance of the study by Heinz Schlaffer (*Faust*), I believe, lies in the fact that by seeing the work as modern allegory he is able to keep its meaning historically rooted and yet not deny its essentially imaginative and poetic character. I cannot agree with Jane K. Brown that the concern in Act IV remains 'epistemological' rather than 'ethical,' though I think this a good distinction to make in an understanding of *Faust II* as a whole (*Goethe's Faust: The German Tragedy* [Ithaca, 1986], p. 217). I use the terms 'thematic' and 'dramatic' to mean much the same thing as 'epistemological' and 'ethical.'

it is true, but stems from the desire for raw experience which was his portion of the agreement with the Devil: 'To know all human weal and woe.'⁹ The challenge he creates for himself is daemonic in its inception, welcomed by Mephistopheles, and yet it produces good, or a vision of it.

He would roll back the sea from the land. This, as no other undertaking, presents a true challenge to him. He is angered by the power of this natural element, by the arrogance of its 'aimless sway.' He describes his reaction:

> I deemed it chance, more keenly eyed the main:
> The billow paused, and then rolled back again
> And from its proudly conquered goal withdrew.
> The hour returns, the sport is does renew ...
> On through a thousand channels it does press,
> Barren itself, and causing barrenness.
> It waxes, swells, it rolls and spreads its reign
> Over the waste and desolate domain ...
> Here would I strive, this force would I control.¹⁰

The confrontation with the sea is the struggle within himself. Only the image of a force as arrogantly impetuous and unclearly purposed as the force within his own breast, which is the breast of mankind, could present a challenge worthy of action. He says to Mephistopheles, who has offered him other goals, 'How knowest thou what man desires? / Adverse thy nature, bitter, keen, / How knoweth it what man requires?'¹¹ Yet there is no mention of purpose in his action. The challenge seems wholly personal, or at least existential, as both the mirror image of himself in the sea and the desire to tame and control its energies would indicate: 'This glorious pleasure for thyself attain.'¹² It is wrong, I think, to see already at this early stage in Faust's return to

9 Line 1773.
10 Lines 10206–33.
11 Was weißt du, was der Mensch begehrt?
    Dein widrig Wesen, bitter, scharf,
    Was weiß es, was der Mensch bedarf?   (ll. 10193–5)
12 Erlange dir das köstliche Genießen,
    Das herrische Meer vom Ufer auszuschließen.   (ll. 10228–9)

reality a conscious wish to be effective in the immediate world.[13] Goethe was too much a psychological poet to put idea before desire in the formulation of motive to action. For all the fantasy, allegory, and symbolism that *Faust II* employs in its attempt to understand the human condition, it remains psychological in its understanding of the individual. Faust must first rage against the sea, spend his rage in the action to overcome it, which is the action to overcome himself, in order to discover the meaning of his initial impulse: he will gain new land in order to create a new society. Like the thought of Gretchen, who comes last in his vision though she was first and most real in his experience, his altruistic desires emerge only after or, rather, through the fact that he has satisfied his desire for power. That is done in Act IV. It is the evolutionist morality in *Faust* that demands the realization of self to set in motion the higher urges in man.

Before Faust has conceived his newest goal, Mephistopheles puts before him other prospects of power and glory, as Satan did in his temptation of Christ. The text itself acknowledges this comparison in a marginal note, 'Matthew 4.'[14] It thereby calls up for us the kingdoms in their glory that the Devil has presented to Faust, though none has pleased or tempted him. 'In boundless space the world thou hast surveyed, / Its kingdoms and their glory, all displayed.'[15] He then presents yet another realm of wealth, leisure, solitude, and superficial pleasures, which after his earlier vain attempts he must know will fail. But the presentation, as always with Mephistopheles, is evilly amusing and has its clear purpose. He describes not an abstract realm of power and munificence, but a sprawling city with its crooked alleys and its poverty and stench and, in deliberate contrast, a pleasure castle that the ruler shall erect 'in grand style in some fair pleasance near.' To the former, where 'at any moment one will find / Stench and activity combined,' the ruler will repair once in a while from his 'velvet lawns and verdurous walls' and his 'sweet, social solitude' to be seen in the streets.

13 In a scenario to Act IV Goethe has Faust 'envying' the inhabitants of the coastal area who would win land from the sea. Beutler, Paralipomena, p. 588.
14 The notation was inserted by Riemer in the manuscript margin, and printed with Goethe's approval.
15 Lines 10130–1.

And let me walk, or let me ride ...
By thousands honored and admired.[16]

It is the world of the old order, the ancien régime, which Faust in his return to reality has entered and cannot escape. The ruler Mephistopheles imagines might be any one and almost all of the monarchs who with equal indifference reigned over the Holy Roman Empire from the Renaissance to Goethe's day. Faust is of course not enticed by the offering. If anything, it is the masses of people, the 'ant swarms running to and fro,'[17] as Mephistopheles describes them, to which he might wish to give direction, as to the purposeless flow of the sea. But as yet he sees little reason that men

> Should multiply, should live at ease,
> Be taught, developed if you please –
> More rebels thus to educate.[18]

Goethe evokes a composite picture, but a striking one. We are in the particular world of Act I, with its ineffectual monarch and stagnated political energies, but it is the repetition of this corrupted model broadcast through history that cries out for change. Goethe would not have changed the system as such. He believed in the powers of the individual, of the great man, to alter history purposefully, as he believed in the power of all individuals to rise through action above themselves. He was *fritzisch*, that is an admirer of Frederick the Great. But it was in Napoleon that he saw in his own time the exemplary great man and it is Napoleon as concept, as we shall see, who is subsumed in *Faust II*.

The war that takes place in Act IV is similarly a composite war that might occur in a composite world. By now the drama has introduced so many different perspectives through its prismatic or cubistic form that we almost expect the action to reflect more than one layer of reality

16 Lines 10152–3. Carl Eugen of Swabia, Schiller's onetime princely benefactor, called his retreat 'Die Solitüde,' Frederick the Great his, 'Sans Souci.'
17 'Zerstreuter Ameis-Wimmelhaufen' (l. 10151).
18 Lines 10156–9.

at once. We have seen evolution and metamorphosis poetisized and actualized in the Classical Walpurgis Night, life and society masqueraded earlier in the play, and we find war allegorized here. The war is a masque, though we do not see it and it is described only from afar. What stands out, indeed, are the details of military maneuver that emerge in the description amid fantastic explosions and other products of magic that accompany the allegorical figures of Bully, Havequick, and Holdfast, who are the causes and the prosecutors of war. Like the details of the vineyard in the bacchanalian celebration, these details make the war seem actual for all its unreality. More important, the parties to the war are recognizable enough in their relation to actuality and history so that their actions take on the aura and the force of a historical moment.

The Emperor of Act I proceeds into battle against an Anti-Emperor who has arisen with the support of various factions to bring order and justice into the chaos that plagues the land. The land has fallen on bad days as a result of the 'false riches' in the form of the paper money that Mephistopheles had earlier created, and the situation demands action:

> The able, they forthwith arose with might,
> And said: Who gives us peace is lord, by right.
> The Emperor cannot, will not! Let us choose
> Another who shall infuse in the realm
> Fresh life, and safety unto each assign ...
> Together peace and justice shall combine.[19]

At the level of humanity, the war is a paradigm of war. The Emperor gains from it for the first time the sense that he is Emperor: 'A rival emperor I hail as gain! / That I am emperor only now I know.'[20] He was too prone to rest, as the Lord of the Prologue in Heaven had said of mankind, and has been sent what he regards as an evil force to goad him to good. He will not achieve good, but rather will postpone its accomplishment for what we feel might be centuries by his failure to recognize the challenge of the times he leads and represents. The Em-

19 Lines 10278–84.
20 Ein Gegenkaiser kommt mir zum Gewinn:
   Nun fühl' ich erst, daß *ich* der Kaiser bin.   (ll. 10407–8)

peror is not one emperor but the epitome of emperorship in the Holy Roman Empire which is about to end. In his innate ineffectuality he is the personification of the inability of this traditional political order, for all its avowed idealism, ever to effect change in the real world. As it has so often been said, the empire was neither holy, Roman, nor an empire. The Anti-Emperor is an equal and opposite force of strength, purpose, and determination which has come into being as a direct product of the reigning confusion. Like the Emperor, he is a composite figure, one standing for many, whence the abstract name. Add to this the allegorical figures who prosecute and themselves represent both the causes and effects of war in its aggression, cupidity, and tenacious hold on mankind and we have an acting-out of 'this hereditary disease of mankind,' as Goethe called it.[21]

Yet the Anti-Emperor also surely represents Napoleon. The generalized history and reality that we find throughout *Faust II* seems to have a particular application and a particular purpose here. It is meant to move to action not only Faust, who has now returned to reality, but the supplying mind that will recognize in this masque of war the features of recent and immediate history. Goethe himself remembered from childhood the crowning of the last sovereign of the Holy Roman Empire and later the pretended coronation of his self-proclaimed successor, Napoleon, in 1806.[22] The single remaining space for a portrait of an imperial leader on the wall in his Frankfurt Rathaus as he describes it in *Fiction and Truth* is meant to forebode the end of the empire. The coalition of princes and principalities that rise up against the Emperor in the drama calls to mind the coalition of nations, among them Germany, that formed against Napoleon in the Wars of Liberation and thereby first discovered that they were nations, though in this equation the Emperor would not represent Napoleon.[23] These nations' varying

21 To music historian Johann Fr. Rochlitz, 22 April 1822: 'diese Erbkrankheit der Welt.'
22 *Poetry and Truth*, Bk. I.
23 There is, however, a peculiar resemblance between Napoleon's rise and the uprising against the Emperor in the play. In the France of 1792, the failure of the *assignats* to solve the economic difficulties which were the cause of the dissatisfaction with the Directory led to the acceptance of Napoleon as the new leader and the guide out of the confusion. It is the paper money of Act I that creates the dissatisfaction in Act IV and with it the desire for a new leader. The search for parallels in Act IV to the political situation at the time it was written, 1831, misses this kind

motives, from the desire to expand territory to the need to consolidate
power to the simple thirst for fame in war, are also reflected in the
figures of Havequick, Holdfast, and Bully. I return to this question in
the next chapter. The Napoleon who simply fled from the allied powers
after the defeat at Borodino is the Anti-Emperor who leaves to the
victors an empty tent, not unlike Helen's empty garments. The view
that Goethe held of Napoleon as the potential emancipator of the age
justifies this comparison of the political with the esthetic ideal. I return
also to this question. At yet another level of identification, the Napoleon who rose from the middle class to become emperor of the
French,[24] if not of the Holy Roman Empire, and who proclaimed, and
himself symbolized, an aristocracy of ability, not of birth, is the Faust
who as a vassal of the state presumes to lead its people to a new way
of life. Both are the Goethe who through his talents became *von* Goethe.
'Carrière ouvert aux talents' was a political slogan of Napoleon.[25]

In Act IV Faust returns from the past to the present in the play, from
the ancient to the modern world, from a dream, if one will, to reality,
from art to life, in order to live in the moment and in his time. If we
ask why amid the abuse of the moment and of time that raged in Act
I he stood idly by, we must answer that he was then distracted by a
pursuit of the past through the failure of which alone he could come
to value the present. He steps once again to the dramatic foreground,
the background having now been prepared in such a way that the
moment will no longer exist abstractly or in a vacuum but will be
informed by a past and by the allusive exploration of nature, history,
art, and thought that the poem has made thus far.

As Faust returns to reality, the drama itself begins to relate to political
concerns. The greatest of these was the failure of the old order and
the prospect of a new order to replace it.

---

of relation and so the more palpable connection with Napoleon. See Nicolas
Boyle, 'The Politics of *Faust II*: A Look at the Stratum of 1831,' *Publications of the
English Goethe Society*, n.s. 1981–2, pp. 4–43; Eva Alexander Meyer, *Politische
Symbolik bei Goethe* (Heidelberg, 1949), ch. 3, 'Zeitgeschichte und Vorschau in den
beiden letzten Akten von *Faust II*,' pp. 104–29; most recently, the remarks in John
R. Williams, *Goethe's Faust* (London, 1987), pp. 190–7.
24 The title granted him after he attempted to have himself crowned as the latter.
25 'Dem Talente offene Bahn' was the German version of the Napoleonic slogan.

CHAPTER THIRTEEN

Act IV: The Failure
of the Old Order

Order is a retarding force, not in itself but in its abuse. Yet its abuse
arises naturally. An order that is created to contain and direct the forces
of a given moment tends to perpetuate itself while the forces and the
moment change.

We have seen how Goethe was continually forced to alter the form
of *Faust*, even in the creative process between plan and execution, to
avoid violating the spirit of the different and changing worlds it encompassed. His work was a composition in the truest sense of bringing
together disparate parts. Its order was sacrificed to its completeness.
In an evolving world, order, and our sense of order, must change with
the evolution.

The order which Goethe was willing to upset in the esthetic realm,
for all the apparent barbarism of the act, he was not willing to change
in the real world. From Act I to Act IV, while the rest of the drama
opens up a panorama of developing purposeful activity in nature, history, and thought, and itself evolves artistically, the reality at its base
stagnates. The established order is not altered, although the events of
Act I cry out for change. The Emperor, even in his newfound sense of
emperorhood, refuses to learn. He perpetuates the worst habits and
indulges the worst interests of the society he is meant to lead. Yet
Goethe condemns neither him nor the system he represents. He is 'so
frank, so kind of heart,' Faust says,[1] and his behavior in Act I would

---

1 'Er jammert mich; er war so gut und offen' (l. 10291). On the figure of the Emperor, see Paul Requadt, 'Die Figur des Kaisers in *Faust II*,' *Jahrbuch der deutschen
Schiller-Gesellschaft*, vol. 8 (1964), pp. 153–71. Requadt points out that the tend-

make us agree. But we were also promised, as it were, an education of this prince. It had been planned for Act I and then reduced to a perfunctory, if colorful, test in the masquerade which the Emperor failed, learning nothing from his failure. The process was to be taken up again in a 'continuation of those court scenes,' as notes to the fourth act put it. The question of kingship was apparently to be developed in the motif of the 'foolish emperor' and the 'wise prince.' 'Council to elect the most powerful' is another notation.[2] Yet there is no mention in the actual text of a wise prince or a council or a debate that might have explored the design of an ideal but real political way of life. A better world is barely implied through the indirection of satire.

It is not that art, as art, has the responsibility to realize its subject matter within the context of a political reality. But the education of the prince, which would relate the action in *Faust* to the real or political world, is demanded by the inner logic of the work. Act III had designated the moment, the real world, not the mind, as the arena in which human life was to expand itself. The motif of the imperial court would as such have lost much of its meaning, and hardly have justified the lengths to which it was developed, had it remained simply a location from which Faust might conjure up the shades of Paris and Helen, play a role in a masquerade, and, in the present instance, pose as a general and conduct a war. As we know from the Homunculus and Helen themes, what Goethe took from the legend he heightened. Yet there is no heightening here. Act I, which forms the basis of the action in reality, remains in Act IV what it was and forever might be.

The intent was present and a solution lay at hand, as the paralipomena and sketches for Acts I and IV indicate. Not that an ideal political and social order should have been created in which the hero would successfully carry out his final noble project. *Faust* remains earthly tragic. But it is not despairing, as the unrelieved persistence of the corrupted order renders it. Faust is doomed to fail in his final undertaking in the real world because that world will not allow of a noble act; the Emperor pawns the land to the church before it has been won from the sea. Nor must the resolution be contradictory. The inspira-

---

ency among scholars to see something positive in the Emperor has led to the ignoring of the obvious satire. Deidre Vincent, *The Eternity of Being*, also suggests that a review of the character of the Emperor may be in order (p. 132).

2 Beutler, Paralipomena, p. 588.

tional end of the drama which is intended to move to action must not move *us* and yet fail to move its author beyond a mere *planning* to raise the question of change in the political realm,[3] where all great objective action gains its ultimate meaning. *Faust* had forced Goethe in Act IV to test his philosophy of commitment to the moment and to the immediate world against a real background and he seems to have avoided the challenge.

Time, it is true, was a factor. He hurried to complete his work in what he must have sensed was the short time he had left to him. And Act IV was the last act to be written. Yet he did not treat certain other motifs that were intended for the same act 'too laconically,'[4] such as the satire of the policies and manners of the ancien régime which takes up a considerable part of the action. It is as though this were the easier task. The greater difficulty lay in the motif of the wise prince, which would have forced the question of leadership and posed the dilemma that had been waiting for Faust upon his return to reality. Does the established order itself not corrupt the individual who like Faust would work in the real world to change it? The new land he gains from the sea will be virgin land on which he can build an ideal society, but that land will have been bought at a high moral price of lies and magical connivances. Must the established order itself then be overthrown?

Faust in its evolution had brought Goethe to a radical position not only in the esthetic and the moral but also in the political sphere. The failure to address the political question in fact makes the final resolution even more subjective than the conditions of the pact with the Devil already render it. For if the perfect moment is to be experienced only in anticipation, and if that anticipation is never to be realized in any form in the real world, then the purpose of individual striving is inwardly, not outwardly directed. The imperative becomes to live within. And that was not the intent.

The reasons for avoiding the political question in *Faust* were as personal, I believe, as they were related to the times. Goethe had chosen

---

3 Gundolf asks the interesting question why Goethe did not use the Alexander the Great motif for this purpose; Alexander as the great leader appears in many versions of the Faust legend (*Goethe*, p. 764).
4 In a diary entry for 24 January 1832: 'in Rücksicht größerer Ausführung der Hauptmotive, die ich, um fertig zu werden, allzu lakonisch behandelt hatte.'

monarchy when at age twenty-five he accepted the invitation from the Duke of Weimar to live at his court. It was a move Schiller was never to make, though he had the opportunity. Schiller was more esthetically timid than Goethe, as we can see in retrospect, but not politically. Yet Goethe was not really choosing. The French Revolution was still more than a decade in the future when he moved to Weimar, and when it came it offered an alternative to the old order at least as seemingly repulsive in its widespread violence as was the latter in its systematic abuses. Goethe could tolerate injustice, it is often said, but not disorder. The observation is based on an incident he himself describes in the *Siege of Mainz* where he stopped a crowd from attacking a rich citizen who was attempting to leave the city, his carriages filled with possessions and plunder. 'These are the quarters of the Duke of Weimar and the area before the house is sacred. If you want to create disorder and wreak vengeance, there is room elsewhere.'5 Yet in the companion piece on the war of 1792, *Campaign in France*, he recognized the new order that would inevitably result from the success of the revolution when he made the famous pronouncement in the face of the victorious attack by its forces at Valmy, 'From here and now begins a new epoch in world history.'6 It is doubtful that he would have foreseen the particulars of subsequent events from the French occupation of Germany through the Napoleonic Wars to the Wars of Liberation, all of which and more political turmoil he witnessed in his lifetime, but his remark does suggest an acute awareness of rather than a resistance to the dynamics of change. Yet what drew his understanding to the course of history might not have drawn his sympathy.

He had also met the great nobility of his day and a great man in Napoleon. In the acquaintance he enjoyed with the greater and lesser leaders of nations and in his knowledge of their ways he might still have believed that events are made by man and not by the abstract force we call history. In Napoleon he had found the great individual who through the power of his person could change history, and he had followed his achievements in war and his attempts at massive political and social reform until they too had gone, though the effects

5 In the entry for 25 July. See the *Seige of Mainz* in the Suhrkamp edition, vol. 5, eds. Thomas P. Saine and Jeffrey L. Sammons.
6 In the entry for the night of 19 September, the eve of the surrender of the allied forces to the revolutionary army.

of the revolution itself were still felt in the unsteadily restored monarchies after 1812. Repercussions continued into the 1830s, where we find Goethe making himself put aside *Le Globe* and *Le Temps* from Paris with their daily political news and discussions of royalist and republican sentiments in order to return to his work on *Faust*.[7]

Napoleon, in turn, admired Goethe as a great man,[8] which might have served in the eyes of both to reaffirm the belief in a human order guided by vision, intelligence, and ability rather than by the infirm process of hereditary power. However, years of dedication and loyalty to the nobility in daily life and in his ministerial duties made it impossible for Goethe to express openly, and so perhaps not inwardly truly know, what in the last analysis he felt about the daemonic rise and fall of the French emperor, who was after all the enemy of the German people.[9] In *Epimenides' Awakening*, the festival play he wrote in 1814 when the allies entered Paris and Europe was restored to the status quo ante, he admonishes or castigates himself allegorically in the figure of Epimenides for having in his political apathy or ' sleep' too long ignored the great upheavals of his day. He had too passively stood by while tyranny and degradation overcame his country. The Demon of Oppression in the play bears almost no resemblance to Napoleon but only he would have been understood in that figure at the time.

The nobility, Wilhelm von Humboldt said, had once been a necessary

---

7 To Eckermann, 21 February 1830. This contradicts the notion that Goethe had no concern for political matters. He followed the events of the July Revolution daily in *Le Temps* and *Le Globe*, both of which journals he read regularly. *Le Globe* became political in 1828. For Goethe's daily reaction to the political events in France, see G.C.L. Suchard, 'Julirevolution, St. Simonismus und die Faustpartien von 1831,' *Zeitschrift für deutsche Philologie*, vol. 60 (1935), pp. 240–74. Nicolas Boyle, in a new biography, *Goethe: The Poet and His Age* (Oxford, 1991), stresses the importance that the social and political tensions of his own world had for Goethe even in the early years of his development. See, especially, the excellent discussion of the reasons for Goethe's going to, identifying with, and eventually spending the whole of his mature life in the Duchy of Weimar (pp. 239–51).

8 Fr. von Müller describes the meeting in Erfurt between Napoleon and Goethe, 2 October 1808, where the emperor on seeing the poet enter the room is reported to have said to those beside him: 'Voilà un homme!'

9 On the older Goethe's view of Napoleon, see the excellent summary in Ilse Peter's 'Das Napoleonbild Goethes in seiner Spätzeit,' in *Jahrbuch der Goethe-Gesellschaft*, vol. 9 (1944), pp. 140–71.

and now become an unnecessary evil.[10] Goethe, who was not of the
nobility himself, wished to replace the old with a new aristocracy of
ability and talent, as is clearly indicated in Faust. But two things were
needed, he said, for great individuals to achieve greatness, 'a good
head and a large inheritance. Napoleon had inherited the French Revolution ..., Luther the obscurantism of clerical rule.'[11]

But what has Faust inherited? The inheritance of a mass of erudite
knowledge would have been a challenge worthy of his abilities to
reconstruct and imbue with meaning, but he has discovered, or soon
will discover, that the very purpose of knowledge is to issue in action,
not in further thought. He has similarly put behind him the pursuit of
beauty in order to involve himself actively in the objective world. Yet
the real world that confronts him and almost begs in its own incon-
sequentiality to be reordered and remade, he leaves to become whatever it will be. The philosopher who raged against the contradictions
and inadequacy of speculative thought in Part I is now the man of
activity who is moved neither by injustice nor disorder. For the Emperor, who in all his goodness is the identified cause of the evil, Faust
has only the admonition that ruling and pleasure do not mix: 'He who
would command, / His highest bliss must in commanding find.'[12]

Again, the point is not to demand of Faust that it create a new
political order to house and sustain its grand visionary project for a
new mankind. We accept the failure, and the part in it Faust plays in
his own tragedy. But in the light of the evil he causes and will further
cause in Act V, his ultimate salvation would then become a salvation
or success beyond good and evil, not only in the sense that his higher
end justifies his means but in an absolute sense. For there is no objective
end to his actions except in his own mind. He dies not knowing the
truth. We cannot say that in his 'dark' way he has accomplished good,
for no good will have been accomplished. Faust then becomes a tragedy
of the utter self-deception of man, and the salvation and absorption
of the hero into a transcendental order of things a mere wishful and
wholly otherworldly resolution. The moment will have been emptied
of its meaning. I also think that was not the intent.

10 Quoted in G.P. Gooch, Germany and the French Revolution (rev. ed., London,
   1920), p. 107.
11 'Die Finsternis der Pfaffen' (to Eckermann, 2 May 1824).
12 'Wer befehlen soll, / Muß im Befehlen Seligkeit empfinden' (ll. 10252–3).

Goethe had created an action in which the hero as the representative of man evolves and the world remains still, at least in its social and political aspects. He himself seems to have been aware of this inherent contradiction when he at least planned in Act I and again in Act IV for an education of the prince. This could not have been a full exploration of the question as Shakespeare had undertaken in the Henry plays, and hardly an attempt to make of his own Emperor a Prince Hal, but it would have satisfied the logic in *Faust* by its simple recognition of the problem.[13] The motif, as we said, would have raised, if not solved, the question of change in a prospective future. The prospective view is the Faustian view. There are in fact a dozen lines that Goethe wrote but did not include in Act IV which directly approach the question. They would have occurred just before the point where the Emperor makes his antiquated challenge to the Anti-Emperor of a duel to resolve their differences of power. The Emperor:

The people never stand against the emperor.
It is treason, rebellion, would they separate themselves from
    him.
Always beneath him would they live
Did he not raise them to him through love,
Not press them in his heart with paternal care.
Now he curses them as degenerate, undutiful creatures.
– But let a man step firmly forth
And declare: I am Emperor,
That sounds quite different, sounds personally great.[14]

The challenge then follows: *So sei's denn Kaiser gegen Kaiser frisch gewagt!* We cannot reasonably speculate on what Goethe originally intended with these lines but we can see that the issue of monarchy and republicanism was to be joined, and joined in the immediate wake of the violent political events that had given rise to the issue. This is

13 Other conflicting developments in Acts IV and V remained unresolved, such as the 'antifeudal' and 'profeudal' sentiments that are reflected in the actions of the hero. Marxist criticism tends to see a triumph of the new over the old order in the play which is not entirely borne out by the action. Cf. Hans Rudolf Vaget, 'Faust, der Feudalismus und die Restauration,' *Akten des VI.* Internationalen Germanistenkongresses (Basel, 1980), p. 345.
14 Beutler, Paralipomena, pp. 613–14; my translation.

not the world of the historical but of the contemporary Faust whom Goethe had created. And we can assume that much of related concern to the Emperor, who can answer only 'after some thought,'[15] would have preceded these lines. We can further assume that in the self-declared emperor whom the present one regards as evil and challenges, Goethe did not see an empty pretender but the representative leader of the future. The image is too close to Napoleon to suggest otherwise,[16] and our Emperor too much the representative of the ancien régime to have a future. We can assume, finally, that it was not want of time that made Goethe abandon his original plan to set the action actively rather than merely passively in conflict with the established order, but the difficulty in his own relationship to that order in his position at the Weimar court that caused him to postpone the question to the end, when there would be no time.[17]

What was left in Act IV in default of the motif of the education of the prince was a continuation from Act I of the social and political 'danse macabre,' as it has been called,[18] in which the affairs of life are presented fantastically and in masquerade. Now the focus is on war and on the larger rather than everyday matters. But if the war is meant to represent all war, the eternal strife between 'Guelfs and Ghibellines,'

---

15 'Nach einigem Nachdenken' (Paralipomena, p. 613).

16 Perhaps important in this regard is the phrase from the lines just quoted, 'Tritt aber *tüchtig* ein Mann hervor ...' The words are a metathesis of 'ein tüchtiger Mann,' an expression Goethe used to describe men of quality and leadership, indeed of genius, as he implied in a discussion of Napoleon with Eckermann, 11 March 1828 (second series).

17 The finest indication of his loyalty to Karl August of Weimar is found perhaps in his *Venetian Epigrams*, 34, 'Augustus and Maecanas': 'For he has given me that which is seldom vouchsafed by the mighty, / Friendship and leisure and trust, meadow and garden and house' (trans. Gooch, *Germany* p. 446). Katarina Mommsen sees Goethe as indirectly and posthumously 'addressing' Karl August in the masquerade scene in Act I as well as Act IV, and in detail: '*Faust II* als politisches Vermächtnis des Staatsmannes Goethes,' *Jahrbuch des Freien Deutschen Hochstifts*, 1989, pp. 1–26.

18 Lukács, Faust Studies,' p. 184, and further: 'Even the distribution of this material [in Acts I and IV] is not fortuitous or determined solely by technical considerations ... What we find in the fourth act, depicted in a historically accurate manner as a privileged feudal "intermundium" at the very heart of feudalism, is its real grave-digger: capitalism ... However, this ideological explosion also has its real economic prehistory which Goethe correctly understood: the invention and introduction of paper money by Mephistopheles.'

in all its mutation and metamorphoses,[19] and if the larger affairs are all political affairs, in the context of the time in which *Faust II* was written they take on specific meaning, or rather a variety of specific meanings. The masquerade figures who conduct the war are images or symbols of its root causes and at the same time reflect more immediate history and reality. Historians have seen in Friedrich Wilhelm III of Prussia, Goethe's contemporary, a mirror image of Maximilian I, the procrastinating and obstructionist Holy Roman Emperor at the time of the historical Faust.[20] The political action that on the one hand represents the inane injustice that must have been perpetuated throughout time represents as well the most recent events. Francis II, the last emperor of the Holy Roman Empire, was crowned just one year before Napoleon was made brigadier general in the French army, in 1793.

The root causes of war are natural aggression, cupidity, and steadfastness, represented in the figures of the bully, the predator, and the conservator – *Raufebald, Eilebeute,* and *Haltefest.* The one desires the vivid excitement, the other the gain, and the last the challenge, of war. Together they create and feed the conflict and, with the help of magic in this case, overcome the forces of the Anti-Emperor. Thus, they begin to resemble the coalition of European powers that formed against the revolution that had caught fire in France and would itself be king. This is the force to which Goethe at Valmy had assigned the future, for good or for ill. When at the same time we see in the Anti-Emperor, as in a telescoping of time, the person of Napoleon who was the creature and the leader of the revolution in its later stages, we begin to sense in the play a sympathy for the supposed enemy, who after all has come in the name of justice and order: 'Let us choose / Another who in the realm shall infuse / Fresh life, and safety unto each assign ... / Together peace and justice shall combine.'[21] When we see in the allegorical figures the coalition of nations that opposed Napoleon in their own

19 Schon schallt's von ritterlichen Prügeln,
   Wie in der holden alten Zeit.
   Armschienen wie der Beine Schienen,
   Als Guelfen und als Ghibellinen,
   Erneuen rasch den ewigen Streit. (ll. 10769–73)
20 E.g., Geoffrey Barraclough, *The Origin of Modern Germany* (2nd ed., London, 1957), p. 409.
21 In einer frisch geschaffnen Welt
   Fried' und Gerechtigkeit vermählen. (ll. 10283–4)

interests of attaining glory, acquiring territory, or restoring borders, we begin to see history from the opposite side in the play. Whether in the forces that earlier attempted to destroy the revolution or in those that later stopped Napoleon at Waterloo, the motives seem to have been much the same. In peace, the Congress of Vienna, in its formal and celebratory way, with feasts and balls and excursions for royal and ambassadorial dignitaries, ratified the acquisitions of the war, honored the victories, and conserved the old order. The sense of the future remained unchanged. The Duke of Weimar, Goethe's own prince, had earlier been at Valmy in search of military glory for himself and his own tiny state, if not in search of territory.

The political picture remains unclear in Act IV. The allegorical figures themselves are seen so much in the round that the specific meaning they take on to one way of thinking, they lose again in the depth of their conception. Bully is young, Havequick of middle years, and Hold-fast elderly, so that there seems to be at work as well a natural law that levels the characters of men and nations in war to a simple bio-logical process. Young Bully, lightly armed and colorfully dressed, is eager for war for its own sake, and mature Havequick, armed and richly clothed, for what it will bring. The aged Holdfast, heavily armed and otherwise unadorned, a grossly pathetic, almost tragic figure, holds firm. They are in war what they are in life. Here the present, the immediate past, and the deep past are one. Through the very nature of his poetic genius, in other words, Goethe makes even caricature, which is intended to move to action, into a vehicle for wisdom, which has a tendency to passivity. He seems, in fact, to have tacitly attributed to his hero the same profound insight into the immutable nature of things that he himself possessed as poet but which was hampering in the man of action that Faust was to become. The 'aimless sway' that Faust sees around him in Act IV should, like the senseless movement of the sea, challenge him to act, and yet he seems also to possess with his author a deeper awareness of the futility of change. *Faust II* is sometimes numbing in its greatness, like the quality I believe Goethe must have found in Raphael.

It was all the more important, therefore, that the satire of the ancien régime that occupies the last part of the act be unambiguous. We must be brought unmistakably to recognize the abject failure of the old order both in its monarchy and, as so often, in its monarchs. For there will not be a dramatic transition to Act v but, again, only a juxtaposing of alternative worlds for the supplying mind to weigh and resolve. What Faust learns through his experience in these worlds and absorbs unconsciously, we learn through observation.

First of all, the verse form changes. The sentiments and policies of the ancien régime, its classicism and formality and rigid order, are expressed in the meter that epitomizes the spirit of that world, the alexandrine verse. It is the language of the great French classical drama at the time of Louis XIV and of its imitators in the eighteenth century. It is the verse form used to express its very theory and justify its own practice, as in Boileau's *L'Art poétique*. It has a parallel in Restoration England, and restoration is in fact the content its form embraces here.

The Emperor calls together the victorious allies who have supported him in the war and rewards them for their loyalty by an increase in their land, power, and profitable responsibilities. He restores himself and them to the position held before the war, and enhances it.

> The bounds of your possessions I forthwith expand.
> You faithful ones, be yours fully many a goodly land,
> Also the lofty right, should time the occasion send,
> Through purchase, chance, exchange, their limits to extend ...
> As judges be it yours to speak the final doom,
> From your high stations none will to appeal presume.
> Then, tribute, tax, and tithe, safe conduct, toil and fee,
> Mine salt and coinage dues, your property shall be.[22]

It is not only this bland presumption of power, itself an emptiness upheld by a nobility of form, but the historical and political context in which these words are spoken that creates the satire. We are no longer simply in the world of the historical Faust, for all the outmoded language and trappings of power, but in that of restoration Europe after the Napoleonic Wars. Yet few anachronisms result. For the powers at

22 Lines 10938–48. 'The sums expended in obtaining the ratification of the Golden Bull ... had been amassed by keeping a market in which honors and exemptions, with what lands the crown retained, were put up openly to be bid for' (James Bryce, *The Holy Roman Empire* [New York, 1968, first published 1864], p. 246).

the Congress of Vienna in 1815 were themselves attempting to recover
the monarchial powers established by imperial authority in the late
Middle Ages. Goethe had researched the Golden Bull of 1356 in preparing Act IV,[23] not so much to refresh his memory of detail, one
suspects, for he knew the history of the Holy Roman Empire, as to
confirm his suspicions that history was repeating itself. These great
powers are not now invested, as in *Faust*, in four princes but in the
nations that comprised the peoples of Europe. We may even say that
there were four, in the main: Austria, Russia, Germany, and Italy.
France was to be protected from the outside against forces that might
arise from within and spread beyond, as in 1789. England remained
an interested party only. Not that these nations were *granted* judicial
power and the authority to extend boundaries, impose taxes, exact labor
and tithes, and punish dissent as treason, as were the original bene-
factors of the Golden Bull. They would simply *retain* what they believed
from the beginning was their right to hold.[24] Goethe might well have
experienced in the events of 1815 and again in 1830, when there was
a renewed attempt to overthrow the old order, that sensation he described as a 'repeated mirroring,' the perception of something 'in the
history of art and of science, of the church and surely in the political
world that has repeated itself time and again and still repeats itself.'[25]
The depth of the perception might, again, have removed something
from the outrage at what has occurred. The detached Olympian was
no more to be suppressed in Goethe than the passionate Faust. But
that he disliked disorder does not mean that he liked injustice. That
he abhorred the Revolution does not mean that he worshipped monarchy.

For the restoration of order is presented not only as unjust but as
empty and ridiculous. The titles awarded to the four princes, those of

23 Goethe charged out a book on the Golden Bull, *Erläuterungen zu der Goldenen
   Bulle* (1766), from the Weimar library while working on Act IV. This further belies
   the contention that he had no interest in the facts of history as he composed
   Faust.
24 Like the Golden Bull 'it did no more than legalize a condition of things already in
   existence, but which by being legalized acquired new importance' (Bryce, *Holy Roman Empire*, p. 385).
25 'Wiederholte Spiegelungen' (1823). The title is borrowed from a concept in optics
   which Goethe mentions in the essay.

Arch-Marshal, Arch-Chamberlain, Arch-Steward, and Arch-Cupbearer, suddenly take on their literal meanings as they are assigned
their respective responsibilities. The seemingly exalted titles, except for
that of Arch-Marshal as protector of the monarch and the land, entail
duties that bear so exact a resemblance to their original functions that
they undermine and ridicule the importance later attached to their
names. In Gilbert and Sullivan fashion, the Arch-Chamberlain is thus
enlisted: 'With valor who, like thee, doth courtesy unite, / Arch-Chamberlain shall be. The duties are not light.' Chief among his duties is
the supervision of the servants, who are 'still to inner strife inclined,'[26]
which in 1830 can only mean political and not personal discord. One
is reminded of those in power at the time in various nations and prin-
cipiates whose task it was, whatever their titles, to search out sedition.[27]
The Arch-Steward, a title still in use after centuries of acquiring for
itself more and more dignity and power, is here charged with the
straightforward duty of getting a good meal onto the table of the Emperor. 'Therefore, henceforth to thee, / The chase, the poultry yard,
the farm shall subject be. / Choice of my favorite dishes still for me
prepare ...'[28] The Arch-Cupbearer is addressed: 'Since festivals [i.e., in
celebration of the victory] perforce alone engage us now, / To Cup-
bearer transformed, young hero straight be thou! ... henceforth the duty
shall be thine / To see our cellars stored richly with generous wine'[29]
Both would have been amply employed at the Congress of Vienna.
The whole concern in the creation of these offices is the protection and
pleasure of the prince and not the responsibilities of leadership. The
Emperor who proclaims that 'a young and joyous prince, of time may
waste the dower, / Him years will teach at last the importance of the
hour,'[30] has in fact learned not one thing from the war and remains
mired in the ease and pleasure he has sought from the beginning. It
was often said of the emigrés and ultraroyalists after the revolution

---

26 'Bei deren innerm Streit ich schlechte Diener finde' (l. 10886).
27 The most notorious was Joseph Fouché who between 1792 and 1815 both helped
   and intrigued against the French political leader Javert.
28 Lines 10899–900.
29 Lines 10909–12.
30 Ein junger, muntrer Fürst mag seinen Tag vergeuden,
   Die Jahre lehren ihn des Augenblicks Bedeuten. (ll. 10869–70)

that they had forgotten nothing of the past and learned nothing from it, and the same may be said of the Emperor. The satire in Act IV is one of the few occasions in *Faust* where Goethe is Mephistophelean outside the character of Mephistopheles.

The harshest criticism of the ancien régime is reserved for the established church, as though here there would be no question of mere modification and compromise. From the beginning Goethe had seen the church in a negative light. Whatever the initial reason for this reaction, whether the revolt of his free spirit or simply the fashionable attitude of the time, when he came at the end of *Faust* to include this powerful institution in his vision of life he did so deliberately and with wholly conscious reasons for his summary rejection. It was no longer a mere disdain for *das Pfaffentum*, as it had been in *Urfaust*. The greatest and, as it were, most fundamental enemy of a philosophy that had come to focus on the moment and the immediate world were the professors of eternity. The things above and the things below had already been the topic of Act I. But not only does the church distract from the world in theory, in practice it expands in the here and now. Thus, the Archbishop, who shares temporal powers in the Holy Roman Empire and is at the same time Arch-Chancellor,[31] demands of the Emperor a tract of land in recompense and atonement for his consorting with the forces of magic in his victorious war: 'Back to our holy church some little share repay.'[32] The land is 'where the Prince of Lies did late thine ears abuse.'[33] In this 'space defiled,' with its 'verdant slopes which yield rich pasture ...., its clear lakes, alive with fish, and brooks unnumbered,' the Archbishop will erect a church to consecrate the land, 'by sin so desecrated.'[34] So described, the action seems not only usurpation of property but an abuse of nature. Yet when the Archbishop creates the structure in his imagination, the effect is no longer satire.

Swift, to the spirit eye, the massive walls aspire;
The morning sun's first light already gilds the choir.

---

31 It was to lessen the power of papal authority in the naming of the emperor that this compromise was incorporated in the Golden Bull. The Archbishop of Mainz, for example, remained an elector until the end of the empire, in 1806.
32 Lines 10991–2.
33 'Wo [du] dem Lügenfürst ein horchsam Ohr geliehn' (l. 10995).
34 Lines 10997–11005.

Crosswise the structure grows, the nave, in length and height
Expanding, straightway fills believers with delight.
Through the wide portal now they throng with ardent zeal
While over hill and vale resounds the bells' first peal.[35]

We no longer see a corruption of justice and of the landscape but are confronted with the paradox of the human need for religion and the unreal nature of that need. It was as if poetry could not touch even abuse without rendering it pardonable. The Archbishop, after all, does only what Faust will later do when he wrenches land from Philemon and Baucis to build his dam in the cause of a paradise on earth. As the last item of business in the scene, he demands 'tithe and dues, with rent and taxes'[36] from the land that Faust will gain from the sea, though like the buried treasure that supports the paper money in Act I, 'the land is not yet there.'[37]

The tent, and the throne in it, are empty when the victorious Emperor enters the camp of the Anti-Emperor. There was a similar emptiness or vacuum of power in Europe when Napoleon fell, and the allied nations moved immediately and with little thought to fill it. They restored the old order. Goethe himself was more cautious. In the old order, which in the play had 'limped, fell, rose again, tripped over itself and landed in a heap,'[38] as was surely the case in 1830, he could no longer place faith, as the action in Act IV indicates. But he had not answered the question how a system that seemed by its own instincts to create the 'bed of ease,' which his drama rejected, could come to change without the violent upheaval of revolution that he would not accept. Faust thus enters the final act with a vision of the future which is doomed in a world that has remained what it is.

---

35 Lines 11007–12.
36 And that forever: 'Zehnten, Zinsen, Beth,' / Für ewig' (ll. 11024–5).
37 'Das Land ist noch nicht da, im Meere liegt es breit' (l. 11039).
38   – es hinkte, fiel, stand wieder auf,
Dann überschlug sich's, rollte plump zuhauf.   (ll. 10272–3)

CHAPTER FOURTEEN

Act V: Preparing
for the End

What is interruption, what continuity in *Faust II*? The question might well have been asked already in Part I, where we are likewise often distracted from the dramatic action proper by the demands of thought. In Part II, however, thought comes into being in the drama and not merely in the mind. The play itself is a conversion of thought into an apparent action, which all drama is, except that *Faust II* makes us aware of the fact.

The Wanderer at the beginning of Act V is one such thought. He comes from nowhere in the play and has in effect nowhere to go, as his name implies. As a character he is of little importance. But as a thought, like the thought and presence of the rainbow that leads Faust to re-see life or the vision of the clouds in which he comes to understand human understanding, the Wanderer in his simple being serves equally to cast the whole of the action into new perspective. If we are right in saying that Goethe saw things always in the round, he will at one point have come to the recognition that the world as it presents itself to Faust even after he has come to see so many other worlds and times is after all only one side of the whole. The Wanderer represents the other side, and coming as he does at the end, his symbol is the more unsettling.

He is wandering Man, unsheltered and undirected, who yet survives and is grateful for his survival. He had once been shipwrecked, we know, and has now come to thank those who saved him. This simple, ungainful act, by its sheer human simplicity, puts into question not only the moral aspect of the driving force in the drama but its philosophical base as well. The Wanderer does not strive, he is. He is not

Wagner, whom we can dismiss as simply misdirected; he is not the Student, who mistakes the will to power for profundity of insight. Of all the figures in the play thus far, he alone comes close to Gretchen. He lives in her spiritual world, though he is much traveled.

The Wanderer by his being provokes the question of the purpose of human striving. We know nothing of his life except for this one act of gratitude, but like a biblical character he gains meaning in the contemplation. He seems to partake of an existence deeper than Faust has yet touched, except in speculation. He is not innocence, like Gretchen, but pure resignation. Significantly, he gazes upon the sea with acceptance and recognition of its powers, whereas Faust had angered: 'Forward let me step, and gazing / Forth upon the boundless sea, / Kneel [with] thankful prayers ...'[1] He will be destroyed by the achieving nature that is Faust, outwardly as an apparent victim of circumstance but inwardly or symbolically as the counterforce to striving and achievement. The gratuitousness of both his appearance and destruction suggests an unconscious factor. Though not aware of the existence of the Wanderer, Faust is aware in his own being of the retarding influence of simple humanity.

The Wanderer raises a philosophical question. The destruction of Philemon and Baucis raises the same question but in a social rather than philosophical framework. The figure of Care will raise the same question of action and retardation psychologically. For the drama has reached the point where, having opted for action, its enemy has become inaction in any form.

Philemon and Baucis, Goethe said, are not intended as the original old couple of Ovid's *Metamorphoses* but only as persons in a similar state; they were merely convenient names.[2] But it is also true that the reward the old couple receives from the gods for their act of hospitality takes a form that has new meaning in its new context. In Ovid, before they are granted their wish to die together (which Goethe, with vicious irony, also grants them), their little hut is made into a palace. The surrounding land has been flooded so that the structure stands magnificently alone.[3] What Faust would accomplish in the modern world,

1 Lines 11075–6.
2 To Eckermann, 6 June 1831.
3 *Metamorphoses*, Bk. 8.

the gaining of land from the sea, the ancient gods of legend had once accomplished in reverse. When one reads Ovid from *Faust* and not *Faust* from Ovid in this scene, the gods' act, though generous in intent, seems wasteful and seignorial. Mercury and Jupiter join the Archbishop in abusing land, which has now become the symbol of earthly existence, for a higher purpose. Philemon and Baucis, of course, have no conscious part in this design. In their simplicity they have made their hut into their palace and wish no more. Yet it is this simplicity that is the opponent of change, metamorphosis, and evolution.

The dilemma for Faust in removing the old couple in order to complete his plan is not essentially moral, but tragic. He does not seek power, but completion and perfection. Nor does he desire fame: 'The deed is everything, fame naught.'[4] The issue at its base is not even ideological, though the old couple with their chapel and church bell are a symbol in the drama for energies directed toward another world while this world remains intractably the same. Philemon and Baucis together with the Wanderer close the opening scene of Act V walking toward the chapel, where they will sound the bell, kneel and pray, and 'trust in the God of old.'[5]

Faust's desire is the human desire for completion and perfection, which cannot be satisfied. The removal of the old couple does not mean for Faust an extension of the land for the inhabitancy of a greater number for the greater good, it means the opportunity and pleasure of contemplating his achievement which alone completes the conscious goal of human action. He will build on this last small piece of land a tower lookout from which to observe what he has accomplished. This is the Faust who has sought absolute beauty and now seeks absolute completion, which are perhaps the same thing. He remains the idealist, and must finally be brought, not to accept the world as it is, which is not the imperative of the historical moment, but to redefine the ideal. For the ideal in an evolving world is not a preconceived notion to which one seeks to make the things of life and of art conform, but a projected image, always imperfectly conceived, which the experience of life and of art modifies to make apparently attainable. The ideal is what conduces to action.

4 'Die Tat ist alles, nichts der Ruhm' (l. 10188).
5 Laßt uns läuten, knieen, beten
Und dem alten Gott vertraun! (ll. 11141–2)

It is the titan in Faust who wishes to achieve the ideal in the real world. It was the frustration with this desire that prompted his pact with the Devil. 'The god who deep within my breast resides, / Deep in my soul can stir the springs; ... [but] he cannot move external things.'[6] Yet the power that provides the ability to move external things through magic must move them within time. The ideal may still conflict with what surrounds it in reality. To change the world for one man, one would have to change the whole world.

Yet an alternative exists, though less for Faust than in the abstract. A further thought, that is, occurs to the poem at this point, if not to the hero. Like the motif of the Wanderer, it is part of the thematic rather than the dramatic development that prepares for the final resolution. It takes the form of Lynceus, the tower watchman of Act III. He sees the world from above, clearly and aloofly, in the manner that is often wrongly attributed to Goethe himself in his later years. His view encompasses all, but at a remove. He has no other part in the action but in its description. His view represents the alternative to action, and it renders the contradictory aspects of life equally acceptable and beautiful.

> I gaze on the distant,
> I look on the near,
> On moon and on planet
> On wood and on deer.
> The beauty eternal
> In all things I see,
> And pleased with myself,
> All bring pleasure to me.[7]

It is the view from eternity, but now placed on earth, which the Archangels commanded in the Prologue in Heaven. It includes, here as there, what from an earthly point of view we must call evil, such as destruction and death. It is Lynceus who is called upon to describe the destruction of Philemon and Baucis at the end of the scene. But he evokes as well the lovely sight of ships in the harbor: 'The sun sinks

6 Lines 1566–9.
7 Lines 11292–9.

down ... A stately galley, deeply freighted / On the canal now draweth near.'[8] Just as the angels after viewing the swiftly and violently changing atmosphere that envelops the earth can still praise the 'mild procession of [the] day,' Lynceus can find 'all that has been' beautiful.[9] He takes no action and utters no word against the destruction of the aged couple.

Lynceus is Goethe the poet. He contains what Faust could not absorb in his person and yet had to be personified in the poem. We saw him earlier express the wonder, fascination, and passion that Helen aroused in men and yet which seemed to render his master speechless. He stands again at his side, like another self, an alter ego that cannot occupy the body of Faust, who has turned to action. For Lynceus represents observation without participation. He is the symbol of resignation in the special sense of renouncing the world, not in its beauty, splendor, and immediacy, but in the demands for action that it makes upon the individual. The poet is by nature 'resigned'; he celebrates what is but does not cause it to be. The tower Faust plans to build in order to observe what he himself has created is a presumption of this position. It is an internalization of fame, the fame he himself had rejected as idle. The tower, one senses, was conceived and would better have been built for Lynceus. It is somehow right that it fails of completion.

The esthetic position will not be destroyed through the destruction and failure in the real world. Goethe's voice will not be silenced in the play. Unlike the Boy Charioteer who is banished to solitude to 'create his own world' in default of a real world of purpose and accomplishment to praise, he will not invent a fiction to celebrate but will sing, through Lynceus, his affirmation of life – 'no matter what it has been.' It is just that this voice and position are not for Faust, who is called upon to decide, to act, and not to accept. Goethe himself, we might say, had to resign his resignation in order to finish his *Faust*, with all its contradictions and incompleteness, so that the greater project of life

---

8 Die Sonne sinkt, die letzten Schiffe,
   Sie ziehen munter hafenein.
   Ein großer Kahn ist im Begriffe,
   Auf dem Kanale hier zu sein.   (ll. 11143–6)
9 Es sei wie es wolle,
   Es war doch so schön!   (ll. 11302–3)

might in some way be furthered. He was called upon in that sense as poet to act. Ancient tragedy had not attempted to change the world; *Faust* in its new position in time and historical circumstance was set the task of arranging its events and characters and symbols to reflect the world as it is in truth and yet move to action.

The final retardation of action in the play takes the form of Care. Faust can overcome the Guilt,[10] also here personified, which he has incurred in the deaths of Philemon and Baucis and the Wanderer, not because his part in their destruction was unintentional, but because the realm of action entails error and evil. Time and nature forgave him the Gretchen tragedy and now the play itself in its great physical and historical panorama that serves to redefine the meaning of good and evil can forgive him his presumptuous attempt to realize perfection in an imperfect, because always incomplete, universe. But Care is amoral and cannot be so overcome. When she enters with the Gray Women, she will not, like her sisters Guilt, Want, and Need, be dismissed by clarity of conscience or by purpose of will, indeed not by action itself, which the poem otherwise tells us is the realization and salvation of man. Care seems to represent the dissoluting inner force that accompanies and opposes all resolution, like the doubt that increases with the emerging certainty. She persists, as if she were not merely one of the inner obstacles to action, such as indolence or idleness, of which we have been warned from the outset, but the opponent of last resort. She is the final obstacle but one, which is death. 'There comes he, our brother, there cometh he – Death.'[11]

Faust has not known Care. 'Hast thou [Care] never known?'[12] Nor has he known Want or Need. Magic has served to fill his wants. His life of passion and unweighed action has in turn protected him from thought. 'I have but hurried through the world, I own.'[13] Guilt he has overcome, though it may weigh upon him. But Care has no regard for the moral and social, the inner or the outer orderings of life and of the mind. It stifles, retards. It causes inaction, which causes Care.

10 The German word is *Schuld*, which can mean either *debt* or *guilt*. In assuming the latter meaning, I am not in line with what might be called the prevailing view, though the question is still vexed. See Arens, *Kommentar*, pp. 886–8.
11 'Da kommt er, der Bruder, da kommt er, der – Tod' (l. 11397).
12 Line 11433.
13 'Ich bin nur durch die Welt gerannt' (l. 11434).

To him whom I have made my own ...
Eternal gloom around him lies.
For him suns neither set nor rise.
With outward senses perfect, whole,
Dwell darknesses within his soul.
Though wealth he owns ...
He nothing can possess ...
Be it joy, or be it sorrow,
He postpones it till the morrow.
Of the future thinking ever,
Present action he ignores ...[14]

Nor is it surprising that Goethe placed this allegorical figure only at the end of the play, in anticipation of the completion that would mean not only the death of the hero and, symbolically, of the work as artistic creation, but his own, real death as well. He had postponed his death in order to complete *Faust*, we might say, or completed Faust in order to postpone his death. What ravaged his mind in either case ravages the mind of his hero as he comes to complete his life and his work. It is not the end that is threatening, it may even be welcome, but the completion in the knowledge of its imperfection. Faust will in fact in his final stage of understanding choose not the completion he might attain through magic, but a further beginning. In place of the classical perfection he had sought to gain in the conscious awareness of the completion of his work, he looks to begin anew. He will open new land for millions. There is no mention in his future plan of a tower from which to observe what he will have accomplished. His vision is an open-ended, evolutionist vision.

The power that Care exerts over Faust results from his renunciation of magic. He stands 'before nature, a man alone,'[15] when Care blinds him. Yet even magic is not meant to be capable of dispelling this demon

14 Wem ich einmal mir besitze,
   Dem ist alle Welt nichts nütze ...   (ll. 11453ff.)
   There is an extensive literature on the elusive figure of Care. See Klett, *Der Streit*,
   pp. 57–63; Arens, *Kommentar*, pp. 897–914. The article most often cited in discussions of problems presented by this allegorical figure is Konrad Burdach's 'Faust
   und die Sorge' (*Deutsche Vierteljahresschrift*, vol. 1 [1923], pp. 1–60).
15 Line 11406.

who is wholly internal. Faust is old. Age engenders inaction, inaction Care. Against this penultimate shatterer of resolve – Death is the ultimate dissolution – he pits what he must experience as sheer will but which the drama envisions as the will of mankind. Faust has now become so surrounded by allegorical and mythical figures that he has become allegorical himself, or so we see him. The drama, moreover, has reconceived the foundations and antecedents of will in such broadly historical and natural terms that we now see its expressions against a background of the whole. Like his guilt, his will seems lodged in nature. Faust, blinded, continues to strive, not because he has now discovered the higher purpose of life, but because he has as yet, like mankind, to be satisfied. In and through his striving he will come to clarity and understanding, just as in and through his inactivity he would have come to despair. The age-long struggle between light and darkness, as Mephistopheles sees it, between good and evil in the Christian view, between life and death in the scientific understanding, continues in this newly understood way.

If the genius of *Faust* lay in its concept of development and evolution, its greatness lay in its reluctance to conclude. It would not be denied growth. Against the advantages or, better, the temptations that the traditional forms of concluding in art and in thought presented, the drama went its own way and in its own time. When it could not go back to new beginnings, as it had so often in its course, it went deeper. As it approached the end, it raised its greatest doubts. The figure of the Wanderer, created so far as we know *after* the conclusion had been written,[16] undermines the philosophy of life that Faust is about to express, as if he were the deeper antagonist in thought to the protagonist, the other side of the Goethe who is in Faust, much as he is in Mephistopheles. And doubt is the enemy of form. What could have been a straight line, as it were, from the Helen adventure to the conclusion, from the search for beauty to the search for purpose (and the action is often so interpreted),[17] is interrupted by the most basic of

16 Of course, we cannot know what was in Goethe's mind as he carried *Faust* with him through the years like an 'inner fairy tale.' The Wanderer may have been there in intention much earlier, as a conversation with Eckermann, 2 May 1831, suggests: 'The intention of these scenes as well [the opening scenes of Act V, which had not as yet been written] is over thirty years old.'
17 After the example set by Rickert, *Goethe's Faust*, in the search for dramatic unity in the work.

questions and the most insidious of fears. The destruction of Philemon and Baucis morally compromises the conclusion, just as it is philosophically compromised, or challenged, by the Wanderer in his simple being and psychologically by Care.

Goethe wrote to Count Reinhard, 7 September 1831, when *Faust* was finally completed, 'Don't expect a revelation. As always in the history of the world and of man the last resolved problem only uncovers a new problem to be resolved.' When he attempted a conclusion to *Faust*, it was, as with his hero, as much an act of will as an act of thought.

CHAPTER FIFTEEN

Act v: The Earthly Resolution

'Nature never creates a whole in the individual, although, to be sure, the species is a whole.'[1] This concept underlay the final resolution in *Faust*. Faust can be forgiven his sins and errors which are the result of his incompleteness. It is this incompleteness striving for completion and perfection that impels the human race. It is the urge, tragic in the individual, which is all saving in the species, as we said. Even the truth, as Goethe conceived it, might contain error, as does nature: 'the useless, indeed the harmful, were absorbed into organic life as binding agents that in turn affected the whole.'[2] And man is a part of nature. Faust, this new everyman, conceived in time and not as an absolute being, will attain not to a complete but to a sufficient truth, a truth in and for his time. He knows 'enough of earth, enough of men,' to act.[3] Action, now as in the beginning, is knowledge unthought: 'In the beginning was the deed.'

The final act that Faust undertakes must be understood within this economy of knowledge and of truth. He must be moved to action from within. 'The view beyond is obscured,' that is, the religious and metaphysical justifications for action no longer obtain. The result of action in the real world cannot be foreseen. Faust, indeed, is now blind. Nor is his continued striving in the face of age, uncertainty, fear, and death guided by an inner light which somehow in a classical paradox illuminates his physical darkness. The darkness is maintained on stage, emphasizing the blindness and anticipating death, and is dissolved in

---

1 To Fr. von Müller, 8 June 1821.
2 Quoted in Georg Simmel, *Goethe* (Leipzig, 1923), p. 24.
3 'Der Erdenkreis ist mir genug bekannt' (l. 11441).

light only when he is about to enter another world. His inner radiance derives less from faith than from defiance; the Prometheus, the Lucifer, within him remains. This is not a Faust who has been humbled or whose concerns are now turned outwardly and away from selfish interest, but one who has been thrust back again upon himself by the failure to attain what the present seems always to offer, to recapture and hold what the past has achieved, or to know the future. His revelation and resolution in the moment is not the sudden desire to aid mankind, which it appears he has already formulated as a plan on a more limited scale, but the recognition finally of how such a grand scheme is to be executed and completed. It is through one mind in an initial creative effort that will provide the impulse for the continuous, endless achievement that alone can satisfy a man, and a species, that is nevertheless 'every moment unsatisfied.'4 The action of Part II is so designed as to bring Faust to this realization not through cumulative, hierarchical understanding, but by default. Faust is not learning (it is we who learn), but being taught. For all his Promethean and daemonic characteristics he is after all the servant of God, as he is called in the Prologue in Heaven, and the creature of time.

To that end, all his undertakings and conclusions are made to fail, of action, of continuity, or of completion. His resolve at the outset to see the world in 'colorful reflection' is undone in the end by his recognition of the ineffective and obstructive nature of passivity in a universe of constant motion. His colorful reflection fails of action, as the colorful celebration of what is fails to affect the world in the case of Lynceus the poet and seer. The education of the prince, which might bring about the creation of a society that could justly allow of the celebration of man and nature within its ideal confines, fails of effect by its indirection. The Emperor has not been taught by the end of the play, has not been moved to action. In Helen Faust pursues beauty, he does not create it, with the result that it can only serve him as model for his own creation and then must leave him, for it is he who must act and create. He must put aside the crutch of classicism, both its manner and its thought, and conceive a new ideal. His reclamation of land from the sea, which challenges his deepest and most defiant creativity, fails of a purpose beyond the satisfaction which its achievement

---

4 'Er, unbefriedigt jeden Augenblick!' (l. 11452).

can bring and, in bringing it, end it. There must be for him a purpose that is continuous and endless, the effects and traces of which will remain 'after eons of time.'[5]

This purpose is provided by his final undertaking. It entails a humanity that will repeat and carry on his experience, in his spirit, and which will complete itself only when the human race has been completed.

> Freedom alone he earns as well as life
> Who day by day must conquer them anew.
> Enclosed by danger, childhood bravely here,
> Youth, manhood, age shall dwell from year to year,
> A people free, standing on free soil ...
> Then to the moment I might say,
> Linger awhile, thou art so fair.[6]

Goethe had not forgotten the wager with the Devil throughout Part II and only now in the resolution returned to the proposition and its terms. Rather, through the resolution we first understand the design of the action. The world, or worlds, he creates are not there to tempt Faust by the glories or values they offer, but represent the experience in multiple conscious and subconscious form which he as a creature of time must encounter in his era in the broadest sense and which may or may not satisfy him. Mephistopheles, who in his immortal state has no sense of time and thus no understanding of its meaning for man, can no more create a successful agenda of action for his purposes than can Faust imagine, request, and experience realities beyond his own understanding, which itself is formed by his culture and his era, again in the broadest sense. Faust's passivity, his dramatic or dramaturgical irrelevance at times, is the product of his having been conceived in Part II as being acted upon rather than acting, until such time as he has found his only and proper course. His passivity is not a proper ingredient for drama, we might say, except that in the larger context it provides for the breathing-in and breathing-out of experience which

5 Es kann die Spur von meinen Erdetagen
  Nicht in Äonen untergehn. (ll. 11583–4)
6 'Verweile doch, du bist so schön' (the operative clause in the agreement with the Devil; ll. 11575–82).

alone rounds out existence. After Shakespeare we have come to accept the comic in the tragic through the same recognition and might well accept the digression with the dramatically pertinent, the interruption with the continuity, in the hands of genius and in the interest of the whole. *Faust II* is more like life than like art in this regard as well.

The moral question has not been answered. There are those who believe it should not be raised,[7] in that Faust has reached in the end a level of comprehension that is beyond good and evil in its commitment to action in an absolute sense. The Philemon and Baucis motif does in fact appear to be a deliberate attempt to shock morally. The coastline from which the new land is to be gained is an imaginary one and might have been imagined as initially devoid of a humanity that would have to be removed, especially of an innocent, devout, and eternally resident humanity which the old couple symbolizes. Moreover, the moral barbarism might be seen as commensurate with the esthetic barbarism that Goethe felt he was committing, and had to commit, in completing *Faust*. The traditional morality, like the traditional artistic forms, would have to be destroyed and overcome in order to move into a new world. The struggle with the poem is the struggle in the poem. The resolution, far from being the harmonious reconciliation in the mind of opposing forces and factors that we might have expected and which indeed we demand from a traditional work of art, becomes instead the defiant step into the future that solves the problems created or conceived in the past by ignoring them, like the Gordian knot that was never unraveled but simply slashed.

Faust itself would then be the earthly product that persists through eons and moves to action a humanity outside itself so long as the work continues to be read. The new land need never have been gained from the sea, the new society never built, as in fact it was not. Faust's failure even through magic to attain to perfection now becomes the failure of the work to achieve harmony and completeness of form, and the failure in both cases the instrument of salvation. Faust the person fails to learn the lesson of his experience, which is that the striving for completion

---

7 'Nicht eine moralische Schuld Fausts ... wird hier dokumentiert, sondern ein Schicksal des Weltlaufs, das unlösbar mit allem Herrschen und Arbeiten verknüpft ist' (Emrich, *Die Symbolik*, p. 400).

and perfection is futile, and is thereby saved. *Faust* the work rejects the strictures of art, not merely in its classical standards but in its very roots in order and imitation, and thereby saves itself for the future where a more complex human consciousness will need a more open artistic prism to picture its world.

Not that Goethe created a new form in *Faust* in the sense that it could be imitated. But he opened up the consciousness that demanded a new form. An education of the artist takes place in the play alongside the education of the hero. From its *Sturm und Drang* beginnings through its objective and balanced middle years of composition to the triumphant sense of freedom it gains at the end, the work undergoes a development which, again like the experience of its hero, is not a process of cumulative understanding so much as a meeting of obstacles and obstructions that are survived more than they are wholly surmounted. At this level or in this mode of identification of author and work the moral question seems moot. The morality in the work would derive in the deepest sense from the morality of the work, if one can speak at all of a morality in the creative process. If we do, it is usually in terms of restraint, order, and the other classical artistic values, whereas in *Faust* the imperative is freedom, as is the moral imperative in its final resolution.

But Goethe does not ultimately subsume morality under the virtue of creativity. It is a measure of the depth of the work that he does not. Rather, there is a further presupposition underlying the action which subsumes both. It is the evolutionist principle. The same force that compels the artist to seek perfection moves the man of action to completion. Yet what compels forward is projected in the mind as an attracting force. The idea of an afterlife, which sustained and motivated an earlier age, now emerges in the new era, or is struggling to emerge, as a sense of endless creative continuity that outlasts, as indeed it has preceded, the individual and of which he is a part. Evolution is the new god. Goethe does not make that pronouncement as such, but the evolving perspectives in which the action of *Faust II* is conceived and presented force us to see the final resolution as partaking of an endless movement and not of an eternal and absolute form. If the resolution is final, and in that sense complete, it is only because at this point the author knows no more than his hero and so in essence has nothing more to say. The play adjourns to heaven. But Goethe speaks of a new God outside the play. Of the contemporary controversy between Cuvier and Geoffroy Saint-Hilaire on the development of plant and animal life, in which he sided with the latter, he remarks: 'no organic being wholly matches the idea that has created it. Behind each is a higher idea. That is my God, that is the God we all seek eternally and hope to discover, but we can only sense, not envision him.'[8]

Faust is the Renaissance man newly conceived because historically understood. The Renaissance for Goethe was not the age that preceded his own or modern times but the beginning of a new era yet to be completed. Renaissance man was not the whole man he might seem in his vitality and humanity, but potentially inwardly conflicted. His great accomplishments in art were not repeated in the moral realm. The influence of the ancient Greek and Roman spirit that had reopened the world of the senses and the mind so long obscured by the otherworldly concerns of the medieval mentality was not put to use in the real world as it was in art.[9] The senses and nature were abused. The golden mean of antiquity was sacrificed to the extremes of an inner, and perhaps false, piety and, moreover, a frivolous and corrupted outward life. The living in the moment had become a living for the moment in the fear, and yet the hope, of death and a better existence: thus, Act I. The things of this world, so valued and celebrated in antiquity, had not at all been reconciled with the otherworldliness of Christianity. Both had simply been neglected. It took in turn the Reformation and then the French Revolution to challenge this abuse in the spiritual and the temporal worlds and to bring the underlying tension that was created in the Renaissance by the meeting of Chris-

8 'Das ist mein Gott, das ist der Gott, den wir alle ewig suchen und zu erschauen hoffen, aber wir können ihn nur ahnen, nicht schauen' (in a conversation with F. von Müller, 7 May 1830).

9 Burckhardt, speaking of the Renaissance in Italy, sees a different world than Goethe envisioned in Germany: 'a new fact appears in history – the State as the outcome of reflection and calculation, the State as a work of art' (Jacob Burckhardt, *The Civilization of the Renaissance in Italy*, trans. S.G.C. Middlemore [New York, 1960], p. 2). Harold Jantz, *Goethe's Faust as a Renaissance Man* (Princeton, 1951) concentrates almost exclusively on the Faust of Part I, the unpolitical Faust. But Löwith makes the point that Goethe was the last thinker to consider the difference between the ancient and the modern, the pagan and the Christian, to be a problem demanding a 'decision' (Karl Löwith, *From Hegel to Nietzsche* [New York, 1964], p. 197).

tianity with the ancient world to the breaking point: thus, Act IV. This was the state of the issue, as he seems to have seen it, when Goethe was completing his *Faust*.

A living *toward* the moment, which combines in a state of mind the two dominant influences on modern man in Western culture and is the silent voice of evolution, thus becomes the earthly resolution in the drama. It is in anticipation, in the motion toward, that Faust experiences the highest moment: *im Vorgefühl*.[10]

The moral act for Goethe himself came with the writing of Act IV. He must have been tempted at the end to complete *Faust* without reference to the world and time in which it was created. He had completed Act V, we assume with the inclusion of the figure of Care who represented the final great obstacle to human striving that man must overcome. The allegory of his own creative life that is inherent in the work would thus also have come to an end, and the ideals and ambitions of a future humanity would have been delineated at least in spirit. There would be little reason to continue in an effort that was in effect completed.

But if the morality in *Faust* was to be new, it was nevertheless to be moral. It would have to come from necessity. Act IV, in a last effort, had shown that necessity. It not only returned the action to the real world, but through its motif and allusions that called up the politics and actuality of contemporary history it also placed the drama in a confrontational relationship to its times. What Goethe could not say at court, he could, and did at the last minute, say in *Faust*. In Act IV he demonstrated the futility of the efforts of cunning, might, the objective lessons of reality or the powers that be, to effect change, and so created the necessity from which the new action, the new morality, arose. It matters little whether we see in the Anti-Emperor Napoleon in particular or merely a challenge to the established order that resuscitates it momentarily, whether we sense in its political atmosphere the atmosphere of Europe in 1830 when Goethe was writing the act or a more abstracted outcry for change, but only that we recognize forces and circumstances that compel Faust forward. The destruction of Philemon and Baucis serves after the fact to suggest the possibility of unforeseeable destruction and error in a future that is only partly

10 Line 11585.

illuminated. The Philemon and Baucis scene was in fact written only later, though it might have been conceived earlier.[11] Without Act IV the final resolution would seem not only formulated in a vacuum but conceived in the spirit of a morality of superior strength – a *Herrenmoral*. With Act IV the struggle that Goethe himself underwent in rejecting and vilifying the old order, which had been his sustenance and in which he had placed his political faith, comes to the fore and again makes the morality *of* the play, of the creative act, a part of the morality in the play. We said that Goethe failed to effect an education of the prince which would have changed the social order. It is possible that by the time he came to develop the motif in the fiction that was *Faust*, the political events of his day had convinced him of the impossibility of such an eventuality in life and there was no longer a viable reason to include it. For Goethe the moral decision, the step into the future, was taken as much in regret as in hope.

For it was not like him to break with the past, but to build on it. Not since his *Sturm und Drang* period had he been anything but a champion of tradition. He criticized its institutions but he would not have abolished them. In the *Wanderjahre*, written together with *Faust II* in his closing years, the opposite of a radical solution is offered. It proposes resignation. Its subtitle is: 'Or, the Resigned.' If it holds out a hope more in the spirit of *Faust*, it is in the vision of the new land of America, where a beginning might be made again on new soil, as on the land gained from the sea, and to which the protagonists in the novel are given the choice to emigrate, as it were from the back door of Europe.[12] In 1848, when the old order in Germany in fact once more suppressed an uprising in the name of reform, that was the choice of many of the young. But the inner logic of *Faust* would allow of no choice. An action conceived within frames of time that determined its broadest course and against whose forces the individual will is as nothing could not as it approached its end deny to these forces a decisive effect. The action, in essence, could *not* end and had itself to be resolved in an eternal continuing. Faust is not strong in himself but in his instinctive and deep tapping of this source which lends him strength.

11 See, again, the conversation with Eckermann of 2 May 1831.
12 Those who stay, however, can say with Lothario, 'Here, if anywhere, is America.'
   – 'Hier oder nirgends ist Amerika.'

He moves with time and with the forces of history and of nature, and in this represents mankind.[13]

He must, of course, fail in his final endeavor. What is made for the real world must be made in the real world. All that Faust has achieved, at least in Part II, has been achieved outside of time through the powers of magic. All that he has imagined to achieve has been imagined without regard to reality, as if in accustoming himself to magic he has developed the habit of thinking independently of cause and effect, of thinking outside of time. His idealism is of a piece with his addiction to magic, a fact Goethe intuited in the legend. European man, or rather northern European man, as he saw it, suffered not from too little but too much idealism.[14]

Faust himself suffers from an excess of idealism even at the very end. His spirit remains undampened. But he must not be made to succeed. To have the 'traces of his earthly existence' in fact outlive him would be to avoid the tragic consequences of the dramatic action, an evasion of which, as we mentioned, Goethe is sometimes accused in general. Faust will be saved but not pampered. He has lived outside of time and the real world through magic, and time and the real world avenge themselves. He has ignored time but not it him. He has aged, and in one sense it is simply time and age that now put an end to his one endeavor that has been conceived in and for the real world. Mephistopheles says when Faust dies: 'Who me so stoutly did withstand / Time conquers ... The old man lies upon the sand.'[15] Nor does the Devil play a part in this failure. His misguided sense, first of triumph, then of defeat at the very end, is itself hardly made convincing. The mixture of humor and infernal stage figures and properties (e.g., the open maw of Hell) that closes the penultimate scene is clearly intended

13 Goethe's view of the average human being, as opposed to the more abstract entity, man is quite different, as witness the contrast between the two fictional heroes he lived longest with, Wilhelm Meister and Faust. See, again, Schrimpf, *Das Weltbild*, ch. 4.
14 'Idealism in human beings, when the object of it is taken away or atrophies, withdraws into itself, becomes more refined and heightened, and as it were self-destructs. Most Northerners have much more idealism than they can use, than they can process. Hence the strange occurrences of sentimentality, religiosity, mysticism and so on' (to Riemer in conversation of August [n.d.], 1808).
15 My italics. 'Die Zeit wird Herr, der Greis hier liegt im Sand' (line 11592).

as pendant to the dramatic moment and not as its culmination: It has been suggested that the whole scene is in essence a comic scene.[16] Goethe seems not to have known quite what to do with his Devil once he was robbed of the object it was his challenged and function on earth to obstruct, destroy, and negate. For it is not Mephistopheles, but time and the real world, that have had their revenge. The new land to be gained from the sea has already been precorrupted in the commitment to the old order of the tithes and taxes and rights that the Emperor has relinquished to the church. The world has not changed. The revolution necessary to effect change in the real world, which Faust has ignored and Goethe has avoided except by implication, is left to us to undertake who possess the only traces of the earthly existence of this Faust. This is what Goethe intended, I believe, by having his hero die in the illusion of great accomplishment, by having him mistake in his blindness the digging of the grave that marks his end as the excavation for his final, ideal project that marks a new beginning. There is an earthly tragedy in *Faust* that occurs despite the salvation of the hero and independent of all magic and the Devil, which is the tragedy of an idealism that with its gaze forward and upward does not easily see before it the ground on which all things, present *and* future, must be built.

16 Eudo Mason, *Goethe's Faust: Its Genesis and Purport* (Berkeley, 1967), p. 353. Even Mephistopheles' claim to Faust's soul is not earnestly debated, but rather gets lost in satirical allusions to how the soul leaves the body, when, and by which channel, so that the Devil may wait to snatch it. See the extended discussion of the scene in Arens (*Kommentar*, pp. 955–95), where its questionable humor, apparent blasphemy, and baroque intricacies are gone into in detail. On the vexed question, *whether* Faust should be saved, which has somewhat abated, see Klett, *Der Streit*, pp. 83–96.

CHAPTER SIXTEEN

Act v: Heaven
and Beyond

The world in *Faust II* is reflected not as reality but as image. Reflected images juxtaposed constitute the work. Behind the images stands a reality that must have existed at one time but which is transmitted to us only through the form or forms it has assumed in history and the development of culture; or if not a reality a need, which is a reality in another sense.

The Christian heaven that opens up at the end of the play is similarly an image made up of mind and imagination reflecting the need to project a life beyond mortal existence. Like the other worlds or spheres of existence we encounter in the play, it is a projection in time, although of eternal things. If we can see in the metamorphosing mythical creatures that are the imaginings of the early Greek mind an anticipation of Darwin, we can see in the Christian heaven an early unworldly projection of the eternal life to come that the evolutionists had newly uncovered, but in nature and in time. Just as the biblical concept of a young earth gave rise to the fear of its imminent end, the new concept of a seemingly ageless universe gave rise to an anticipation of its virtually eternal future. The concept of evolution had created not only a new god in the idea of progress and progression but a new eternity on earth. It is a surprising feature of *Faust II* that it actualizes and defines the past not through attention to detail but by placing it opposite other worlds that are in turn reflected in its light. So it is with the future and with the heaven into which Faust is now assumed at the end of the play.

Faust would seem to have been saved on a mere technicality, but the technicality in fact is the heart of the matter. He experiences the highest moment only in anticipation. 'Then to the moment *might* I say: / Linger awhile, thou art so fair.' But anticipation, a living *toward*, is the disposition of the human condition in the historical moment. The energies Faust has spent in search of an abstract or more obtuse truth, which is the truth he substituted for the otherworldly reality of the religion of his youth, he now employs *in* the moment, to be sure, but toward a purpose in the future. His idealism will not be denied. Whether one sees him in the setting of the legend as Renaissance man striving to reconcile the sentiments of a religious tradition with his newly acquired classical heritage, or as modern man attempting to adapt the absolute values from his past to the newly understood relativistic laws of nature, the model remains the same. Two souls reside within him. It is often assumed that Faust through his experience of Helen has come to live in the moment. He lives in the moment, but as modern, not as classical man.

The inner logic that persuades Goethe to save Faust compelled him to conceive a heaven for his salvation. He had to have somewhere to put him, so to speak. The concept of a natural universe in which Faust has his being allowed of no life beyond except in terms of a material future. Goethe might have crete a new heaven, which he did in a sense in envisioning an ideal earthly existence, but it was not the instinct of the poem to create anew but to uncover in the past the modes of thought and forms of things that corresponded in essence to what presents itself as eternally new. 'Everything transitory / Is but a metaphor.' Hence the traditional Christian, indeed extremely Catholic, heaven he presents at the end in which neither he nor Faust can be said to believe.[1]

He chose what he called an 'ecclesiastical' heaven[2] in order not to lose himself in poetic vagueness. The making of poetry, like the making of history, is a concretizing. Yet Goethe takes the clearly defined celestial hierarchy and turns even this projection of the absolutist mind into a process, as though everything he touched in *Faust*, even as he attempted to conclude, had to have its own beginning, middle, and end. It has often been noted that the individual acts in Part II are dramas

---

1 See Konrad Burdach, 'Das religiöse Problem in Goethes *Faust*' (*Euphorion*, vol. 33 [1932], pp. 1–83).
2 To Eckermann, 6 June 1831: 'christlich-kirchlich.'

in themselves, each with its own theme and resolution. The final scene of the drama fits the model perfectly.

Faust has already been saved in nature, in the background of the play, as it were, where the conflicted world of which he as man is a part inevitably resolves itself in purposeful harmony: the inconclusion of the individual life is the salvation of the species. In that sense his salvation in the foreground is a formality. He has only to strive and that he does instinctively. A line from a defunct poem that was intended to accompany the publication of Faust reads: 'Let him strive on, it is the will of nature.'³ We know from the Prologue in Heaven that he has been saved in his own nature, for all his transgressions. 'A good man in his dark urge / Is yet conscious of the way.' This apprehension, purified and clarified, is the subject of the final scene. That the clarification takes the form of a Christian apotheosis results from the fact that it is the only vision of Utopia that has withstood the test of poetic, let alone political, reality. One may not believe in heaven but it is the only image of an afterlife available in Western culture should the thought cross the mind.

Because the salvation is a formality, it is not the less, but the more, poetic for that. The ritual enacts the separation of the 'united dual nature' that is man.⁴ The movement is toward the purest harmony, in sound and in the becoming oneness of thought and reality that culminates in the Chorus Mysticus at the very end. But at first the struggle resembles the struggle on earth. The soul here being separated from the earth is not conceived as an abstraction, any more than Goethe thought of body and soul as separate in living man.⁵ At the lowest order in the panoply of saints and holy figures, ranged as if painted above the altar on the ceiling of a church,⁶ the earth still intrudes:

3 'Er schreite fort: so will es die Natur' (Beutler, Paralipomena, p. 530).
4 From l. 11982: 'geeinte Zweinatur.'
5 In this final scene Goethe is clearly allowing for a life of the spirit beyond the grasp of human intellect. He spoke of this 'soul' as an 'Entelechie.' But it is not to be conceived of as static (Joachim Müller, 'Die letzte Szene von Goethes Faust,' in Etude Germanique, vol. 38 [1983], pp. 147–55). Staiger speaks of a 'Weiterdauer der zeitlichen Existenz [Entelechie] auf unbemessene Zeit' (Goethe [Zurich, 1959], vol. 3, p. 454).
6 The arrangement seems to have been suggested by a fresco in Pisa a copper engraving of which is titled 'Anchorites in Egyptian Thebes.'

Forests are waving here,
Rocks their huge fronts uprear,
Roots round each other coil,
Stems thickly crowd the soil.
Wave gushes after wave,
Shelter yields deepest cave.
Lions in friendly silence roving,
Honor the hallowed ground,
Refuge of love.7

Nature bears the same formidable aspect we have seen throughout, here in the repeated image of the roaring waterfall whose 'sound the heart appals / Yet lovely in its plashing brings / The wealth of water to the deep, / Refreshment to the valley.'8 The angels in the Prologue in Heaven had likewise seen beauty and purpose in the tumultuous atmosphere surrounding Earth. A Pater Ecstaticus, hovering, 'floating up and down,'9 in his mind mutilates his body in an attempt to rid himself of his material being, like one who feels pain in an amputated limb. It is as if he were granted in heaven the only happiness he experienced on earth, which is pain. 'Darts pierce me through and through, / Lances my flesh subdue ...'10 He stands in contrast to the Pater Profundis who accepts nature and the flesh unchanged and sees divine love in all earthly things. 'So love, almighty ... doth all things mold, doth all sustain.'11 In a middle region, somewhat farther removed from the world and thus by implication closer to God or divine knowledge, is the Pater Seraphicus to whom come a chorus of young souls seeking their way. These children, 'born at midnight,'12 that is between light and darkness, between good and evil, having died unbaptized in the world and in the church bear no traces of human

---

7 Lines 11844–53.
8 Und doch stürzt, liebevoll im Sausen,
Die Wasserfülle sich zum Schlund,
Berufen, gleich das Tal zu wässern.   (ll. 11876–8)
9 After l. 11853: 'auf und ab schwebend.'
10 Lines 11858–9.
11 So ist es die allmächtige Liebe,
Die alles bildet, alles hegt.   (ll. 11872–3)
12 'Mitternachts Geborne' (l. 11898).

experience on their souls. From the glimpse they are granted of the earth through the eyes of the Pater Seraphicus, who like God naming for Adam the things of Creation presents the world to them, they turn away. 'Grand the scene, but fear awakening ... Hold us not, kind father, here!'[13]

We see in this heaven the familiar deep patterns of the earthly existence we find throughout *Faust*, but they are now bathed in a new light. It is the light of pure poetry. It seems to suggest the element in creation that informs all things and is here described as divine love. The word 'love' occurs time and again throughout the scene. Only the blessed innocents seem to have no need for the word, as if experience of the world and of suffering were necessary in uncovering its meaning and revealing its strength. As the progression develops upward toward the highest region and the highest forms of knowledge and love, the images seem to fall away and are replaced by the purest abstraction. This process is epitomized in the Chorus Mysticus, where the concentration of abstractions seems to transform itself into sheer poetic sound and yet in fact conveys the whole experience and meaning of the drama in essence. Even now, in the approach to the end, in the region where the saintliest of souls and the holiest of sinners reside, feeling is evolving into thought, adjective into substantive, verb into noun. German lends itself to this process. It is as if in some underlying movement the attempt is being made to hold fast in the mind what in nature and on earth is always in motion, to make constancy of change, to suggest a sphere of existence outside of time. Faust is the 'early loved,' the Virgin Mary 'the incomparable' and the 'rich in grace,' Faust 'the no longer troubled,' the forgiven sinners, among them Gretchen, 'the easily seduced,' all as substantive denominations and capitalized, as they would have to be in the original.[14] Some of the appellations are repeated,

13 Das ist mächtig anzuschauen,
   Doch zu düster ist der Ort ...
   Edler, Guter, laß uns fort! (ll. 11914–17)
14 *Der früh Geliebte* (l. 12073), *Du Ohnegleiche* (l. 12035), *Du Gnadenreiche* (l. 12036),
   Nicht mehr Getrübte (l. 12074), *die leicht Verführbaren* (l. 12022). This substantiating of adjectives, surely in imitation of medieval Latin, is of course common in church liturgy. 'Ach, neige, / Du *Schmerzenreiche*,' Gretchen says in her prayer to the Virgin already in *Urfaust*.

furthering the impression of a general tendency to abstraction. We are being separated from the body and from the material world, as is Faust.

He does not partake of the action as conscious spirit. He is the subject of the ritual, not a participant. Yet what he experiences in the separation, we experience through the poetry. His 'united dual nature,' bound together by a spiritual force, can only be unbound by an equal power. The angels alone cannot effect the change. 'Where joins strong spirit force, / Elements blending, / No angel can divorce ... Eternal Love alone the union ends.'[15] This suggests that love in the poetry, which itself strives by its nature to be eternal, becomes the object of the words and sounds that comprise the scene. They accompany the assumption of Faust's 'immortalness' (again a quality substantiated)[16] into heaven and yet cannot wholly divest themselves of the memory of earth. Two souls are being separated, not merely a soul from a body which might be forgotten. And to speak is to remember the earth. From the point where Mephistopheles is driven off from his claim to Faust by the rose-pelting angels to the point in the higher reaches of an afterlife, the imagery and poetry, despite the attempt to shed the physical world, must remain attached to it. Two souls reside in poetry as well and the attempt to separate them parallels the movement in the action to separate the two souls in Faust. The divine love that alone truly joins and separates becomes the spirit of the words on the page.

The need that Goethe felt at the end of *Faust* to state his sense of an ineffable force or spirit that informs all things brought with it the necessity of using words, although what was to be expressed was unsayable. The Chorus Mysticus that closes the action succeeds in expressing the inexpressible by making that theme, and its variant expressions in the attaining of the unattainable, the accomplishing of the indescribable, into its subject. All that is denied to human experience except in anticipation is given in heaven. Thought and the objective world become one outside of time. Faust asked that the perfect moment should stop, arrest itself, but it is the moment stopped that is perfection. When Faust dies, the hands of the clock are said to fall, as

---

15 Lines 11959–63. I alter the lines slightly from Swanwick.
16 'Faustens Unsterbliches' (after l. 11824).

he agreed should be the case in the wager,[17] but the stopping of time does not mean his death but his passage into a timeless and unfathomed sphere of existence that seems to have its being not only beyond words but beyond the farthest regions of the heaven we have been given to see. When Faust meets Gretchen, or that which was 'once called Gretchen,' in the highest celestial region, she is told to rise to even higher spheres and that 'when he senses your presence, he will follow.'[18] There is still movement to come when the action ends.

'Everything transitory / Is but a metaphor.' The play itself, all that is in and outside of it through its suggestion, is only an image behind, beneath, or beyond which exists a state of being, constant and balanced, but only sensed, not grasped or attained as yet by man and that the Chorus Mysticus attempts to evoke. Heaven, by definition, is where the unattainable is attained, where that which as yet cannot even be thought is accomplished, and logically and appropriately so. The unattainable is the theme, anticipation the mode of action from the beginning in this play of evolution which itself so strangely evolved. We have no proof of the existence of this heaven except through the poetry that Goethe offers. But there is as much logic and reason in the Chorus Mysticus to persuade the mind as there is sound to persuade the senses. The play throughout had been moving more and more toward sound to convey its meanings, had become more and more an operatic poem, so that the culmination of its abstractions in a final chorus is as expected, as poetically and dramatically motivated, as is the amazing concentration of its sounds. I give the Chorus in the original. Feeling has been abstracted into thought and yet retains through sound the power to move:

> Alles Vergängliche
> Ist nur ein Gleichnis;
> Das Unzulängliche
> Hier wird's Ereignis;
> Das Unbeschreibliche
> Hier ist's getan;

17 Die Uhr mag stehn, der Zeiger fallen,
    Es sei die Zeit für mich vorbei! (ll. 1705–6)
    And here, l. 11594, 'Der Zeiger fällt.'
18 'Wenn er dich ahnet, folgt er nach' (l. 12095).

Das Ewig-Weibliche
Zieht uns hinan.[19]

So too with the Eternal Feminine, we may say, which is the final word
and thought of the Chorus. It does not arrest us in conscious recognition
but, rather, 'draws us on.' It is that which in the changing images of
the material Gretchen through the imagined Helen to the ethereal
Mothers and the holy sinner in the highest regions of heaven seems
to have the power to separate or to join, but only for the good. It is
the force of life, change, and evolution purified, forgiven, and blessed.

19 My literal translation:
   Everything transitory
   Is but a metaphor.
   The unattainable
   Is here attained.
   The indescribable,
   Here it is done.
   The Eternal-Feminine
   Draws us on.

CHAPTER SEVENTEEN

The Prologue
in the Theater
as Epilogue

Goethe must have known from the beginning that he had chosen a
theme and subject matter in *Faust* that he could not readily control. In
the early period the unwieldiness of the material can only have attracted him, and he did in fact create in *Urfaust* a drama freer and more
truly volatile than anything his *Sturm und Drang* contemporaries had
produced. Even when he had outgrown the attraction, at least superficially, and could distance himself from both the style and the matter
of what he had written, rather than abandon the early beginnings or
alter them to fit a new concept of life and of art, he retained what he
had and continued. His poem grew as he grew. It accumulated, like
life, but not like art. As he persisted in his approach, always retaining
and accumulating, it was as if he had made an unconscious experiment
to discover what would result if one were to allow into art what is
allowed into the life of the mind. It was not unlike the wager Faust
had made with the Devil, which was likewise an experiment with the
outcome unknown.

The process had begun early on. The sequence he added to the first
Walpurgis Night had already broken the illusion of art by introducing
satire and parody of contemporary life and letters into the most dramatic, indeed most highly tragic, moment in the play. Gretchen, preg-
nant, has just fainted in the cathedral when the first Walpurgis Night
begins. This kind of Romantic irony is neither unique, nor for us in
itself important. In the year that Goethe wrote the Walpurgis Night,
1797, with its salute to the stage manager of the Weimar Theater,[1]

---

1 The reference to Mieding would of course be understood only by the inner group

Tieck wrote *Der gestiefelte Kater*, in which the audience takes part in
the dialogue and the action. Important is the fact that upon this initial
break with illusion Goethe erected the formal concept of Part II. Literature had become part of the consciousness of the drama; art had
become part of the life that was to be imitated in art. As paradoxical
as this development may seem, it was in fact inevitable. Art, having
begun as an imitation of reality, soon became to the extent that it
succeeded as art a part of the imagination, thought, and perception
that constitute the conscious reality of a people or a time. The world
to be described was no longer simply a political, social, or physical
reality, but a reality overlaid with the perceptions that had accumulated
through evolving historical circumstance, overlaid, that is, with culture.
The characters from Shakespeare and the Weimar stage manager who
is mentioned in the Walpurgis Night's Dream are as much a part of
the total consciousness of the audience or reader as the illusion that
is presented as reality in *Faust*. But whereas this literary irony had been
employed in the past to shatter illusion, and is so employed in *Faust
I*, in *Faust II* it has become part of the illusion itself. Ariel from Shakespeare, Helen from classical legend, Byron from the contemporary literary world become, through the magic that is here part of the drama
and dispels all disbelief, the realities of the play itself. When Hegel
anticipated that literature, as illusion, would soon be replaced by philosophy in an inevitable natural progression, he failed to take into
account the ability of the imagination to comprehend much more of
an accumulating, developing, and living reality than can be described
in logical thought.

Faust II had reasons for incorporating classical themes, motifs, and
verse forms, but none of these reasons, as we have seen, were classical.
Its instincts were not absolute, but historical. It did not imitate, it juxtaposed. It looked for and found change in all things, as much in the
historically developing mind that imagines and so is responsible to life
in different ways at different times, as in the evolving physical world
and the creatures in it. Illusion, imitation, the surface of reality had to
be gone beyond or beneath in the drama, both in the sense that the

---

in Weimar, but the principle is the same. Benjamin Bennett sees a relation between this 'self-consciousness' and the tragic insufficiency of life in *Faust* (*Goethe's
Theory*, p. 51).

justification for its second part rested upon the deepening rather than the simple extending of the antecedents to its final resolution and in the sense that these antecedents, these explanatory and motivating forces, were of a nature that presented itself not as immediate reality but to the inner mind. I am not speaking of symbolism, which for all its great importance in an understanding of Part II has no inextricable relation to structure or form. Traditional art has always been able to house its symbols without altering its mode of composition. I raise the question of form rather to suggest a view of Goethe against the future, not as guide to action or as model in art, but as a writer expressive of a process that is only now emerging broadly as the consciousness of our own age. In *Faust II* the process is given in the product itself.

There was a peculiar reluctance in Goethe to expound on the conflicting demands of his *Faust*, which expressed themselves not only in the moral realm but in the relation of logic to intuition, thought to fantasy, order to creativity, reason to rhyme, in the composition of the work itself. It is Schiller, not he, whom we find abstracting from the poetry in *Faust*. 'I have again read through *Faust* and it makes me almost dizzy thinking about a solution.'[2] Only in the Prelude in the Theater are these artistic difficulties and conflicts raised in the play itself, indirectly, to be sure, but significantly. It is because of what I believe is its significance that I have reserved a discussion of the scene to the very end.

Read in anticipation of what is to come, the Prelude in the Theater might seem little more than an entertainment. It has been argued that the piece was originally not intended as an introduction to *Faust* but had been written earlier for another purpose and later attached to *Faust* with the publication of Part I.[3] Such utilitarianism was not unlike Goethe. But it matters little whether he originally intended the Prelude as a general or a specific introduction to his play, it matters most how he resolved the conflicts he deliberately or unconsciously raised in it.

His conscious intent was clear. He presents, in lively fairness, the opposing demands made on drama by a public as eager for entertain-

2 To Goethe, 26 June 1797.
3 Oscar Seidlin, 'Is the "Prelude in the Theatre" a Prelude to *Faust*?' (*Studies in German and Comparative Literature* [Chapel Hill, 1961], pp. 60–9).

ment as for enlightenment, and casts the arguments in familiar terms. The very liveliness and fairness to the presentation suggest a classical intent, which is to please and to instruct, as does the simple fact that a prelude should precede the drama. It permits the audience into the inner sanctum and yet preserves the social order on which the classical in art is founded. When the Director, who represents the interests and demands of the public on whom he relies for an audience, makes a plea for popular themes and novel presentation, his words seem the less shallow and self-serving when we hear in turn the Poet speak, who in his lofty demands appears less attached to life than to the sacred practice of his art. The two extremes should strike between them the exact balance desired. We are not surprised when the Director asks, 'How make our entertainment striking, new, / And yet significant and pleasing too?'[4] This had been the aim of classical art from Horace through Boileau to the culmination of the theory in the eighteenth century. The Prelude was also written when Goethe was at the height of his classical period and it shows him 'coming to terms as best he can with his classical conscience.'[5] Wieland said of him at the time, 'Clarity is his favorite word. Genius has settled to the bottom and now clear water swims above.'[6]

Read in retrospect, however, the Prelude presents itself quite differently. After we have observed *Faust* in its development not only beyond the confines of the stage but beyond the principle of imitation and reaching toward a new form of dramatic art, we no longer see the conflicting demands that the Director, the Poet, and the Merryman in turn make upon the drama as happy tensions that forebode a future harmony. The intimations of classicism recede. The Director in his insistence upon action and entertainment no longer seems to provide a legitimate balance to the Poet in his supposed remove from the reality, but comes to represent a kind of tyranny of art over life which is inherent in the principle of imitation. It is not simply the 'motley multitude ... the noisy crowd, whose vortex rude / Still draws us downward with resistless might'[7] that now opposes the Poet in his attempt to be

---

4   daß alles frisch und neu
Und mit Bedeutung auch gefällig sei.   (ll. 47–8)
5 Eudo Mason, *Goethe's Faust: Its Genesis and Purport* (Berkeley, 1967), p. 26.
6 The archeologist K.A. Böttiger quoting Wieland, 15 July 1798.
7 Lines 59–62.

heard in his own right, but the weight of a tradition which demands that he express his new vision in a form that was designed for an earlier age. The Poet only appears to flee the real world. In fact he is looking to create an even larger world in his art, to open up much more of the universe to conscious human awareness and in so doing make it part of conscious human reality. Only those caught up 'in the wild tumult of the hour'[8] ignore his efforts or mistake his explorations for flights of fantasy, as *Faust II* itself was often mistaken. When the work was completed more than three decades later this 'tumult of the hour' had in fact become the 'absurd and confused times' of which Goethe spoke in his last letter and to which he felt he was abandoning the work. A classical fusion of purposes had to his mind not at all taken place.

The posterity for which the Merryman mocks the Poet in his supposed concern with unreal and ethereal things now seems similarly misunderstood. Fame and posterity are not the whim of the ambitious mind, and a distraction from the present, as the Merryman argues, but the expression of that same evolutionary force that projects itself in different forms always toward the future. What compels the Poet seems to him, like the Eternal Feminine, to 'draw him on.' The result of his success is not that his name will be revered in vague generations to come but that he will have added through word, image, and symbol to the reality that can exist in the future mind. It is the tragedy in Act I that its world in its abuse of time has produced nothing of substance for the Poet to celebrate and thus create as a reality for a future world, and he is thus 'banished to solitude.' The Poet of the Prelude prefers solitude, apparently in the confidence that the same world will be there should he choose to return. He thinks classically. The Poet in his various guises in *Faust II* exists in a different world, in the changing, changeable, and irretrievable world of evolution.

Yet nothing is resolved by the Prelude, whether read or seen before or after the fact of the completed drama, and that is the point. No final rhyming couplet sums up its demands on art. The Director and the Merryman, who together represent the means of communication between the esthetic and the social realm, no more convince the Poet of the rightness of their position than he convinces them of his needs.

8 From l. 70: 'des Wilden Augenblicks Gewalt.'

The play of *Faust* can commence not because the parties to the conflict have come to agree, or have agreed to disagree, but only because the Director in his impatience demands a beginning: 'Sufficient speeches have been bandied, / Now let me see some deeds at last.'[9]

'In the beginning was the deed.' The same moral and philosophical impulse that had begun the poem, in other words, and was conceived as having begun the universe itself, also served to usher the play onto the stage when it too had to begin. Nor was it thought that led to action in the conclusion of the work, but act or deed that ordered thought and feeling and first made them intelligible.[10] The challenge to the sea had already begun before it was given purpose and direction in 'opening room for millions.'[11] The Prelude, composed between this beginning and this end, thus could not deny in its own principles and its own action what was operative in the work as a whole. *Faust* had to *be* what it would mean. When the Director says somewhat cynically that the audience for whom the consummate work of art is created will in fact only devour it piecemeal for its own purposes, he is saying more than he knows: 'You give a piece, in pieces give it, friend!'[12] But the completed *Faust* will not be taken in pieces, it will already be given fragmented and with the demand that the supplying mind form a whole from its parts. Whether Goethe was conscious that this would be the case when he composed the Prelude is not the point and is highly doubtful. But that such a progression would be necessary is indicated by the decision of the Director to act in default of complete knowledge, to act, like Faust, *in order* to know. This esthetic resolution is the same as the moral resolution in the play, though it occurs long before the latter obtains.

The world is a stage, Shakespeare said, but he did not say that the stage is the world. What is offered in the theater as representing the ways of the world and the actions of man is more often a representation

9 Die Worten sind genug gewechselt,
   Laβt mich auch endlich Taten sehn! (ll. 214–15)
10 Goethe placed his faith in this idealistic pragmatism in the belief that 'nature could not be so designed that the goals of the individual would contradict the purpose of the whole, indeed would not serve to sustain it' (to Riemer, 3 February 1807).
11 'Eröffn' ich Räume vielen Millionen' (l. 11563).
12 'Gebt Ihr ein Stück, so gebt es gleich in Stücken' (l. 99).

of the ways and actions of the time. We find already in *Urfaust*: 'And what the spirit of the times men call / Is merely their own spirit after all, / wherein ... the times are mirrored.' Only an absolutist or classical view of man as a constant nature created whole from the beginning could presume to represent the universal in the particular, the world in a single period of time. While Goethe rejected the absolutist fallacy, he did not accept the alternative view which expressed itself in historicism and relativism. He did not create an image of the world seen and measured through the eyes of his hero in a kind of cultural solipsism. Out of his very awareness of history and the relativism of values and perceptions, he imagined a series of worlds, or images of worlds, each bound in its times by its own understanding, each true to itself in its speech forms and sentiments, and yet, juxtaposed with other worlds, suggesting a comprehensive whole that not only is and has been but will be in an unending progression. *Faust* does not represent the world in fact, but in anticipation. It does not appropriate experience itself but provides a means of appropriation. In its own inevitably incomplete and contingent movement always toward an end, it acts out esthetically its position in the moral realm and resolves it in the same way. When the Prelude in its failure to compose its differences nevertheless calls for the play to begin, it acts in the spirit both of the hero who in his human incompletedness is yet condemned to act and of the author who only in creating his drama uncovered its deepest meanings. The moral resolution in *Faust* has its attraction in the modern world because it speaks to the creative, not the *negative* side of man.

Once begun, the play in the latter part of its composition took the radically unique course we have described. Not only are the changing literary and esthetic movements of its own age reflected in its inner development but those of the past as well, and not only do the phases of this development themselves in turn exert an artistic influence in the contemporary world, but the many forces combine, as it were, to create a history of art in anticipation. The fact that Goethe produced a body of work in his remarkably varied artistic development more suitable to an age than to a single author already suggests that he had taken more from his times than is usually given to one man and was already unknowingly processing the materials of the future. The fact that this remarkable development was encompassed in the single product *Faust* and not merely expressed broadcast in diverse forms only added to the intensity and importunity with which the forces of the age played against one another in the work and so forced this future into being. Pressed from all sides, the surface of the drama erupted, creating a literary cubism, as I have called it, in which background and foreground no longer served as perspectives but had become one as they do in the thinking mind. But it was not only through this esthetic disjunction that the vision of a multilayered reality emerged. The same vision invaded the moral realm and found the natural cause beneath the spiritual accounting for it, the pagan beneath the Christian belief, the anthropology beneath cultural diversity and change. Myth was uncovered in science. No absolutes remained but only metaphors for our changing perceptions of a reality that itself constantly changes.

This sense of things, or mode of perception, which we must allow is itself a projection of our time and for our times, is now vindicated in the poem through its own resolution which is likewise consciously a resolution for its time. The worlds it evokes were never intended to form a chain of progressive enlightenment, so that the present of which it makes us aware also need not stand philosophically triumphant. The very manner in which the work came into being would belie a resolution of completeness and completion. It had to end, as it had begun, in action. It would never have reached that point, we might say, had not the Director in his own incompleteness and rootedness in time called for the play to go on.

Select Bibliography

The list includes only those titles to which I have referred in the text and some few that I have used in comparing the English renderings of various lines in *Faust*.

Goethe's Works

Beutler, Ernst, ed. *Gedenkausgabe der Werke, Briefe, und Gespräche*. Artemis edition, 24 vols. Zurich, 1949–62.
Lange, Victor, ed. *Goethe's Collected Works*. In English translation. Suhrkamp edition, 12 vols. Boston and New York, 1983–9.

Faust

Beutler, Ernst, ed. *Die Faustdichtungen*. Artemis edition, vol. 5. Zurich, 1950.
Trunz, Erich, ed. *Goethe. Faust*. Der Tragödie erster und zweiter Teil. *Urfaust*. Munich, 1982.
Witkowski, Georg, ed. *Goethes Faust*. 2 vols. Leipzig, 1907. Reprint Leiden, 1949–50.

Faust in English Translation

Arndt, Walter, trans. and Hamlin, Cyrus, ed. *Faust: A Tragedy*. New York, 1976.
Atkins, Stuart, ed. and trans. *Faust I and II*. Suhrkamp edition, vol. 2. Boston, 1984.
Fairley, Barker, trans. *Faust*. Toronto, 1970.
Passage, Charles, ed. and trans. *Faust*. Part I and Part II. Indianapolis, 1965.

Swanwick, Anna, trans. *Faust: A Tragedy by Goethe in Two Parts*. New York, 1882.

Taylor, Bayard, ed. and trans. *Faust: A Tragedy*, 3rd ed. London, 1890.

Reference, Commentary, and Critical Analysis

Arens, Hans. *Kommentar zu Goethes Faust II*. Heidelberg, 1989.

Atkins, Stuart. *Goethe's Faust: A Literary Analysis*. Cambridge, Mass., 1964.

– 'Goethe, Calderon and *Faust II*.' *Germanic Review* 28 (1953): 83–98.

– 'The Evaluation of Romanticism in Goethe's *Faust*.' *Journal of English and Germanic Philology* 54 (1955): 9–38.

Bahr, Ehrhard. *Die Ironie im Spätwerk Goethes*. Berlin, 1972.

Barraclough, Geoffrey. *The Origins of Modern Germany*, 2nd ed. London, 1957.

Bennett, Benjamin. *Goethe's Theory of Poetry: Faust and the Regeneration of Language*. Ithaca, 1986.

Bielschowsky, Albert. *Goethe: Sein Leben und seine Werke*. 2 vols. Munich, 1907.

Boyle, Nicolas. *Goethe: The Poet and the Age*. Oxford, 1991.

– 'The Politics of *Faust II*: Another Look at the Stratum of 1831.' *Publications of the English Goethe Society*, n.s. 52 (1981–2): 4–43.

Brown, Jane K. *Goethe's Faust: The German Tragedy*. Ithaca, 1986.

Bryce, James. *The Holy Roman Empire*. New York, 1968 (first published 1864).

Buchwald, Reinhard. *Führer durch Goethes Faust*. Stuttgart, 1964.

Burckhardt, Jacob. *The Civilization of the Renaissance in Italy*. Trans. S.G.C. Middlemore. New York, 1960.

Burdach, Konrad. 'Faust und die Sorge.' *Deutsche Vierteljahresschrift* 1 (1923): 1–60.

– 'Das religöse Problem in Goethes *Faust*.' *Euphorion* 33 (1932): 1–83.

Burwick, Frederick. *The Damnation of Newton: Goethe's Theory of Color and Romantic Perception*. Berlin and New York, 1986.

Butler, E.M. *Byron and Goethe*. London, 1956.

Crum, Ralph B. *Scientific Thought in Poetry*. New York, 1931.

Darwin, Charles. *On the Origin of Species*, 2nd ed. New York, 1860.

Diener, Gottfried. *Fausts Weg zu Helena*. Urphänomen und Archetypus. Stuttgart, 1961.

Elias, Julius, ed. and trans. *Schiller's 'On Naive and Sentimental Poetry' and 'On the Sublime.'* New York, 1966.

Emrich, Wilhelm. *Die Symbolik von Faust II*. Bonn, 1957.

Ergang, Robert. *The Renaissance*. New York, 1967.

Fairley, Barker. *Six Essays on Faust*. Oxford, 1953.

– *A Study of Goethe*. Oxford, 1947.

Friedländer, Paul. *Rhythmen und Landschaften im zweiten Teil des Faust*. Weimar, 1953.

Gearey, John. *Goethe's Faust: The Making of Part I*. New Haven, 1981.

– ed. *Goethe's Essays on Art and Literature*. Trans. Ellen and Ernest von Nardroff. Suhrkamp edition, vol. 3. New York, 1986.

Gille, Klaus F. *Wilhelm Meister im Urteil der Zeitgenossen*. Assem, 1971.

Gillies, Alexander. *Goethe's Faust: An Interpretation*. Oxford, 1957.

Gode-von Aesch, Alexander. *Natural Science in German Romanticism*. New York, 1941.

Gooch, G.P. *Germany and the French Revolution*, rev. ed. London, 1920.

Gray, Ronald. *Goethe, the Alchemist*. Cambridge, 1952.

Gundolf, Friedrich. *Goethe*. Berlin, 1918.

Haile, H.G., trans. *The History of Doctor Faustus*. Urbana, 1965.

Hardy, Swana. *Goethe, Calderon und die Theorie des romantischen Dramas*. Heidelberg, 1965.

Heller, Erich. 'Goethe and the Avoidance of Tragedy' in *The Disinherited Mind*. Cambridge, 1952.

Henkel, Arthur. *Entsagung: Eine Studie zu Goethes Altersroman*. Tübingen, 1954.

Himmelfarb, Gertrude. *Darwin and the Darwinian Revolution*. Garden City, NY, 1962.

Hinderer, Walter. *Der Mensch in der Geschichte: Ein Versuch über Schillers Wallenstein*. Königstein, 1980.

Hoeffler, Otto. *Homunculus: Eine Satire auf August Wilhelm Schlegel*. Vienna, 1923.

Jantz, Harold. *The Mothers in Faust*. Baltimore, 1969.

– *Goethe's Faust as a Renaissance Man*. Princeton, 1951.

– *The Form of Goethe's Faust*. Baltimore, 1978.

Jung, C.G. *Psychologie und Alchemie*. Zurich, 1944.

Klett, Ada. *Der Streit um Faust II seit 1900*. Jenaer germanistische Forschungen 33, 1939.

Kommerell, Max. '*Faust II*: Zum Verständnis der Form' in *Geist und Buchstabe der Dichtung*. Frankfurt, 1939.

Kuhn, Thomas S. *The Structure of Scientific Revolutions*. Chicago, 1970.

Lévi-Strauss, Claude. *The Savage Mind*. Chicago, 1966.

Lohmeyer, Dorothea. *Faust und die Welt*. Munich, 1975.

Löwith, Karl. *From Hegel to Nietzsche*. Trans. David E. Green. New York, 1964.

Laine, Barry. 'By Water and Fire: The Thales-Anaxagoras Debate in Goethe's *Faust*.' *Germanic Review* 50 (1975): 99–110.

Lyell, Charles. *Principles of Geology*. 3 vols. London, 1831–3.

Lukács, Georg. *Goethe and His Age*. Trans. R. Anchor. New York, 1968.

Mandelkow, Karl R. *Goethe im Urteil seiner Kritiker*. Munich, 1977.

Martin, Günter. 'Goethes evolutionärer Sinn.' *Goethe-Jahrbuch* 105 (1988): 247–69.

Mason, Eudo. *Goethe's Faust: Its Genesis and Purport*. Berkeley, 1967.

Marx, Karl. Preface to *A Contribution to the Critique of Political Economy*. New York, 1970.

May, Kurt. *Faust, Zweiter Teil: In der Sprachform gedeutet*. Berlin, 1936.

Meding, Karl. *Goethe als Naturforscher in Beziehung zur Gegenwart*. Dresden, 1861.

Meyer, Eva A. *Politische Symbolik bei Goethe*. Heidelberg, 1949.

Miller, Douglas, ed. and trans. *Goethe: Scientific Studies*. Suhrkamp edition, vol. 12. New York, 1988.

Mommsen, Katharina. *Natur- und Fabelreich in Faust II*. Berlin, 1968.

– 'Faust II als politisches Vermächtnis des Staatsmannes Goethe.' *Jahrbuch des Freien Deutschen Hochstifts* (1989): 1–36.

Morris, Max. *Goethe Studien 2*. Berlin, 1902.

Müller, Joachim. 'Die letzte Szene von Goethes *Faust*.' *Etudes Germaniques* 38 (1983): 147–55.

Nisbet, H.B. *Goethe and the Scientific Tradition*. London, 1972.

Palmer, P.M., and More, R.P. *The Sources of the Faust Tradition: From Simon Magus to Lessing*. New York, 1965.

Peter, Ilse. 'Das Napoleonbild Goethes in seiner Spätzeit.' *Jahrbuch der Goethe-Gesellschaft* 9 (1944): 140–71.

Pniower, Otto. *Dichtungen und Dichter: Essays und Studien*. Berlin, 1912.

Powell, Jocelyn. 'Reflections on Staging Faust, Part II.' *Publications of the English Goethe Society*, n.s. 48 (1978): 52–80.

Requadt, Paul. 'Die Figur des Kaisers in *Faust II*.' *Jahrbuch der deutschen Schiller-Gesellschaft* 8 (1964): 153–71.

Rickert, Heinrich. *Goethes Faust: Die dramatische Einheit der Dichtung*. Tübingen, 1932.

Saine, Thomas P., and Sammons, Jeffrey L., eds. *Goethe's Campaign in France 1792* and *Seige of Mainz*. Suhrkamp edition, vol. 5. New York, 1987.

Schanze, Helmut. 'Szene, Schemen, Schwammfamilie: Goethes Arbeitsweise und die Frage der Struktureinheit von Faust I und II.' *Euphorion* 178 (1984): 383–400.

Schlaffer, Heinz. *Faust zweiter Teil: Die Allegorie des 19. Jahrhunderts*. Stuttgart, 1981.

Schöne, Albrecht. *Goethes Farbentheologie*. Munich, 1987.

Schrimpf, Hans-Joachim. *Das Weltbild des späten Goethe*. Stuttgart, 1956.

Seidlin, Oscar. 'Is the "Prelude in the Theatre" a Prelude to *Faust?' PMLA* 64 (1949): 462–70.

Sharpe, Lesley. *Schiller and the Historical Character.* London, 1982.

Simmel, Georg. *Goethe.* Leipzig, 1923.

Staiger, Emil. *Goethe.* 3 vols. Zurich, 1959.

Suchard, G.C.L. 'Julirevolution, St. Simonismus und die Faustpartien von 1831.' *Zeitschrift für deutsche Philologie* 60 (1935): 240–74.

Traumann, Ernst. *Goethes Faust.* 2 vols. Munich, 1914.

Treitschke, H. von. *Kulturhistorisch-Literarische Bilder*, vol. 2 of *Bilder aus der deutschen Geschichte.* Leipzig, 1914.

Trevelyan, Humphrey. *Goethe and the Greeks.* Cambridge, 1941.

Vaget, Hans Rudolf. 'Faust, der Feudalismus und die Restauration.' *Akten des VI. Internationalen Germanistenkongresses* (Basel, 1980): 345–51.

Vincent, Deirdre. *The Eternity of Being: On the Experience of Time in Goethe's Faust.* Bonn, 1987.

Watson, Francis. *Wallenstein.* New York, 1938.

Wells, George. 'Goethe and Evolution.' *Journal of the History of Ideas* 28 (1967): 537–50.

– 'Goethe's Scientific Methods and Aims in the Light of His Studies in Physical Optics.' *Publications of the English Goethe Society*, n.s. 38 (1968): 69–113.

Wenzel, Manfred. 'Goethe und Darwin: Goethes morphologische Schriften in ihrem naturwissenschaftlichen Kontext.' Dissertation, University of Bochum, 1982.

Williams, John R. 'Die Rache der Kraniche, Goethe, *Faust II* und die Julirevolution.' *Zeitschrift für deutsche Philologie* 103 (1984): 105–27.

– *Goethe's Faust.* London, 1987.

Index